Camper's Guide to TEXAS

Parks, Lakes, and Forests
Where to Go and How to Get There

THIRD EDITION

McKittrick Canyon, Guadalupe Mountains National Park

Mickey Little

Lone Star Books®

A Division of Gulf Publishing Company/Houston, Texas

Third Edition

Library of Congress Catalog Card Number 77-73561
ISBN 0-88415-097-6

First Edition—May 1978   **Second Edition**—August 1983   **Third Edition**—July 1990
Second Printing—May 1982   Second Printing—September 1986
                                  Third Printing—August 1988

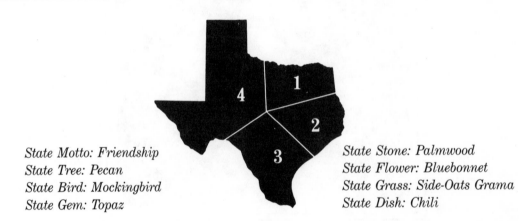

State Motto: Friendship
State Tree: Pecan
State Bird: Mockingbird
State Gem: Topaz

State Stone: Palmwood
State Flower: Bluebonnet
State Grass: Side-Oats Grama
State Dish: Chili

Enjoy the best of Texas with these Lone Star Books:

The Alamo and Other Texas Missions to Remember
Amazing Texas Monuments and Museums
Backroads of Texas/2nd Edition
Beachcomber's Guide to Gulf Coast Marine Life
Birder's Guide to Texas
The Best of Texas Festivals
Bicycling in Texas
Camper's Guide to Texas Parks, Lakes, and Forests/
    3rd Edition
Diving and Snorkeling Guide to Texas
From Texas Kitchens
Frontier Forts of Texas
Great Hometown Restaurants of Texas
A Guide to Fishing in Texas

A Guide to Historic Texas Inns and Hotels/2nd Ed.
A Guide to Hunting in Texas
A Guide to Texas Lakes
A Guide to Texas Rivers and Streams
Hiking and Backpacking Trails of Texas/3rd Edition
Historic Homes of Texas
A Line on Texas
Pocket Guides to Speckled Trout and Redfish
Rock Hunting in Texas
Texas—Family Style/2nd Edition
Traveling Texas Borders
Unsung Heroes of Texas
Why Stop? A Guide to Texas Historical Roadside
    Markers/2nd Edition

Contents

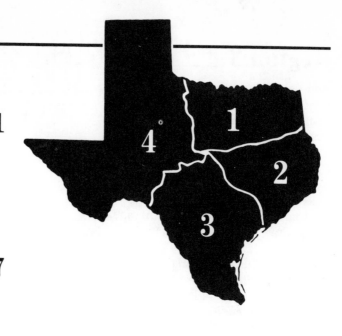

Introduction — 1

Region 1 — 7

Region 2 — 50

Region 3 _____ 87

Region 4 _____ 120

Appendix 1— Camping Supplies Checklists _____ 146

Appendix 2— Facilities Summary of State Parks _____ 148

Index _____ 151

I went to the woods because I wished to live deliberately, to front only the essential facts of life, and see if I could not learn what it had to teach, and not, when I came to die, discover that I had not lived.
—Henry David Thoreau

This third edition of the *Camper's Guide* includes detailed maps and camping information on 13 new parks/ lakes, comprising 8 state parks, 1 large city park, and 4 campgrounds/lakes administered by various water authorities. There's also a new "Facilities Summary of State Parks" on page 148 that quickly shows you the key facilities and accommodations of state-operated parks and recreation areas. At a glance you can tell which parks have screened shelters, primitive camping, group accommodations, swimming pools, equestrian/ bike trails, golf courses, etc. Correspondence with each of the parks, lakes, and forests has made possible a complete update of maps, facilities, addresses, phone numbers, etc. Because reservations can be made at all Texas state parks, the latest reservation system is included in order to further publicize the procedure.

I am indebted to and wish to thank the following agencies and individuals for information—in the form of maps, brochures, books, articles, telephone conversations, and personal interviews—without which this book would not have been possible:

City of Fredericksburg
City of Waco, Parks and Recreation Department
Colorado River Municipal Water District
Corps of Engineers, U.S. Army Engineer District
Forest Service, U.S. Department of Agriculture
Franklin County Water District
Guadalupe-Blanco River Authority
Lavaca-Navidad River Authority
Lower Colorado River Authority
National Park Service, U.S. Department of the Interior
Sabine River Authority
San Jacinto River Authority
Texas Parks and Wildlife Department
Travel and Information, State Department of Highways
  and Public Transportation
Trinity River Authority
U.S. Government Printing Office

May this third edition of the *Camper's Guide* con-
tribute to your quest for many happy camping days
in the Lone Star State!

Mickey Little
Johnson City, Texas

Introduction

One of the greatest things about camping in Texas is that you can choose exactly what appeals to you: rugged mountains, placid lakes, thorny deserts, flowing rivers, sandy beaches, and lots more in between. The number of campgrounds located at our Texas parks, lakes and forests appears to be almost countless. The purpose of this *Camper's Guide* is to suggest places to go and provide directions to get there. You will discover information about the popular, well-known campgrounds as well as the lesser used—where you will find everything, except crowds!

These public campgrounds, provided and operated by federal, state, county, or city agencies, afford varied options for outdoor recreation. You can hike, swim, canoe, sail, fish, water ski, or backpack. You can pursue your favorite hobby as a bird watcher, shell collector, photographer, geologist, botanist, or naturalist. You may choose to rough it at a primitive campsite or to enjoy all of the comforts of home in a recreational vehicle. You can spend a day, a weekend, or an entire vacation doing what you like best, no matter how active, or inactive, it is.

...or you can enjoy all the comforts of home in a mobile camper.

Let's look more closely at the state of Texas and what it has to offer to the camping enthusiast. In elevation, the surface of the state varies from sea level along the coast of the Gulf of Mexico to 8,751 feet at the summit of Guadalupe Peak. Terrain varies from the subtropic Rio Grande Valley to the Great Plains in the far north, from the lush pine forests of East Texas to the mountainous Trans-Pecos region of West Texas. In straight-line distance, Texas extends 801 miles from north to south and 773 miles from east to west. The tidewater coastline extends 624 miles.

The weather is generally characterized by mild temperatures. Average annual rainfall varies sharply, from more than 56 inches along the Sabine River to less than eight inches in the extreme west. Included in Texas' 26 million acres of woodland are four national forests with 658,023 acres. The most important forest area of the state is the East Texas pine-hardwood region, known as the "Piney Woods." It extends over 43 counties.

Texas has 91 mountains a mile or more high, all of them in the Trans-Pecos region. Guadalupe Peak, at 8,751 feet, is the state's highest mountain. The longest river in the state is the Rio Grande, which forms

Texas parks offer all kinds of camping facilities—you can rough it in a tent...

the international boundary between Texas and Mexico and extends 1,248 miles along Texas. The next longest river is the Red River, which extends 726 miles.

Of the 50 states, Texas ranks second only to Alaska in the volume of its inland water—more than 6,000 square miles of lakes and streams. Toledo Bend Reservoir, on the Sabine River between Texas and Louisiana, is the largest reservoir in Texas or on its borders, with 181,600 surface acres at normal operating level. The largest body of water wholly within the state is Sam Rayburn Reservoir, with a normal surface area of 113,410 acres.

Texas is fortunate, indeed, to have so many agencies vitally interested in providing and maintaining such excellent camping facilities for the public. There are five parks administered by the National Park Service of the U.S. Department of the Interior that provide camping facilities. They are: Big Bend National Park, Guadalupe Mountain National Park, Padre Island National Seashore, Lake Meredith Recreation Area, and Amistad National Recreation Area. The Big Thicket National Preserve does not operate campgrounds in any of the 12 units at the present time.

The Texas Parks and Wildlife Department presently operates over 70 parks and recreation areas that have camping facilities, and more are being added each year. Their continuing goal is to provide a state park within a two-hour drive of every major metropolitan area in Texas.

Many Texas lakes are under the jurisdiction of the river authorities in Texas; many other lakes are under the jurisdiction of water districts, municipalities, and counties. Provisions for outdoor recreation development and administration vary greatly with each agency. However, numerous parks with camping facilities are located along the shoreline of more than 20 lakes under the jurisdiction of the U.S. Army Corps of Engineers. Most of the parks are operated by the Corps of Engineers, but state and local agencies may lease project land to provide specialized facilities. On the other hand, the Lower Colorado River Authority, with its chain of seven lakes, has land designated for park development but has done little to develop campgrounds. Their stated function is merely "to not prevent free use [sic]."

The four national forests in Texas are open to the public for a wide variety of uses and pleasures. Presently, there are 16 recreation areas with camp facilities. These are designed and managed for families or small groups wanting "elbow room" in a natural forest setting. Backpacking is permitted any-

where in the national forests in Texas, but detailed information regarding the area to be visited should be obtained from the District Ranger.

Other public campgrounds included in the *Camper's Guide* are operated by county and city agencies. Major coverage has been given to the Lady Bird Johnson Municipal Park of Fredericksburg, and Wolf Creek Park because of size, available maps, etc. The author apologizes for any parks of this size omitted and welcomes information on them for future inclusion. Over 100 parks are included in the section entitled "Other Parks" appearing at the end of each of the four divisions of this guide. This information was obtained from several publications of the State Department of Highways and Public Transportation.

Many of the parks operated by the Texas Parks and Wildlife Department are located at lake settings.

Texas Tourist Bureaus

Travel Literature Maps	Information
Amarillo—I-40 East	806/335-1441
Anthony—I-10, New Mexico State Line	915/886-3468
Austin—State Capitol	512/463-8586
Denison—US 75 and 69 North	214/465-5577
Gainesville—I-35 North	817/665-2301
Langtry—US 90 (Loop 25)	915/291-3340
Laredo—I-35 North	512/722-8119
Orange—I-10, Louisiana State Line	409/883-9416
Texarkana—I-30, Arkansas State Line	214/794-2114
Valley—Junction US 77 & US 83 (Harlingen)	512/428-4477
Waskom—I-20, Louisiana State Line	214/687-2547
Wichita Falls—I-44 North	817/723-7931

How to Use the Camper's Guide

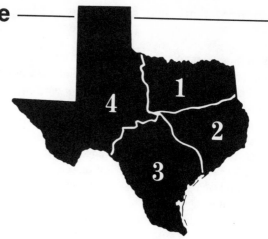

The state has been divided into four geographic regions shown in the illustration. The parks, lakes and forests within each region are arranged alphabetically. A list of "Other Campgrounds" in each region appears at the end of the section devoted to that region. All campgrounds, parks, lakes and forests are cross-listed by name and city in the index.

All information reported in this *Camper's Guide* has been supplied by the respective operating agency, either through literature distributed by them, through verbal communication, or through secondary sources deemed reliable.

The maps showing the location of facilities within a park should be of considerable help. These maps are often available to you at the park headquarters, but they can also aid you in planning a trip to an unfamiliar park. Those of you who have attempted to meet up with friends at a predetermined spot at a large campground can readily appreciate the value of possessing such a map.

The maps showing the location of the numerous parks around a lake should also be of tremendous help to all campers. Perhaps this information will help to better distribute the visitors to the various parks. Far too many campers stop at the first campground they see when they arrive at a lake—later they're disappointed because of the crowded conditions. The major roads to each park are shown, but remember that many back roads exist. You may eventually choose to obtain a more detailed local map from the reservoir manager. Names and addresses are provided for each park, lake and forest in this book.

Several statistics about each lake have been included, such as water elevation, the size of the area covered (in acres), and the length of the shoreline. These facts can serve as a point of reference as you compare various lakes. Many newspapers carry information on water elevation, and you can thus have some forewarning of extreme water conditions.

Most parks are easily found with the aid of a good road map, but vicinity maps have been included here in some instances. Signs along the way can also be relied upon after you reach the general vicinity of a park.

The facilities available at a campground are always changing, but a change in status usually means the addition of a service rather than a discontinuation. In other words, a camper often finds bet-

ter and more facilities than those listed in the latest brochure.

The average camper usually doesn't need help deciding what activities to engage in. Obviously, water-related sports are the most popular activities at a lake setting. Other possible activities have been listed to indicate the availability of nature trails, hiking trails, swimming pools, horseback trails, etc. In many parks, interpretive programs, including nature walks, guided tours and campfire talks, are conducted by park personnel.

Checklists for general camping equipment, cooking equipment and food are included on pages 146–147 to guide you in planning your camping trips. Careful and adequate planning can mean the difference between the "I wish we had stayed at home" trip and the "Let's go again next weekend" trip.

Since reservations can be made at all Texas state parks, the reservation system has been included on page 5 to further publicize the procedure. Something to remember if your intended park is full and you're too tired to drive to another: One-day stops are permitted in highway picnic and rest areas, limited to a maximum of 24 hours; no tent or other structure may be erected in such areas.

This third edition also contains a "Facilities Summary of State Parks" on pages 148–149 that quickly shows you the key facilities and accommodations of state-operated parks and recreation areas. At a glance you can tell which parks have screened shelters, primitive camping, group accommodations, swimming pools, equestrian/bicycle trails, golf courses, etc.

May this *Camper's Guide* serve you well in the years ahead, whether you are a beginner or a seasoned camper. Take time to camp, to become *truly* acquainted with nature ... and with yourself and your family! Don't put off until tomorrow what can be enjoyed today!

General Policies, Rules and Regulations

There are some rules and regulations often encountered at public campgrounds, whether administered by a national, state, county, or city agency. Please keep in mind that policies, fees, regulations, and available facilities change from time to time. Campers must stay informed by requesting updated information from the parks they visit, by reading the material posted or distributed at the parks, and by reading newspaper articles reporting policy changes.

Rules imposed by campgrounds are common sense rules meant to control actions that may damage natural resources and facilities, and actions that cause unreasonable disturbance to other campers. The following rules are quite general but are common to most campgrounds. More detailed and specific rules are posted and distributed by the agency operating the campground. Observance of these rules will make your visit and the visits of others more pleasant and enjoyable.

▲ Campers should register, upon arriving, at the designated place.

▲ Fee schedules are posted in individual parks and are subject to change.

▲ An entry fee may be charged (usually $2.00 per vehicle).

▲ Campsite user fees vary according to the extent of services provided. (*Note:* Some parks charge a per-campsite fee; others charge a per-vehicle fee).

What better place to stroll barefooted with your grandchildren than at the beach?

▲ Fees are usually charged for concession-operated facilities.

▲ Many individual campsites are available on a first-come first-served basis and cannot be reserved.

▲ The reservation system is in operation at all state parks.

▲ Reservations are usually required for group campsites.

▲ The number of days you may occupy a site is limited during peak seasons (usually to 14 days).

▲ Camping shall be in designated areas only.

▲ Fires shall be confined to grills and fireplaces in established campgrounds and picnic areas.

▲ Before you retire for the night or leave your campsite unattended for any reason, make certain that your campfire is entirely out.

▲ The gathering of wood for fires *may* be prohibited; it is *always* limited to dead materials found on the ground, even when permitted.

▲ Fire danger or wood shortage may make it necessary for a park to place a temporary or permanent ban on open fires.

▲ Keep your campsite clean by placing all garbage and trash in containers provided. Do not bury garbage.

▲ Pets may be allowed if they are on a leash.

▲ Be especially careful not to be noisy late at night or early in the morning.

▲ Leaving camping equipment or other property unattended at a campsite for the purpose of holding the site for future occupancy is prohibited.

▲ Operating or using any audio devices or other noise-producing devices in such a manner and at such times as to disturb other persons is prohibited.

▲ Adults are responsible for the conduct of minors under their supervision.

▲ Possession of loaded firearms is prohibited.

▲ Self-contained recreation vehicles can be accommodated at most campgrounds, but size restrictions are imposed at some campgrounds.

▲ Some parks offering back-country camping require camping and/or fire permits, which may be obtained at park headquarters.

▲ Occasionally, back-country use is prohibited because of emergency conditions such as high fire danger or severe weather conditions.

▲ Horseback riding is permitted in designated areas only.

▲ Swimming is permitted only in designated areas and at designated times.

▲ Swimming, boating, skiing, and other activities are at the participant's sole risk.

▲ Boats may be launched and operated only in designated areas.

▲ All boating and water activities are subject to the rules and regulations of the Texas Water Safety Act.

▲ Texas fishing laws are applicable.

A $25 annual entrance permit to state parks may be purchased and used in lieu of the daily entrance fee where entrance fees are required. A State Parklands Passport exempting persons 65 years of age or over from having to pay an entrance fee at state parks is available. A $25 annual entrance permit to national parks, called the Golden Eagle Passport, is available where entry fees are charged (all persons are eligible). The Golden Age Passport is issued free of charge to persons 62 years of age or older. It provides the same entry privileges as the Golden Eagle Passport, plus a 50 percent discount on federal special-use fees in designated areas.

Flowering dogwood makes spring a lovely time of year to hike the in the piney woods of East Texas.

*Reservation System for Texas State Parks

▲ **Reservations for park facilities** will be accepted daily at the park headquarters where the facility is located, by mail, telephone or in person between the hours of 8:00 a.m. to 5:00 p.m.

▲ **Reservations for cabins, screened shelters and campsites cannot be made more than 90 days in advance of occupancy date.**

▲ **Reservations made more than 10 days in advance of occupancy date for cabins, screened shelters and campsites require a reservation fee for each facility reserved in an amount equal to one day's fee for the type of facility reserved.** Reservations made by telephone will be held five days pending receipt of required reservation fees. If the reservation fee has not been received after five days, the reservation request will be canceled.

▲ **All reservation fees will be applied to the total amount due at the time of registration.** If a reservation or any part of a reservation is canceled 72 hours or more prior to arrival date, the reservation fee will be refunded; otherwise the reservation fee will be forfeited.

▲ **Reservations with no fee will be canceled at 6:00 p.m. on arrival date unless late arrival privileges have been confirmed by the park. Persons requesting late arrival privileges must call the park headquarters either on the day of arrival or the day before during the hours 8:00 a.m. to 5:00 p.m.**

▲ **Reservations for campsites are made according to the type requested with adequate space necessary to accommodate eight persons and a combination of motor vehicles and trailers not to exceed two (2).** (Excludes Enchanted Rock State Natural Area.) Screened shelter occupancy is also limited to eight persons; however, the use of certain types of motor vehicles and/or camping equipment at shelters may be restricted. Persons making requests for screened shelters should ask park staff for more details.

▲ **Specific campsites or shelters cannot be reserved;** however, if a specific location is desired on arrival it will be honored (1) if a user fee has not been paid and (2) if it will accommodate your equipment.

▲ **Reservation requests for adjoining or adjacent camping facilities will be honored subject to availability.**

▲ **Cabin reservations will be confirmed by facility number.** Preference will be honored if available. The department reserves the right to change assignments if confirmed cabin is out of service upon arrival.

* From Texas Parks & Wildlife Brochure 4000-0001/89
For further information contact:
Texas Parks & Wildlife Department
4200 Smith School Road
Austin, Texas 78744
1-800-792-1112   In Austin: 389-4890

Texas scenery is quite diverse; it includes the vastness of Big Bend country . . .

▲ **Facilities that have not been reserved and those for which cancellations have been received will be available on a first-come, first-served basis to persons arriving at the park without reservations.** A waiting list will be maintained if demand exceeds availability.

▲ **On the last day of occupancy, facilities must be vacated by 2:00 p.m.** Incoming visitors cannot be assured of facility occupancy before 2:00 p.m. on scheduled date of arrival. Continuous occupancy of park facilities is limited to 14 days.

▲ **Room reservations at Indian Lodge, San Soloman Spring and Landmark Inn** will be accepted in the same manner as prescribed for cabins, except that reservations will be accepted for as much as 12 months in advance of occupancy date. Check-out time at Indian Lodge and Landmark Inn is 12:00 noon.

Group Facilities

An impartial drawing to determine assignment dates for park facilities designated as group facilities for the 12-month period beginning February 1st and ending January 31st of the following year will be held each year at respective park headquarters on January 11th at 10:00 a.m. Each group wishing to participate in the drawing may enter its name one time only. Participants may include in their reservation request for group facilities a total of four (4) dates in their order of preference which will be considered as alternate choices in the event there is no open date for first choice when the name is drawn. Entry blanks for the drawing (PWD 214) are available from parks that have group facilities. The entry blanks may be left at the park headquarters beginning December 1st prior to the January 11th drawing. Participants in the drawing will be notified as soon as possible if reservation has been confirmed. A reservation fee in the amount of one day's user fee for the type of group facility reserved must be received by the park no later than January 31st after receiving reservation confirmation as a will furnish this information when requested.

result of the annual drawing. If the reservation fee has not been received by 5:00 p.m. on January 31st, the reservation will be cancelled. All reservation fees will be applied to the amount due at the time of registration. If group facility reservations are cancelled 72 hours or more prior to scheduled arrival date, the reservation fee will be refunded; otherwise, the reservation fee will be forfeited. Reservations for group facilities will be taken on a first-come, first-served basis by letter, telephone or in person after the drawing is held. All group facility reservations require a reservation fee in the amount of one day's user fee for the type of group facility reserved if the reservation is made 10 days or more in advance of occupancy date. All groups must comply with occupancy limitations established for each group facility. The park superintendent

State Park User Fee Rates

A user fee will be collected for the privileges, services, accommodations or facilities. The fees range from about $4/day for primitive campsites to about $12/day for screened shelters.

Fees are based on type of site occupied regardless of utilities used. Capacity requirements will be observed; parties requiring larger accommodations must obtain additional facilities. Preferences will be given if desired facility is vacant or not reserved.

. . . and the beauty of the Texas Hill Country.

Region 1

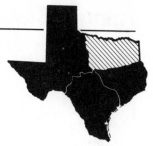

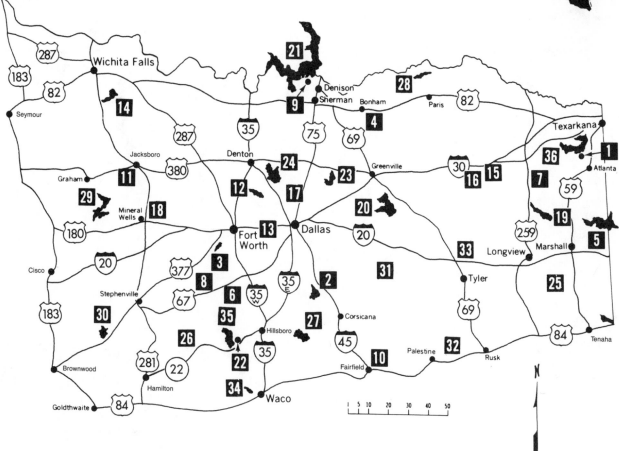

1—Atlanta State Recreation Area, 8
2—Bardwell Lake, 9
3—Benbrook Lake, 10
4—Bonham State Recreation Area, 11
5—Caddo Lake State Park, 12
6—Cleburne State Recreation Area, 13
7—Daingerfield State Park, 14
8—Dinosaur Valley State Park, 15
9—Eisenhower State Recreation Area, 16
10—Fairfield Lake State Recreation Area, 17
11—Fort Richardson State Historical Park, 18
12—Grapevine Lake, 19
13—Joe Pool Lake, 20
14—Lake Arrowhead State Recreation Area, 21
15—Lake Bob Sandlin State Recreation Area, 22
16—Lake Cypress Springs, 23
17—Lake Lewisville State Park, 24
18—Lake Mineral Wells State Park, 25

19—Lake O' the Pines, 26
20—Lake Tawakoni, 27
21—Lake Texoma, 28
22—Lake Whitney State Recreation Area, 30
23—Lavon Lake, 31
24—Lewisville Lake, 33
25—Martin Creek Lake State Recreation Area, 35
26—Meridian State Recreation Area, 36
27—Navarro Mills Lake, 37
28—Pat Mayse Lake, 38
29—Possum Kingdom State Recreation Area, 39
30—Proctor Lake, 40
31—Purtis Creek State Recreation Area, 41
32—Rusk-Palestine State Park, 42
33—Tyler State Park, 43
34—Waco Lake, 44
35—Whitney Lake, 45
36—Wright-Patman Lake, 47
    Other Parks in Region 1, 49

Atlanta State Recreation Area

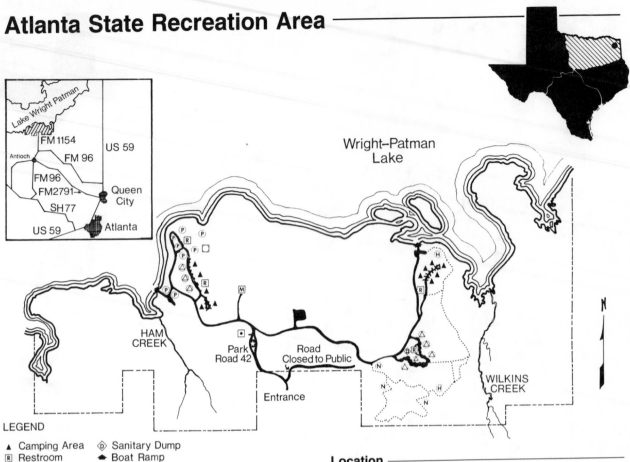

LEGEND

- ▲ Camping Area
- ℝ Restroom
- ☐ Playground
- △ Trailer Camping
- Ⓗ Hiking Trail
- Ⓝ Nature Trail
- Ⓟ Picnic Area
- ◈ Sanitary Dump
- ⬥ Boat Ramp
- ✪ Headquarters
- Ⓜ Maintenance Area
- ⊡ Residence

Facilities & Activities

59 campsites
  8 with water only
  43 with water/electricity
  8 with water/electricity/sewage
restrooms
showers
trailer dump station
group picnic area
amphitheater
picnicking
playground
swimming beach
water skiing
fishing
boat ramps
1.1-mile nature trail
2.4-mile hiking trail

Location

Atlanta State Recreation Area is located on the shores of 119,700-acre Wright-Patman Lake approximately 8 miles northwest of Atlanta. The 1,475-acre park may be reached by driving 2 miles north of Atlanta on US 59 to FM 96, west for 8 miles to FM 1154, north for 2 miles to Park Road 42.

For Information

Atlanta State Recreation Area
Route 1, Box 116
Atlanta, TX 75551
214/796-6476

About the Park

Caddo Indians, the most culturally advanced tribe in Texas, once made this area their home. The Caddos settled the area peacefully as farmers, unlike their nomadic and warlike brothers, the Apaches and Comanches.

Excavations conducted by the Smithsonian Institute produced many graves and artifacts, and archeologists found evidence of a house pattern with post molds still intact.

Bardwell Lake

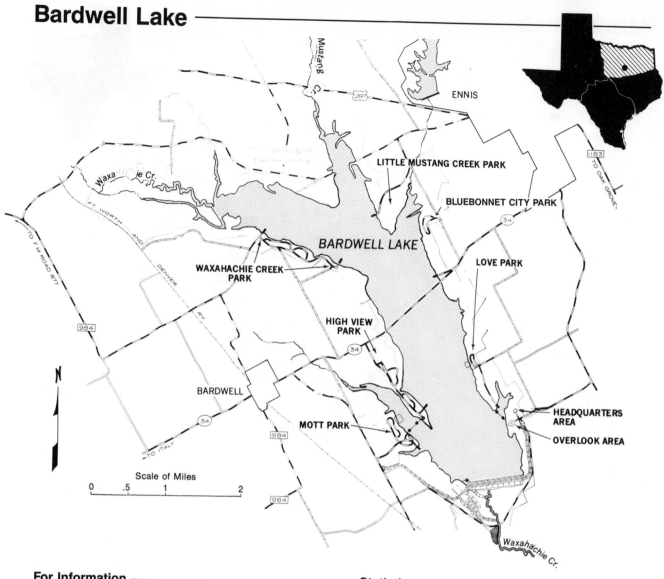

For Information

Reservoir Manager
Bardwell Project Office
Route 4, Box 60
Ennis, TX 75119-9563
214/875-5711

Statistics

Elevation, conservation pool . . . . 421 feet
Elevation, spillway crest . . . . 439 feet
Area, conservation pool . . . . 3,570 acres
Shoreline, conservation pool . . . . 25 miles

Campground	Facilities	Drinking Water	Restrooms	Picnic Facilities	Camping Area	Trailer Area	Boat Launch Ramp	Boat Storage (Rental)	Electrical Outlets	Fish Bait & Supplies
Love Park		X	X	X	X	X	X			
Little Mustang Ck Pk			X				X			
Bluebonnet City Pk		X	X	X	X	X	X			
Waxahachie Ck Park		X	X	X	X	X	X		X	
High View Park		X	X	X	X	X	X	X	X	X
Mott Park		X	X	X	X	X	X		X	

Benbrook Lake

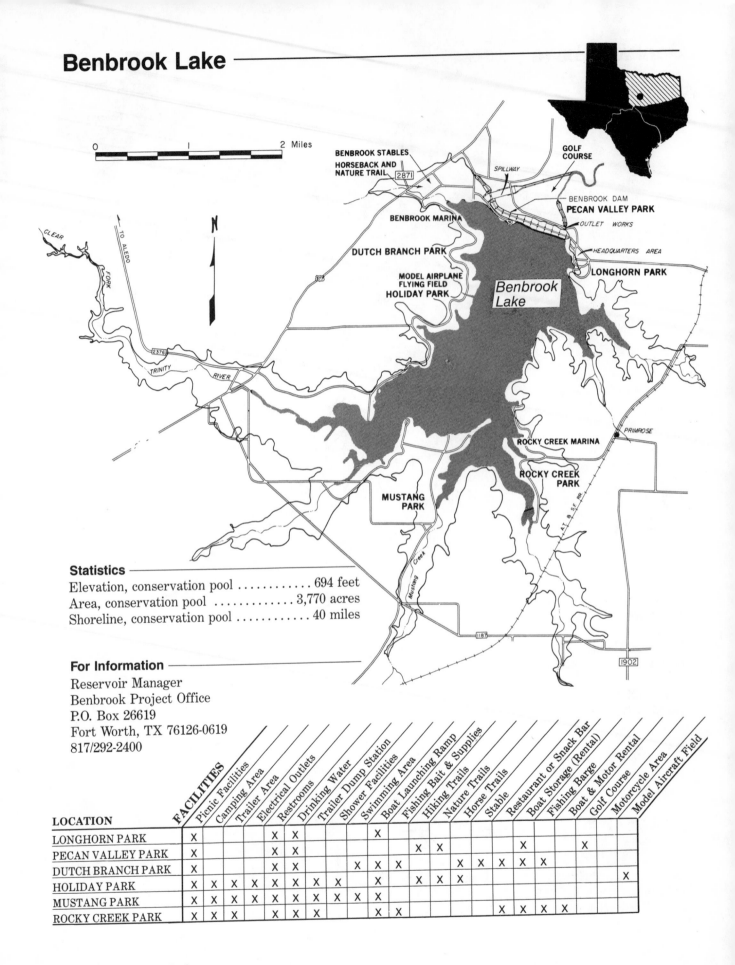

Statistics

Elevation, conservation pool .... 694 feet
Area, conservation pool .... 3,770 acres
Shoreline, conservation pool .... 40 miles

For Information

Reservoir Manager
Benbrook Project Office
P.O. Box 26619
Fort Worth, TX 76126-0619
817/292-2400

LOCATION	Picnic Facilities	Camping Area	Trailer Area	Electrical Outlets	Restrooms	Drinking Water	Trailer Dump Station	Shower Facilities	Swimming Area	Boat Launching Ramp	Fishing Bait & Supplies	Hiking Trails	Nature Trails	Horse Trails	Stable	Restaurant or Snack Bar	Boat Storage (Rental)	Fishing Barge	Boat & Motor Rental	Golf Course	Motorcycle Area	Model Aircraft Field
LONGHORN PARK	X				X	X			X								X			X		
PECAN VALLEY PARK	X				X	X				X	X					X						
DUTCH BRANCH PARK	X				X	X		X	X	X		X	X	X	X	X						X
HOLIDAY PARK	X	X	X	X	X	X	X	X		X	X	X										
MUSTANG PARK	X	X	X	X	X	X	X	X	X													
ROCKY CREEK PARK	X	X	X		X	X	X		X	X					X	X	X	X				

Bonham State Recreation Area

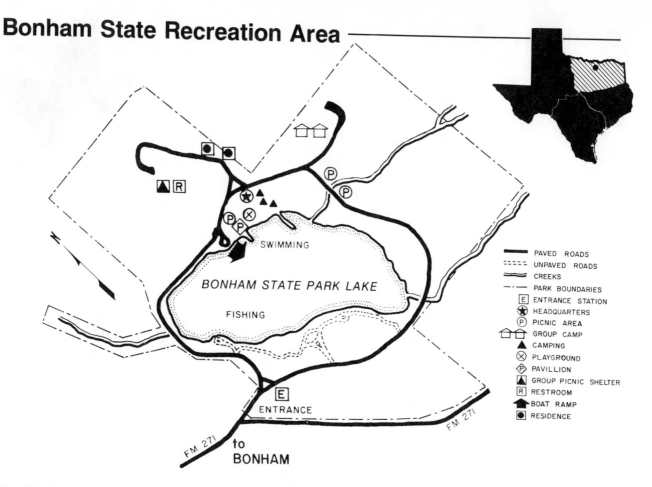

PAVED ROADS
UNPAVED ROADS
CREEKS
PARK BOUNDARIES
E ENTRANCE STATION
★ HEADQUARTERS
P PICNIC AREA
GROUP CAMP
▲ CAMPING
⊗ PLAYGROUND
P PAVILLION
▲ GROUP PICNIC SHELTER
R RESTROOM
BOAT RAMP
RESIDENCE

Facilities & Activities

21 campsites
  10 with water only
  11 with water/electricity
restrooms
showers
trailer dump station
group picnic area
group barracks & dining hall
pavilion
picnicking
playground
swimming
lighted fishing pier
boat ramp and boat dock
boats for rent (seasonal)
concession (seasonal)

Location

Bonham State Recreation Area is located in Fannin County 2 miles southeast of Bonham on SH 78, then 2 miles southeast on FM 271 to Park Road 24. The 261-acre park includes a 65-acre lake.

For Information

Bonham State Recreation Area
Route 1, Box 337
Bonham, TX 75418
214/583-5022

Texas has some great fishin' opportunities, no matter whether you're bank fishing, boat fishing, or doing something in between.

Caddo Lake State Park

PAVED ROADS
PARK BOUNDARY
★ HEADQUARTERS
▲ CAMPING
△ SCREENED SHELTERS
Ⓘ INTERPRETIVE TRAIL
Ⓒ CABINS
Ⓡ RESTROOM
Ⓟ PICNIC AREA
Ⓗ HIKING TRAIL
⚓ BOAT RAMP
◉ RESIDENCE
⊠ PLAYGROUND
▨ PRIVATE PROPERTY
Ⓜ MAINTENANCE AREA
Ⓐ ACCESS TRAIL
Ⓕ FISHING PIER
Ⓖ RECREATION HALL

For Information

Caddo Lake State Park
Rt. 2, Box 15
Karnack, TX 75661
214/679-3351

Location

Caddo Lake State Park is located off of SH 43 north near Karnack via FM 2198 to Park Road 2. The 478-acre park fronts Big Cypress Bayou with access to Caddo Lake.

Caddo Lake State Park near Karnack, Tx. This lake figured prominently in the early history of East Texas, and its beauty has been well preserved. The fishing is superb here; the wildlife, abundant.

Facilities & Activities

48 campsites
  20 with water only
  20 with water/electricity
  8 with water/electricity/sewage
9 cabins
8 screened shelters
restrooms
showers
trailer dump station
recreation hall for group day-use and group
  overnight use
picnicking
playground
swimming
water skiing
fishing pier
boat ramp
canoe rental (seasonal)
concession (rentals & snacks)
¾-mile nature trail
3 miles of hiking trails
exhibits in Visitor Center

Cleburne State Recreation Area

TO US HWY 67

PARK RD 21

PLAYGROUND

CEDAR LAKE

1 in. = 1,500 ft.

- ◣ Paved Road
- Ⓐ Trailer Area
- ▲ Camping Area
- Ⓐ Group Camp
- Ⓟ Picnic Area
- ○ Concession Building
- Ⓜ Maintenance Area
- ◆ Boat Ramp
- △ Screened Shelters
- Ⓡ Restroom
- ✴ Headquarters Building
- ◉ Park Residence
- Ⓔ Park Entrance

Fifteen state parks rent boats in season. . .

Facilities & Activities

58 campsites
  31 with water/electricity
  27 with water/electricity/sewage
6 screened shelters
restrooms
showers
trailer dump station
group barracks with kitchen/dining hall
picnicking
playgrounds
swimming
fishing
boat ramp
boats for rent (seasonal)
park store (seasonal)

Location

Cleburne State Recreation Area is located in Johnson County 6 miles southwest of Cleburne on US 67 to Park Road 21, then southwest on Park Road 21 for 6 miles. The 1,068-acre park includes a 116-acre lake of clear, clean spring water.

For Information

Cleburne State Recreation Area
Route 2, Box 90
Cleburne, TX 76031
817/645-4215

. . .and Cleburne State Recreation Area is one of them; the 116-acre lake is ideal for canoeing.

Daingerfield State Park

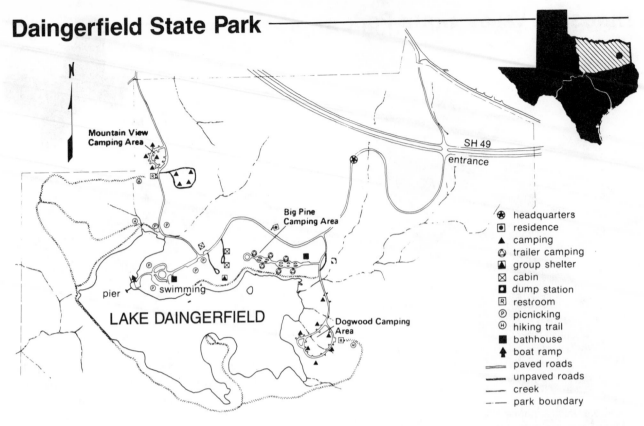

Legend

- ⊗ headquarters
- ⊡ residence
- ▲ camping
- ⌀ trailer camping
- ⬔ group shelter
- ⊠ cabin
- ■ dump station
- Ⓡ restroom
- Ⓟ picnicking
- Ⓗ hiking trail
- ■ bathhouse
- ⬆ boat ramp
- paved roads
- unpaved roads
- creek
- park boundary

Location

Daingerfield State Park is located east of Daingerfield off SH 11 and SH 49 south on Park Road 17. The 551-acre park includes an 80-acre lake.

For Information

Daingerfield State Park
Route 1, Box 286B
Daingerfield, TX 75638
214/645-2921

Facilities & Activities

40 campsites
   15 with water only
   16 with water/electricity
   9 with water/electricity/sewage
3 cabins
Bass Lodge (28 maximum)
restrooms
showers
trailer dump station
group picnic area
amphitheater
picnicking
playground
swimming beach & bathhouse
fishing pier
fish cleaning facilities
boat ramp & boat dock
boats for rent (seasonal)
2½ miles of hiking trails
park store (seasonal)

Mixed pines and hardwoods shade quiet woodland campsites, hiking trails, and picnic areas around a scenic lake in Daingerfield State Park.

Dinosaur Valley State Park

Replica of the 12-foot-high × 50-foot-long Tyrannosaurus rex, at Dinosaur Valley State Park near Glen Rose, Tx.

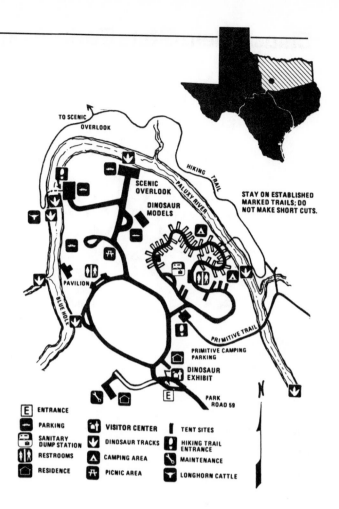

STAY ON ESTABLISHED MARKED TRAILS; DO NOT MAKE SHORT CUTS.

E	ENTRANCE			
	PARKING		VISITOR CENTER	TENT SITES
	SANITARY DUMP STATION		DINOSAUR TRACKS	HIKING TRAIL ENTRANCE
	RESTROOMS		CAMPING AREA	MAINTENANCE
	RESIDENCE		PICNIC AREA	LONGHORN CATTLE

Facilities & Activities

46 campsites
  6 with water only
  40 with water/electricity
7 primitive camping areas for backpackers
restrooms
showers
trailer dump station
group picnic area
picnicking
playground
swimming
fishing
6 miles of hiking trails
horseback trails
dinosaur exhibit at Visitor Center
Texas Longhorn Herd

Location

   Dinosaur Valley State Park is located 4 miles west of Glen Rose via US 67 and FM 205. Along the Paluxy River, this 1,523-acre park was designated as a National Natural Landmark by the National Park Service in 1969.

For Information

Dinosaur Valley State Park
Box 396
Glen Rose, TX 76043
817/897-4588

A dinosaur exhibit is located in the Visitor Center at Dinosaur Valley State Park.

Eisenhower State Recreation Area

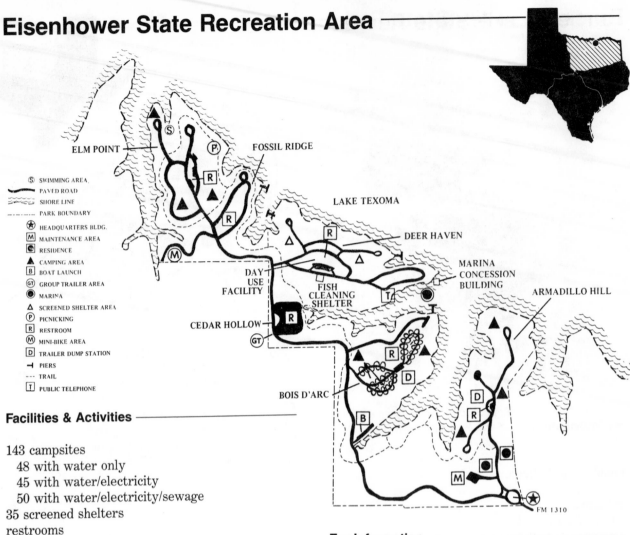

ELM POINT

FOSSIL RIDGE

LAKE TEXOMA

DEER HAVEN

MARINA
CONCESSION
BUILDING

ARMADILLO HILL

DAY
USE
FACILITY

FISH
CLEANING
SHELTER

CEDAR HOLLOW

BOIS D'ARC

FM 1310

Ⓢ SWIMMING AREA
〰 PAVED ROAD
〰 SHORE LINE
--- PARK BOUNDARY
✪ HEADQUARTERS BLDG.
Ⓜ MAINTENANCE AREA
Ⓒ RESIDENCE
▲ CAMPING AREA
Ⓑ BOAT LAUNCH
ⒼⓉ GROUP TRAILER AREA
◉ MARINA
△ SCREENED SHELTER AREA
Ⓟ PICNICKING
Ⓡ RESTROOM
Ⓜ MINI-BIKE AREA
Ⓓ TRAILER DUMP STATION
⊢ PIERS
--- TRAIL
Ⓣ PUBLIC TELEPHONE

Facilities & Activities

143 campsites
  48 with water only
  45 with water/electricity
  50 with water/electricity/sewage
35 screened shelters
restrooms
showers
trailer dump station
recreation hall for group day-use and group
  overnight use
group trailer area for 37
picnicking
playgrounds
swimming
water skiing
fishing piers, including 1 lighted pier
fish cleaning shelter
boat ramps
marina concession
4.2 miles of hiking trails

Location

Eisenhower State Recreation Area is 5 miles
northwest of Denison. Travel on US 75A to FM
1310 then 1.8 miles to Park Road 20. The 457-acre
park is located on the shores of Lake Texoma,
formed by the damming of the Red River.

For Information

Eisenhower State Recreation Area
Route 2, Box 50K
Denison, TX 75020
214/465-1956

*On the shore of Lake Texoma, Eisenhower State Park is a
terrific base of operations for lots of fun, including water
skiing.*

Fairfield Lake State Recreation Area

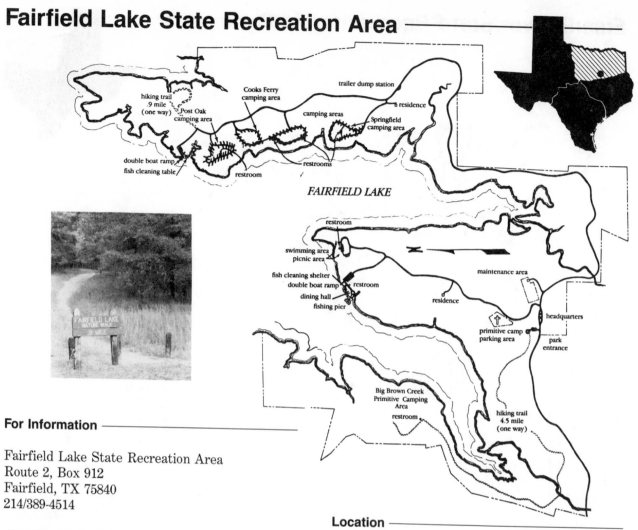

FAIRFIELD LAKE

For Information

Fairfield Lake State Recreation Area
Route 2, Box 912
Fairfield, TX 75840
214/389-4514

Facilities & Activities

135 campsites
  36 with water only
  99 with water/electricity
primitive camping area for backpackers
restrooms
showers
trailer dump station
dining hall for group day-use
amphitheater
picnicking
playgrounds
swimming
water skiing
lighted fishing pier
fish cleaning facilities
boat ramps and docks
9/10-mile nature trail
4½-mile hiking trail leading to the primitive
  camping area
interpretive displays

Location

Fairfield Lake State Recreation Area is located 6
miles northeast of Fairfield. From IH 45 take US
84 east to FM 488 to FM 2570 to the park. The
1,460-acre park is situated on the southern end of
the 2,400-acre Fairfield Lake.

*The picnic area at Fairfield Lake State Recreation Area is
adjacent to the swimming area on the 2,400-acre Fairfield
Lake.*

Fairfield Lake State Recreation Area   17

Fort Richardson State Historical Park

PARK KEY

⊗ HEADQUARTERS
◉ RESIDENCE
Ⓟ PICNIC AREA
Ⓡ RESTROOM
△ GROUP SHELTER
▲ MULTI-USE CAMPSITES
◈ TRAILER DUMP STATION
Ⓝ NATURE TRAIL
Ⓟ PARKING
Ⓗ HIKING TRAIL

HISTORIC SITE KEY

Ⓟ HISTORIC SITE PARKING
① OFFICERS' QUARTERS
② HOSPITAL and MORGUE
③ COMMISSARY
④ BAKERY
⑤ GUARDHOUSE
⑥ MAGAZINE
⑦ BARRACKS
⑧ INTERPRETIVE CENTER

Facilities & Activities

23 campsites with water/electricity
primitive camping area
restrooms
showers
trailer dump station
group picnic area
picnicking
fishing
½-mile nature trail
1.7-mile hiking trail
interpretive center
9 historic structures

Location

Fort Richardson State Historical Park is located 1 mile south of Jacksboro on US 281 and has an 8-acre lake in the park.

For Information

Fort Richardson State Historical Park
P.O. Box 4
Jacksboro, TX 76056
817/567-3506

The Visitor Center at Fort Richardson State Historical Park overlooks the scenic Quarry Lake.

Grapevine Lake

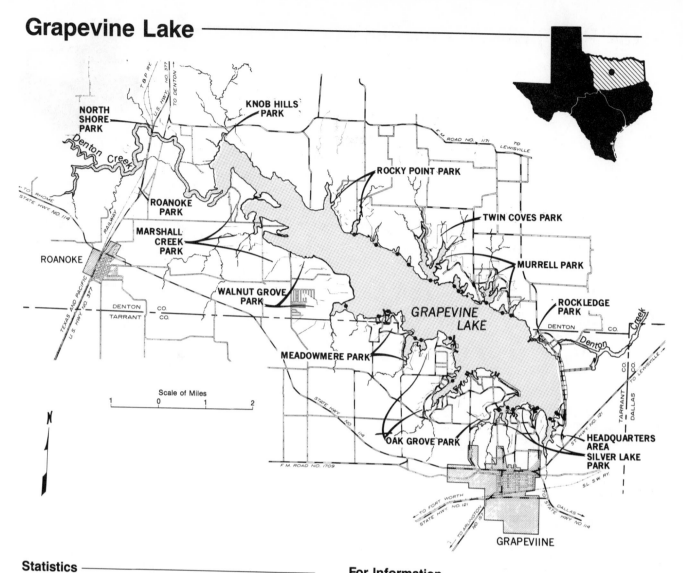

KNOB HILLS PARK

NORTH SHORE PARK

Denton Creek

ROANOKE PARK

ROANOKE

MARSHALL CREEK PARK

WALNUT GROVE PARK

ROCKY POINT PARK

TWIN COVES PARK

MURRELL PARK

GRAPEVINE LAKE

ROCKLEDGE PARK

Denton

MEADOWMERE PARK

OAK GROVE PARK

HEADQUARTERS AREA
SILVER LAKE PARK

GRAPEVINE

Scale of Miles

N

Statistics

Elevation, conservation pool .... 535 feet
Elevation, spillway crest .... 560 feet
Area, conservation pool .... 7,380 acres
Shoreline, conservation pool .... 60 miles

For Information

Reservoir Manager
Grapevine Lake
110 Fairway Drive
Grapevine, TX 76051-3495
817/481-4541

LOCATIONS	FACILITIES	Drinking Water	Sanitary Facilities	Picnic Facilities	Camping Areas	Trailer Areas	Boat Launching Ramps	Shower Facilities	Boat Rental	Fishing Bait & Supplies	Restaurant or Snack Bar
ROCKLEDGE PARK		X	X	X							
MURRELL PARK		X	X	X	X		X			X	X
TWIN COVES PARK		X	X	X	X	X	X	X			
MARSHALL CREEK PARK		X	X	X			X				
MEADOWMERE PARK		X	X	X			X				X
OAK GROVE PARK		X	X	X	X		X		X	X	X
SILVER LAKE PARK		X	X	X	X	X	X	X	X	X	X

Joe Pool Lake

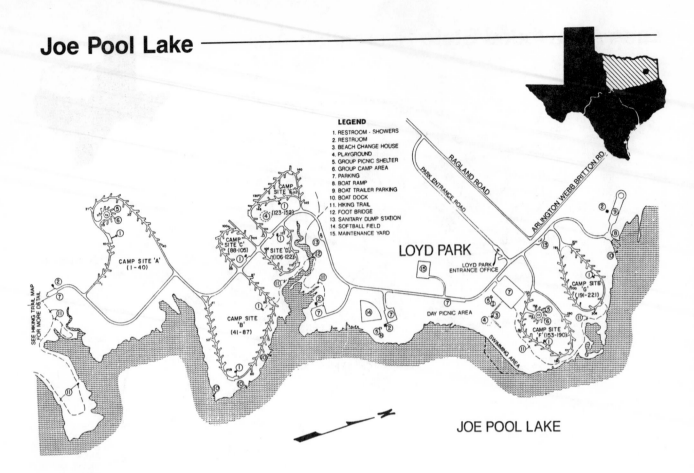

LEGEND
1. RESTROOM - SHOWERS
2. RESTROOM
3. BEACH CHANGE HOUSE
4. PLAYGROUND
5. GROUP PICNIC SHELTER
6. GROUP CAMP AREA
7. PARKING
8. BOAT RAMP
9. BOAT TRAILER PARKING
10. BOAT DOCK
11. HIKING TRAIL
12. FOOT BRIDGE
13. SANITARY DUMP STATION
14. SOFTBALL FIELD
15. MAINTENANCE YARD

JOE POOL LAKE

Location

Joe Pool Lake, created by the impoundment of Mountain Creek and Walnut Creek, is south of IH 20 between Fort Worth and Dallas, east of US 287 and west of US 67 to Midlothian. Loyd Park is on the west side of the western arm of the lake, and Lynn Creek Park, a day-use park, is off of Lakeridge Parkway near the spillway (see location map).

Facilities & Activities at Loyd Park

202 campsites with water & electricity
30 walk-in primitive campsites
2 group camp areas (10 sites each) with shelter
restrooms/showers
trailer dump station
group picnic shelters
picnicking
playgrounds
softball field
swimming beach & bathhouse
boat ramps & docks
hiking trails
*Only group facilities may be reserved
  (817/467-2104)

LOCATION MAP

For Information

Trinity River Authority of Texas
Project Manager
3401 Ragland Road
Grand Prairie, TX 75052
817/467-2104

Lake Arrowhead State Recreation Area

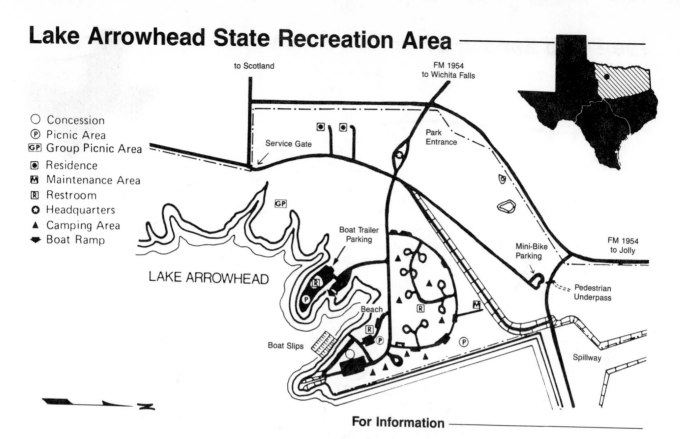

- ○ Concession
- ℗ Picnic Area
- GP Group Picnic Area
- ◉ Residence
- M Maintenance Area
- R Restroom
- O Headquarters
- ▲ Camping Area
- ⬥ Boat Ramp

LAKE ARROWHEAD

to Scotland

FM 1954 to Wichita Falls

Service Gate

Park Entrance

GP

Boat Trailer Parking

Mini-Bike Parking

FM 1954 to Jolly

Pedestrian Underpass

Beach

Boat Slips

Spillway

Facilities & Activities

67 campsites
  19 with water only
  48 with water/electricity
restrooms
showers
trailer dump station
group picnic area
picnicking
swimming beach
water skiing
day-use boat slips
fishing piers
boat ramp
equestrian area
concession

Location

Lake Arrowhead State Recreation Area is located off of US 281, 18 miles southeast of Wichita Falls on FM 1954. The 524-acre park is on the northwest shore of Lake Arrowhead, adjacent to the west end of the three-mile-long earthen dam and spillway.

For Information

Lake Arrowhead State Recreation Area
Route 2, Box 260
Wichita Falls, TX 76301
817/528-2211

This lighted fishing pier at Lake Arrowhead State Recreation Area enables fishermen to try their luck at night.

About the Park

Lake Arrowhead was built in 1965 on the Little Wichita River and covers approximately 13,500 surface acres, with 106 miles of shoreline. The land surrounding the lake is semi-arid, gently rolling prairie, much of which has been invaded by mesquite in recent decades. The lake is dotted with large steel oil derricks, and the waters around these structures frequently yield large stringers of fish.

Lake Bob Sandlin State Recreation Area

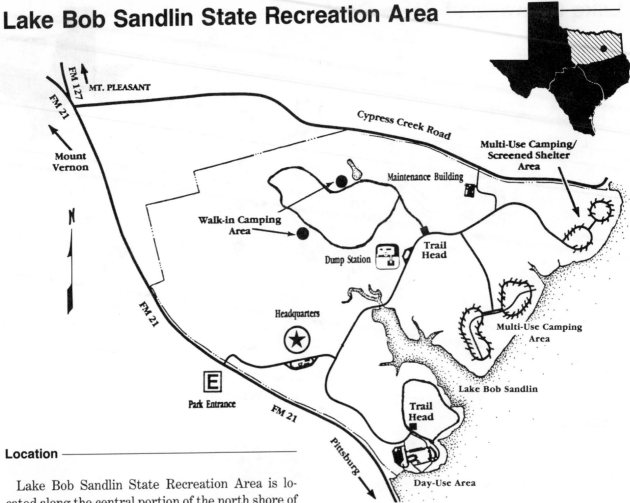

Location

Lake Bob Sandlin State Recreation Area is located along the central portion of the north shore of Lake Bob Sandlin, a 9,460-acre reservoir on Cypress Creek, southwest of Mount Pleasant. The 641-acre park may be reached by FM 21, which bounds the west side of the park.

Facilities & Activities

75 campsites with water/electricity
walk-in primitive campsites (on the 1½-mile hiking trail)
20 screened shelters
restrooms
showers
trailer dump station
group picnic area
picnicking
playground
swimming
water skiing
fishing pier
fish cleaning facility
boat ramps and dock
4 miles of hiking trails

For Information

Lake Bob Sandlin State Recreation Area
Route 5, Box 224
Pittsburg, TX 75686
214/572-5531

Many of the campsites at Lake Bob Sandlin State Recreation Area have covered picnic tables.

Lake Cypress Springs

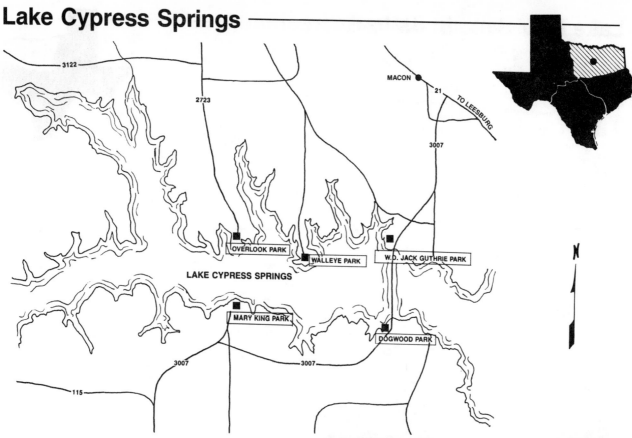

Location

Lake Cypress Springs is located 10 miles south of Mt. Vernon on FM 115 and FM 21. The Franklin County Water District operates 5 public parks at Lake Cypress Springs: 10-acre Dogwood Park; 14-acre Mary King Park; 16-acre Overlook Park; 89-acre Walleye Park; and 30.5-acre W.D. Jack Guthrie Park.

Notes:
Restrooms and drinking water are available at all campgrounds.
Each campground has a swimming area.
Walleye Park has 5 screened shelters available.

The 5 public parks at Lake Cypress Springs are operated by the Franklin County Water District.

Campground	Campsites with water/electricity	Undeveloped Tent Camping	Primitive Sites	Showers	Dump Station	Boat Ramp
Dogwood Park		X				X
Mary King Park	10		X		X	X
Overlook Park		X				X
Walleye Park	52		X	X	X	X
W.D. Jack Guthrie Park	38		X	X	X	

For Information

Franklin County Water District
Lake Cypress Springs
P.O. Box 559
Mt. Vernon, TX 75457
214/537-4536

Lake Lewisville State Park

(Also see page 33, Lewisville Lake)

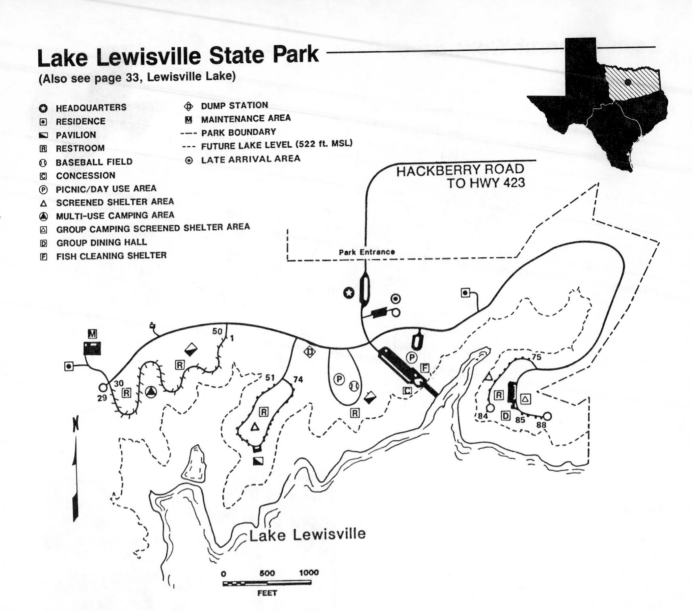

- ⊕ HEADQUARTERS
- ⊡ RESIDENCE
- ◿ PAVILION
- Ⓡ RESTROOM
- Ⓑ BASEBALL FIELD
- Ⓒ CONCESSION
- Ⓟ PICNIC/DAY USE AREA
- △ SCREENED SHELTER AREA
- ▲ MULTI-USE CAMPING AREA
- ◭ GROUP CAMPING SCREENED SHELTER AREA
- Ⓓ GROUP DINING HALL
- Ⓕ FISH CLEANING SHELTER

- ⊕ DUMP STATION
- Ⓜ MAINTENANCE AREA
- --- PARK BOUNDARY
- --- FUTURE LAKE LEVEL (522 ft. MSL)
- ◉ LATE ARRIVAL AREA

HACKBERRY ROAD
TO HWY 423

Park Entrance

Lake Lewisville

0   500   1000
FEET

Facilities & Activities

50 campsites with water/electricity
38 screened shelters
restrooms
showers
trailer dump station
group picnic area
group camping area with 14 screened shelters
group dining hall
picnicking
playgrounds
swimming
water skiing
fishing
fish cleaning facility
boat ramp
softball field
park store (seasonal)

For Information

Lake Lewisville State Park
Route 2, Box 353H
Frisco, TX 75034
214/292-1442

Location

Lake Lewisville State Park is located northwest of Dallas on the east central shore of Lewisville Lake. The 720-acre park may be reached by traveling east from Lewisville on SH 121, then north on FM 423. From Denton, travel east on US 380, then south on FM 423. Turn west on Hackberry Road which leads to the park entrance.

Lake Mineral Wells State Park

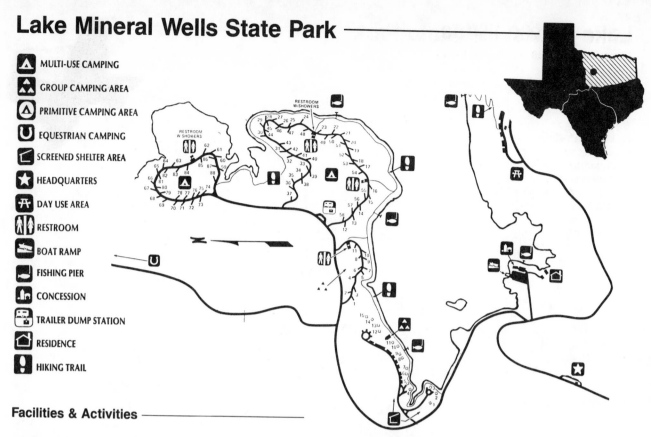

Legend:
- **A** MULTI-USE CAMPING
- **A** GROUP CAMPING AREA
- **A** PRIMITIVE CAMPING AREA
- **U** EQUESTRIAN CAMPING
- **■** SCREENED SHELTER AREA
- **★** HEADQUARTERS
- **🎋** DAY USE AREA
- **🚻** RESTROOM
- **■** BOAT RAMP
- **■** FISHING PIER
- **■** CONCESSION
- **■** TRAILER DUMP STATION
- **■** RESIDENCE
- **🚶** HIKING TRAIL

Facilities & Activities

90 campsites
  10 with water only (tents)
  80 with water/electricity
primitive camping areas for backpackers
equestrian camping area
restrooms
showers
trailer dump station
group camp with 15 screened shelters
group dining hall
picnicking
swimming
fishing piers, including 1 lighted pier
fish cleaning facility
boat ramp and dock
boats, canoes & pedal boats for rent
5 miles of hiking trails
8½ miles of horseback trails
concession

Location

Lake Mineral Wells State Park is situated only 4 miles from the center of town. The park contains 2,809 acres, which include a 646-acre lake, and may be reached by traveling 4 miles east from the city of Mineral Wells on US 180, or 15 miles west of Weatherford on the same highway.

For Information

Lake Mineral Wells State Park
Route 4, Box 39C
Mineral Wells, TX 76067
817/328-1171

When you visit Lake Mineral Wells State Park, don't forget to explore the deep canyons located near the day-use area; steps and a trail, near an overlook, lead to the bottom.

Lake O' the Pines

Statistics

Elevation, conservation pool .... 228 feet
Elevation, spillway crest .... 249 feet
Area, conservation pool .... 18,700 acres

For Information

Reservoir Manager
Lake O' the Pines
P.O. Drawer W
Jefferson, TX 75657-0660
214/665-2336

Campground	Group Camping Area	Trailer Dump Station	Tent/Trailer Camping	Swimming Beach	Shelters	Restaurant	Drinking Water	Picnic Area	Electrical Outlets
Alley Creek	X	X	X	X	X		X	X	X
Brushy Creek		X	X	X	X		X	X	X
Buckhorn Creek Park			X		X		X	X	X
Cedar Springs Park	X	X	X				X	X	
Copeland Park			X				X		
Hurricane Creek			X				X	X	
Johnson Creek	X		X	X	X		X	X	X
Lakeside Park			X	X	X		X	X	
Lone Star Park			X				X		
Mims Chapel			X				X		
Oak Valley Park			X				X	X	
Overlook			X				X	X	
Pine Hill			X				X		
Shady Grove Park		X	X			X	X	X	

Notes:
Comfort stations are available at all campgrounds.
All campgrounds are equipped for boat launching.

As these folks know, when the sun goes down and the campfire starts dancing in the night, it's "marshmallow time."

Sunsets, such as this one at Lake Livingston State Recreation Area (page 67), are especially relaxing after a busy day.

Lake Mineral Wells (page 25) is only four miles from the center of its namesake.

From this tranquil cove on Lake O'the Pines (page 26) it is easy to see how the 18,000-acre lake got its name.

MICKEY LITTLE

Around a campfire is the perfect place to swap stories of the day's adventures.

TEXAS HIGHWAYS

TEXAS HIGHWAYS

A novice may see nothing but trees in this photo, but the experienced hiker/camper may recognize this leg of the Moscow trail of the Texas Woodland Trails System. (See *Hiking and Backpacking Trails of Texas*/Third Edition by M. Little, Lone Star Books, Houston).

TEXAS HIGHWAYS

This scene at Lake Sam Rayburn (page 78) depicts the perfect find for almost all campers and picnickers—an unoccupied, shaded table, down by the water.

Lake Tawakoni

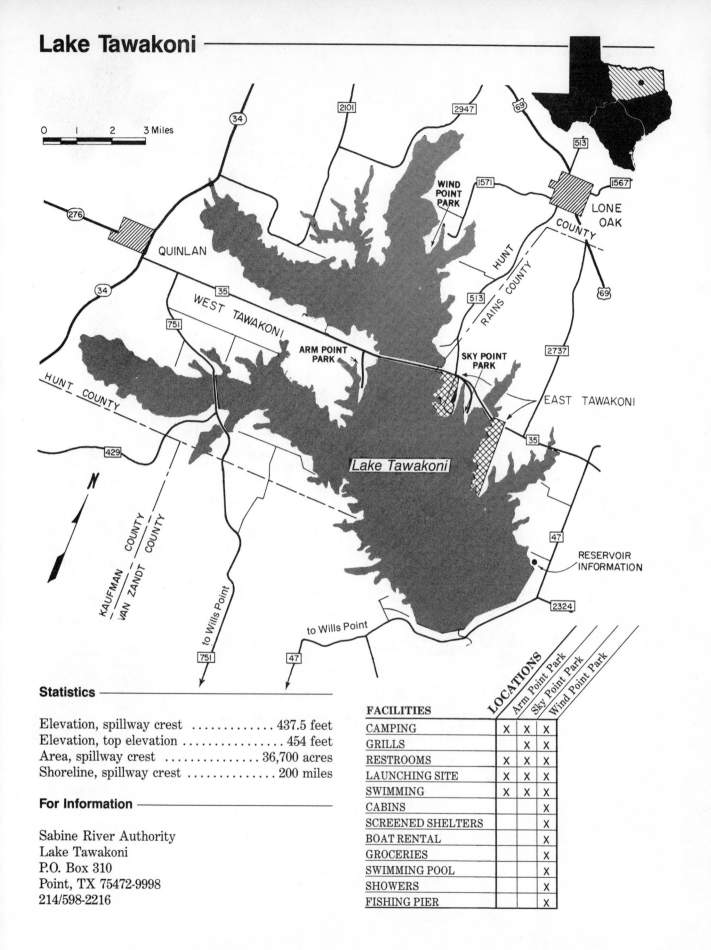

0   1   2   3 Miles

Statistics

Elevation, spillway crest .... 437.5 feet
Elevation, top elevation .... 454 feet
Area, spillway crest .... 36,700 acres
Shoreline, spillway crest .... 200 miles

For Information

Sabine River Authority
Lake Tawakoni
P.O. Box 310
Point, TX 75472-9998
214/598-2216

FACILITIES	Arm Point Park	Sky Point Park	Wind Point Park
CAMPING	X	X	X
GRILLS		X	X
RESTROOMS	X	X	X
LAUNCHING SITE	X	X	X
SWIMMING	X	X	X
CABINS			X
SCREENED SHELTERS			X
BOAT RENTAL			X
GROCERIES			X
SWIMMING POOL			X
SHOWERS			X
FISHING PIER			X

Lake Texoma

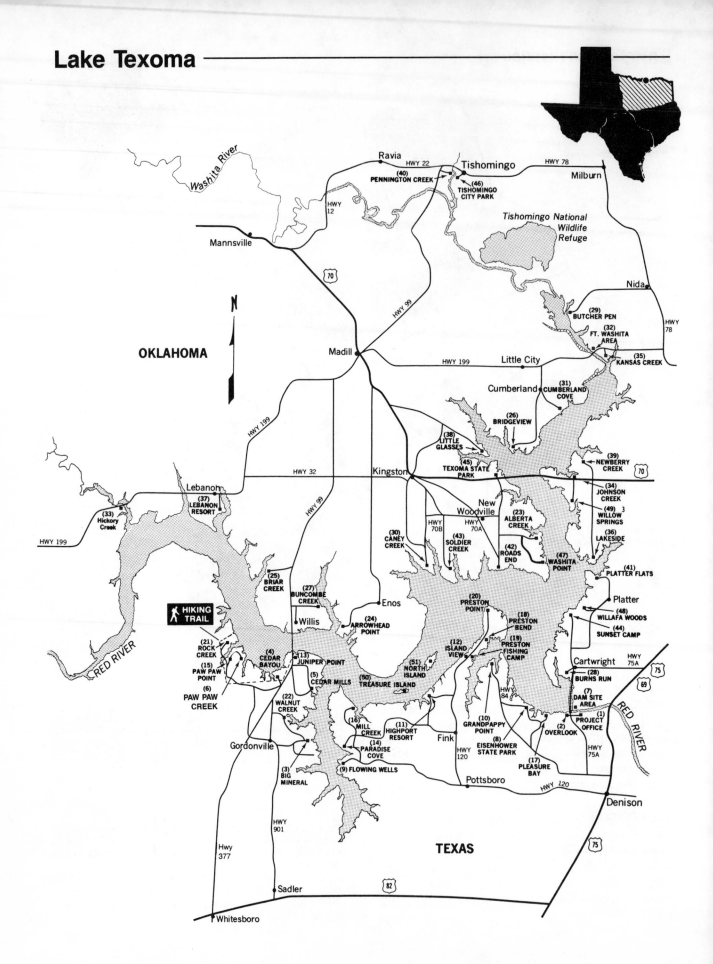

Lake Texoma *(continued)*

Sailboarding has become a popular activity on Texas lakes; it's a challenge at any age.

Campground	Boat Launching Ramp	Picnic Area	Designated Campsites	Drinking Water	Group Shelter	Showers	Swimming Beach	Trailer Dump Station	Concession Service
Big Mineral Camp	X	X	X	X	X				X	X
Cedar Bayou Resort	X	X	X	X	X					X
Cedar Mills Resort	X	X	X	X	X			X	X	X
Dam Site Area	X	X	X	X	X				X	X
Eisenhower State Park	X	X	X	X	X	X	X	X	X
Flowing Wells Camp	X	X	X	X	X				X	X
Grandpappy Point Resort	X	X	X	X	X					X
Highport Resort	X	X	X	X	X					X
Island View Rec. Area	X	X	X	X						X
Juniper Point	X	X	X	X	X	X	X	X	
Mill Creek Resort	X	X	X	X	X			X		X
Overlook				X					
Paradise Cove	X	X	X							X
Paw Paw Point Rec. Area	X	X	X							
Paw Paw Creek Resort	X	X	X							X
Preston Bend Rec. Area	X		X	X	X		X		
Preston Bend Resort	X	X	X	X	X					X
Preston Fishing Camp	X	X	X	X	X	X	X	X	X
Resident Office				X					
Rock Creek Camp	X	X	X	X	X					X
Walnut Creek Resort	X	X	X	X	X				X	X

Notes:
Restrooms are available at all campgrounds.
Eisenhower State Park and Juniper Point are equipped with electrical outlets.
A nature trail is provided at Cedar Bayou Resort, Eisenhower State Park, Juniper Point, Paw Paw Point Recreation Area, Paw Paw Creek Resort, and Rock Creek Camp.

Statistics

Elevation, top power pool . . . . 617 feet
Elevation, top flood control pool . . . . 640 feet
Area, top power pool . . . . 89,000 acres
Shoreline, top power pool . . . . 580 miles

About the Lake

Quasi-public organized camps, private clubs, and individual private cottage sites have been extensively developed at Lake Texoma. There are good camping facilities on both the Texas and Oklahoma sides of the lake. There are also 23 private resorts on the waterfront and dozens of others within a short distance from the lake. The 457-acre Eisenhower State Recreation Area has a large marina and one of the finest camping and public use parks in Texas.

More than 500 species of birds have been sighted at Lake Texoma, including the rare whooping crane. Bird lovers may get a close look at many of the species at the lake's two national wildlife refuges administered by the U.S. Fish and Wildlife Service. The Tishomingo Refuge, three miles south of Tishomingo, contains 13,450 acres, while Hagerman Refuge, 15 miles west of Denison, has 11,430 acres.

For Information

Project Manager
Lake Texoma
Route 4, Box 493
Denison, TX 75020
214/465-4990

Lake Texoma, formed by the Red River between Texas and Oklahoma, is one of the most popular Army Corps of Engineers lakes in the nation. The damsite is near Denison, Tx.

Lake Whitney State Recreation Area

For Information

Lake Whitney State Recreation Area
Box 1175
Whitney, TX 76692
817/694-3793

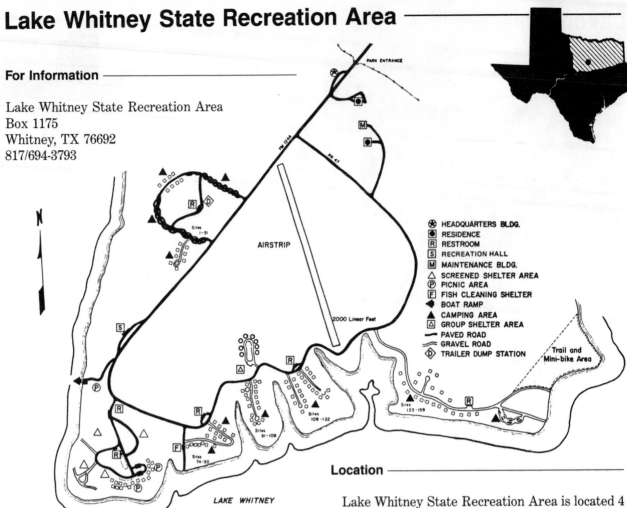

AIRSTRIP

2000 Linear Feet

Sites 1-51

Sites 74-90

Sites 91-108

Sites 109-132

Sites 133-159

Trail and Mini-bike Area

LAKE WHITNEY

PARK ENTRANCE

⊗ HEADQUARTERS BLDG.
◉ RESIDENCE
Ⓡ RESTROOM
Ⓢ RECREATION HALL
Ⓜ MAINTENANCE BLDG.
△ SCREENED SHELTER AREA
Ⓟ PICNIC AREA
Ⓕ FISH CLEANING SHELTER
◀ BOAT RAMP
▲ CAMPING AREA
◬ GROUP SHELTER AREA
— PAVED ROAD
⩙ GRAVEL ROAD
◈ TRAILER DUMP STATION

Facilities & Activities

137 campsites
   95 with water only
   7 with water/electricity
   35 with water/electricity/sewage
48 screened shelters
restrooms
showers
trailer dump station
group screened shelter camp
recreation hall
picnicking
playground
swimming beach
water skiing
fishing
fish cleaning facility
boat ramp
mini-bike area
airstrip

Location

Lake Whitney State Recreation Area is located 4 miles southwest of Whitney on FM 1244. The 955-acre park fronts the east side of Lake Whitney, which extends 45 river miles along the Brazos River.

The picnic area at Lake Whitney State Recreation Area has beautiful shade trees, as well as an excellent view of the lake.

Lavon Lake

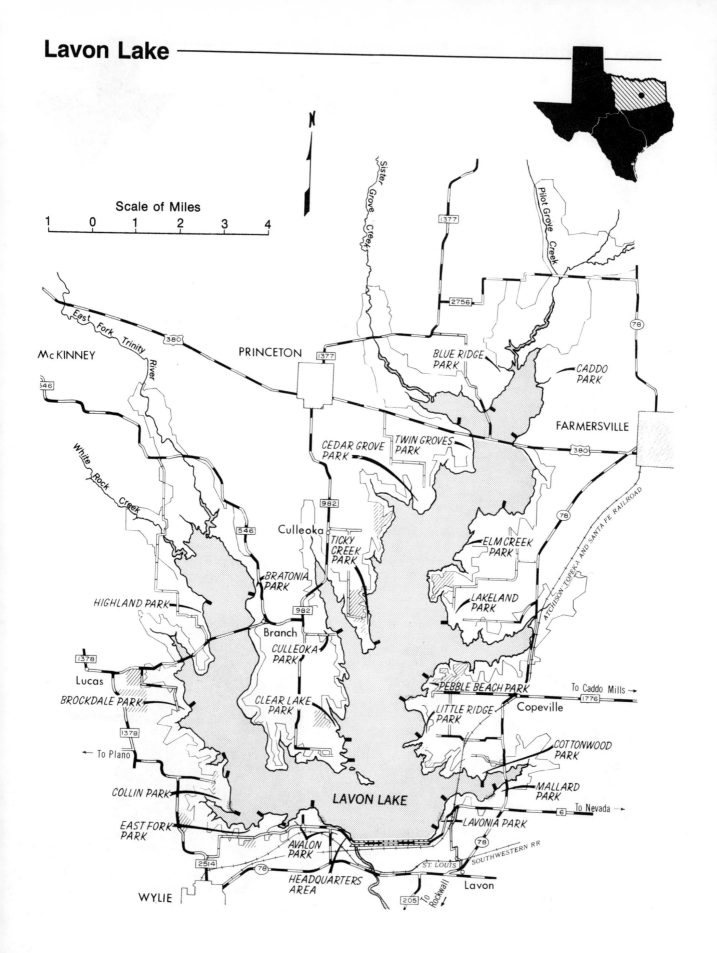

Scale of Miles

1   0   1   2   3   4

N

McKINNEY

East Fork Trinity River

380

PRINCETON

1377

Sister Grove Creek

1377

2756

Pilot Grove Creek

78

BLUE RIDGE PARK

CADDO PARK

FARMERSVILLE

546

White Rock Creek

CEDAR GROVE PARK

TWIN GROVES PARK

380

546

982

Culleoka

TICKY CREEK PARK

ELM CREEK PARK

78

ATCHISON, TOPEKA AND SANTA FE RAILROAD

BRATONIA PARK

LAKELAND PARK

HIGHLAND PARK

982

Branch

CULLEOKA PARK

1378

Lucas

BROCKDALE PARK

CLEAR LAKE PARK

PEBBLE BEACH PARK

To Caddo Mills →

1776

Copeville

1378

LITTLE RIDGE PARK

← To Plano

COTTONWOOD PARK

COLLIN PARK

MALLARD PARK

To Nevada →

6

LAVON LAKE

EAST FORK PARK

LAVONIA PARK

2514

AVALON PARK

78

HEADQUARTERS AREA

ST. LOUIS

SOUTHWESTERN RR

78

WYLIE

205

To Rockwall →

Lavon

Lavon Lake (continued)

FACILITIES	Picnic Facilities	Camping Area	Trailer Area	Electrical Outlets	Sanitary Facilities	Drinking Water	Trailer Dump Station	Shower Facilities	Group Shelter (Picnic)	Swimming Area	Boat Launching Ramp	Fishing Bait & Supplies	Hiking Trails	Restaurant or Snack Bar	Boat Storage (Rental)	Fishing Barge	Boat & Motor Rental	Courtesy Dock	Area for Handicapped
AVALON PARK	X			X	X				X	X	X							X	
* BLUE RIDGE PARK											X	X							
BRATONIA PARK			X								X								X
BROCKDALE PARK				X	X						X							X	X
CADDO PARK				X	X						X								
* CEDAR GROVE PARK	X			X	X			X			X	X		X		X		X	
CLEAR LAKE PARK	X			X	X		X			X	X			X	X			X	
COLLIN PARK	X	X	X	X	X	X	X	X		X	X			X	X			X	
* COTTONWOOD PARK																			
* CULLEOKA PARK											X	X	X	X	X		X	X	
EAST FORK PARK	X	X	X	X	X	X	X	X	X		X							X	
ELM CREEK PARK			X								X								
HIGHLAND PARK			X								X								
LAKELAND PARK	X			X	X			X			X							X	
LAVONIA PARK	X	X	X	X	X	X	X	X	X	X	X							X	
LITTLE RIDGE PARK	X	X	X	X	X	X	X	X	X		X							X	
MALLARD PARK				X	X					X	X							X	
PEBBLE BEACH PARK	X			X	X					X	X							X	
TICKY CREEK	X			X	X						X							X	
TWIN GROVES PARK			X								X								

* Closed to vehicles

Statistics

Elevation, conservation pool .... 492 feet
Elevation, spillway crest 503.5
Area, conservation pool .... 21,400 acres
Shoreline, conservation pool .... 121 miles

For Information

Reservoir Manager
Lavon Lake
P.O. Box 429
Wylie, TX 75098-0429
214/442-5711

This proud fisherman is enjoying one of the many forms of recreation you'll find at Lavon Lake. Twenty public parks around the lake offer a wide range of facilities and activities; four parks have camping areas.

This youngster knows the importance of wearing a PFD (personal flotation device) while enjoying a day at the lake.

Lewisville Lake

(Also see page 24, Lewisville Lake State Park)

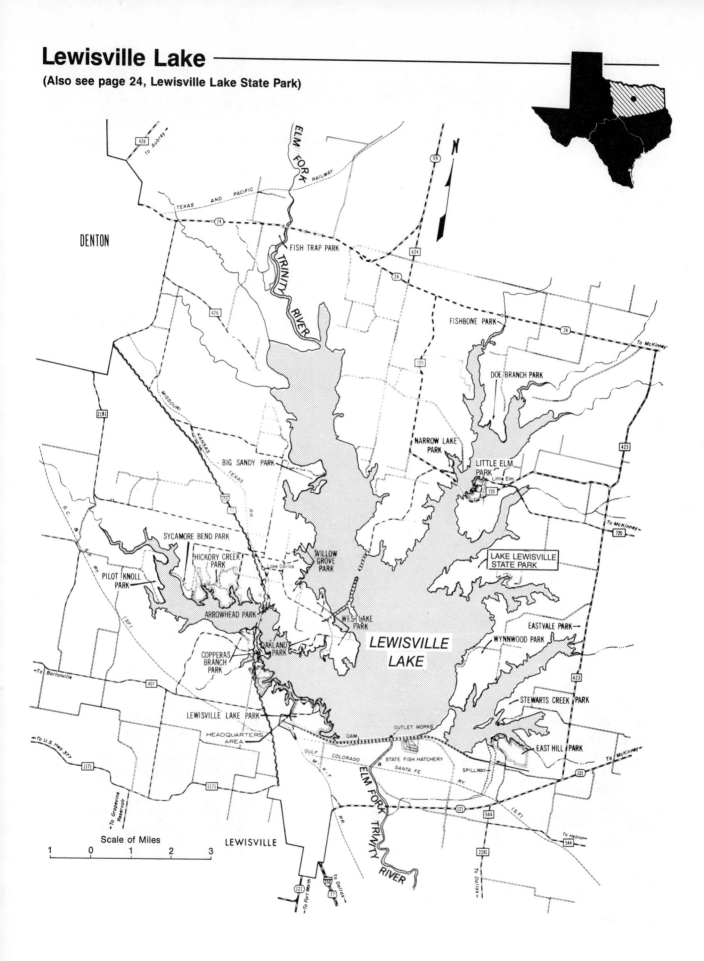

Lewisville Lake (continued)

Fishing from the bank allows you to move around a lot; these young, active boys do plenty of that.

Lots of activity is evident at this marina located on Lewisville Lake.

Statistics

Elevation, conservation pool .... 522 feet
Elevation, spillway crest .... 532 feet
Area, conservation pool .... 29,592 acres
Shoreline, conservation pool .... 250 miles

For Information

Reservoir Manager
Lewisville Lake
1801 N. Mill St.
Lewisville, TX 75067-1821
214/434-1666

LOCATION	Picnic Facilities	Camping Area	Trailer Area	Electrical Outlet	Sanitary Facilities	Drinking Water	Trailer Dump Station	Shower Facilities	Group Shelter	Swimming Site	Boat Launching Ramp	Fishing Bait & Supplies	Boat Storage (Rental)
EAST HILL PARK	X				X	X	X	X	X	X	X	X	
STEWARTS CREEK PARK	X	X	X		X	X	X		X	X	X		
EASTVALE PARK	X	X	X		X						X		
LAKE LEWISVILLE STATE PARK	X	X	X	X	X	X	X	X	X		X	X	
LITTLE ELM PARK	X				X	X			X		X		
BIG SANDY RAMP											X		
WILLOW GROVE PARK	X	X	X		X	X			X		X	X	X
WESTLAKE PARK	X				X	X		X	X	X	X	X	X
OAKLAND PARK		X	X	X	X	X	X	X	X		X		
ARROWHEAD PARK					X	X					X		
HICKORY CREEK RAMP											X		
SYCAMORE BEND PARK	X	X			X	X					X		
PILOT KNOLL PARK	X	X	X	X	X	X	X	X	X		X		
WEST COPPERAS BRANCH PARK	X	X	X		X	X	X			X	X		
EAST COPPERAS BRANCH PARK					X						X		
LEWISVILLE LAKE PARK	X	X	X	X	X	X	X	X	X	X	X	X	X

Notes:
Lewisville Lake Park provides a golf course and fishing barge.
Restaurants or snack facilities are available at Westlake Park and Lewisville Lake Park.
Fish cleaning houses are available at Lake Lewisville State Park and Lewisville Lake Park.

Martin Creek Lake State Recreation Area

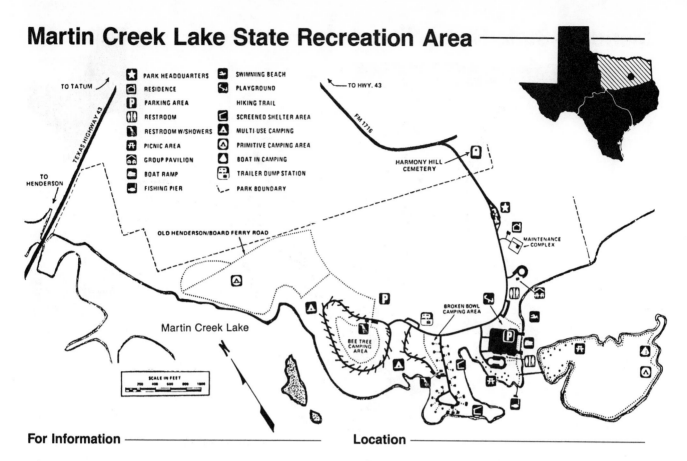

PARK HEADQUARTERS
RESIDENCE
PARKING AREA
RESTROOM
RESTROOM W/SHOWERS
PICNIC AREA
GROUP PAVILION
BOAT RAMP
FISHING PIER

SWIMMING BEACH
PLAYGROUND
HIKING TRAIL
SCREENED SHELTER AREA
MULTI USE CAMPING
PRIMITIVE CAMPING AREA
BOAT IN CAMPING
TRAILER DUMP STATION
PARK BOUNDARY

TO TATUM
TO HENDERSON
TEXAS HIGHWAY 43
TO HWY. 43
FM 1716
HARMONY HILL CEMETERY
OLD HENDERSON/BOARD FERRY ROAD
MAINTENANCE COMPLEX
Martin Creek Lake
BEE TREE CAMPING AREA
BROKEN BOWL CAMPING AREA
SCALE IN FEET

For Information

Martin Creek Lake State Recreation Area
Route 2, Box 20
Tatum, TX 75691
214/836-4336

Facilities & Activities

60 campsites with water/electricity
2 primitive camping areas
hike-in camping
boat-in camping
21 screened shelters
restrooms
showers
trailer dump station
group pavilion
picnicking
playground
swimming beach
water skiing
lighted fishing pier
boat ramps
3 miles of hiking trails

Location

Martin Creek Lake State Recreation Area is located 20 miles southeast of Longview. The 286-acre park may be reached by driving 3 miles southwest of Tatum on SH 43, then turning south on FM 1716. The park is located on 5,000-acre Martin Creek Lake, constructed to provide cooling water for a lignite-fired, electric power generation plant. The plant warms the lake water in cold months, producing excellent year-round fishing for largemouth bass, crappie, channel catfish, and sunfish.

Access to the island at Martin Creek Lake State Recreation Area is via this charming wooden bridge; a picnic area and one of the primitive camping areas are located on the island.

Meridian State Recreation Area

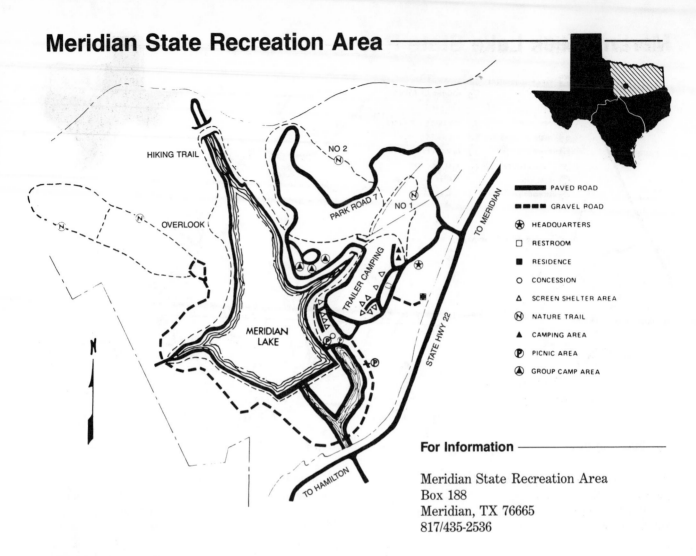

HIKING TRAIL

NO 2

OVERLOOK

PARK ROAD 7

NO 1

TRAILER CAMPING

TO MERIDIAN

MERIDIAN LAKE

STATE HWY 22

N

TO HAMILTON

	PAVED ROAD
	GRAVEL ROAD
✪	HEADQUARTERS
☐	RESTROOM
■	RESIDENCE
○	CONCESSION
△	SCREEN SHELTER AREA
Ⓝ	NATURE TRAIL
▲	CAMPING AREA
Ⓟ	PICNIC AREA
⊕	GROUP CAMP AREA

For Information

Meridian State Recreation Area
Box 188
Meridian, TX 76665
817/435-2536

Facilities & Activities

15 campsites
  7 with water/electricity
  8 with water/electricity/sewage
tent camping area
11 screened shelters
restrooms
showers
trailer dump station
open air pavilion
7 screened shelters in group camp
group dining hall
picnicking
playground
swimming
fishing
boat ramp
paddle boats for rent (seasonal)
5 miles of trails (3 nature & 1 hiking)
concession (seasonal)
scenic drive

Location

Meridian State Recreation Area is located 4 miles southwest of Meridian off of SH 22, north on Park Road 7. There is a 73-acre lake in the park.

Four of the 11 screened shelters at Meridian State Recreation Area are located on the shoreline of the park's 73-acre lake.

Navarro Mills Lake

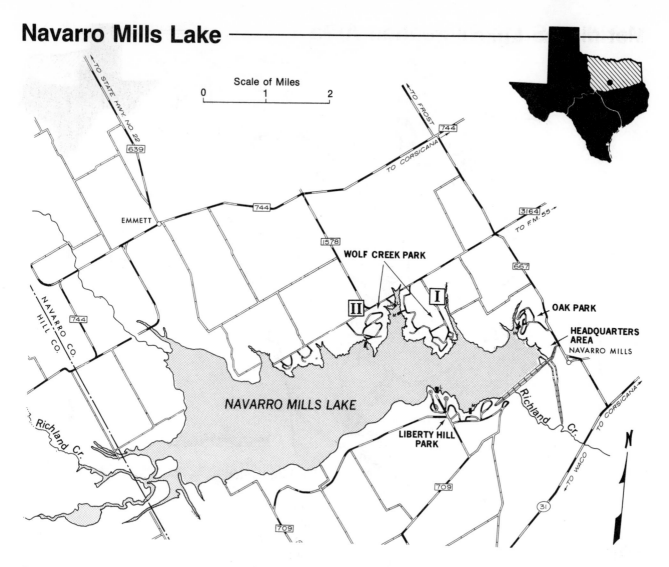

Statistics

Elevation, conservation pool .... 424.5 feet
Elevation, flood control pool .... 443 feet
Area, conservation pool .... 5,070 acres
Shoreline, conservation pool .... 38 miles

For Information

Reservoir Manager
Navarro Mills Lake
Route 1, Box 33D
Purdon, TX 76679-9707
817/578-1431

LOCATION	Drinking Water	Restrooms	Picnic	Camping	Trailer	Fishing Pier	Shower	Group Picnic Shelter	Boat Ramp	Boat Storage	Boat & Motor Rental	Fishing Bait & Supplies	Snack Bar
OAK PARK	X	X	X	X	X	X	X	X	X				
WOLF CREEK PARK I	X	X	X	X	X	X	X	X	X				
WOLF CREEK PARK II	X	X	X	X	X			X					
LIBERTY HILL PARK	X	X	X	X	X	X	X	X	X	X	X	X	X

Pat Mayse Lake

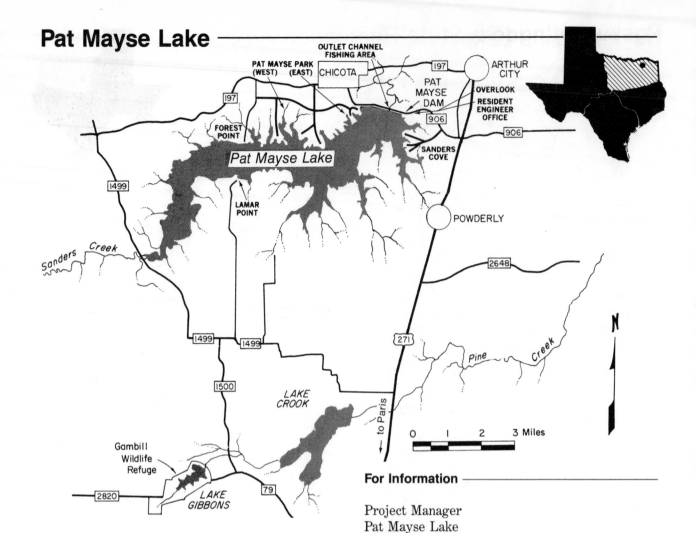

Statistics

Elevation, conservation pool . . . . 451 feet
Elevation, flood control pool . . . . 460.5 feet
Area, conservation pool . . . . 5,993 acres
Shoreline, conservation pool . . . . 67 miles

LOCATION	FACILITIES	Boat Launching Ramp	Picnic Area	Designated Campsites	Drinking Water	Restrooms	Swimming Beach	Trailer Dump Station
OVERLOOK						X		
FOREST POINT		(Area closed)						
LAMAR POINT		X	X	X	X	X	X	X
PAT MAYSE EAST		X	X	X	X	X	X	X
PAT MAYSE WEST		X	X	X	X	X	X	X
SANDERS COVE		X	X	X	X	X	X	X

Notes:
Showers and electrical hookups are available at Pat Mayse West. Sanders Cove provides electrical hook-ups.

For Information

Project Manager
Pat Mayse Lake
Route 1, Box 565
Powderly, TX 75473
214/732-3020

Jet skis are gaining in popularity on the larger Texas lakes.

Possum Kingdom State Recreation Area

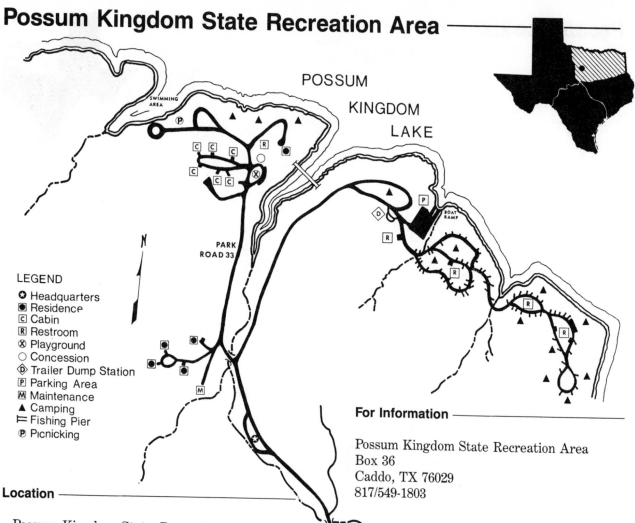

POSSUM

KINGDOM

LAKE

SWIMMING AREA

PARK ROAD 33

BOAT RAMP

LEGEND
- ✪ Headquarters
- ▣ Residence
- ⓒ Cabin
- Ⓡ Restroom
- ⊗ Playground
- ○ Concession
- ◈ Trailer Dump Station
- Ⓟ Parking Area
- Ⓜ Maintenance
- ▲ Camping
- ⊨ Fishing Pier
- Ⓟ Picnicking

Location

Possum Kingdom State Recreation Area is located 18 miles north of Caddo on PR 33 off of US 180. The 1,615-acre park is located on the southwestern shoreline of the 19,800-acre Possum Kingdom Lake.

Facilities & Activities

116 campsites
  58 with water only
  58 with water/electricity
6 cabins
restrooms
showers
trailer dump station
picnicking
swimming
water skiing
lighted fishing pier
boat ramp
boats for rent
park store
Texas Longhorn Herd

For Information

Possum Kingdom State Recreation Area
Box 36
Caddo, TX 76029
817/549-1803

Campers aren't the only ones who enjoy spending a day at the lake; Great Blue Herons enjoy it too.

Proctor Lake

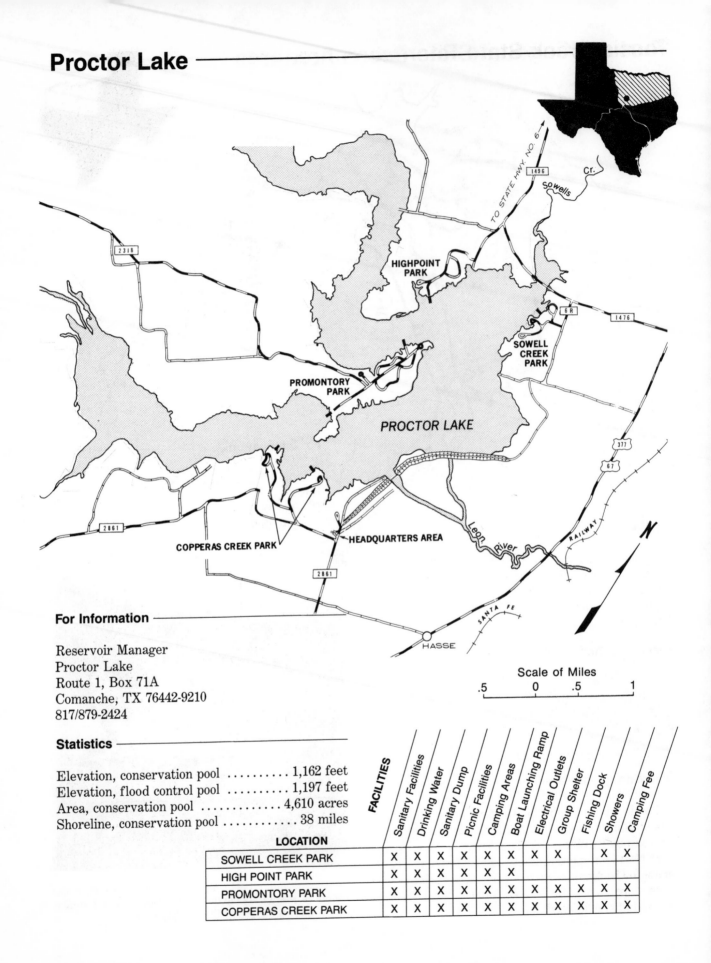

HIGHPOINT PARK

SOWELL CREEK PARK

PROMONTORY PARK

PROCTOR LAKE

COPPERAS CREEK PARK

HEADQUARTERS AREA

Leon River

SANTA FE

RAILWAY

HASSE

Sowells Cr.

TO STATE HWY. NO. 6

For Information

Reservoir Manager
Proctor Lake
Route 1, Box 71A
Comanche, TX 76442-9210
817/879-2424

Scale of Miles

.5   0   .5   1

Statistics

Elevation, conservation pool .... 1,162 feet
Elevation, flood control pool .... 1,197 feet
Area, conservation pool .... 4,610 acres
Shoreline, conservation pool .... 38 miles

LOCATION	FACILITIES: Sanitary Facilities	Drinking Water	Sanitary Dump	Picnic Facilities	Camping Areas	Boat Launching Ramp	Electrical Outlets	Group Shelter	Fishing Dock	Showers	Camping Fee
SOWELL CREEK PARK	X	X	X	X	X	X	X	X		X	X
HIGH POINT PARK	X	X	X	X	X	X					
PROMONTORY PARK	X	X	X	X	X	X	X	X	X	X	X
COPPERAS CREEK PARK	X	X	X	X	X	X	X	X	X	X	X

Purtis Creek State Recreation Area

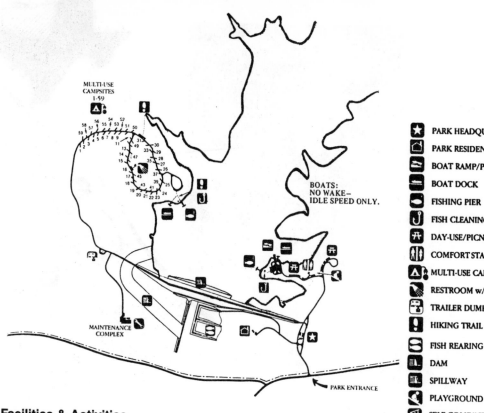

MULTI-USE
CAMPSITES
1-59

BOATS:
NO WAKE–
IDLE SPEED ONLY.

MAINTENANCE
COMPLEX

PARK ENTRANCE

★	PARK HEADQUARTERS
	PARK RESIDENCE
	BOAT RAMP/PARKING
	BOAT DOCK
	FISHING PIER
	FISH CLEANING AREA
	DAY-USE/PICNIC AREA
	COMFORT STATION (NO SHOWERS)
	MULTI-USE CAMPING AREA
	RESTROOM w/SHOWERS
	TRAILER DUMP STATION
	HIKING TRAIL
	FISH REARING PONDS
	DAM
	SPILLWAY
	PLAYGROUND
	SELF-COMPOSTING TOILET

Facilities & Activities

59 campsites with water/electricity
30 primitive walk-in campsites
restrooms
showers
trailer dump station
picnicking
playground
lighted fishing piers
fish cleaning facilities
boat ramp and docks
50 boats maximum allowed on lake at one time (boat
   permits may be reserved in advance)
$5 per day boating fee
fishing bag limits are in effect (including catch-and-
   release-only on all species of bass)
1¼-mile loop hiking trail to walk-in campsites

Location

Purtis Creek State Recreation Area is located
about 65 miles southeast of Dallas and can be
reached by traveling US 175 to Eustace, then north
on FM 316 for approximately 3 miles to the park entrance. The facilities at this 1,533-acre park are designed primarily for recreational fishing on the
park's unique 355-acre lake.

For Information

Purtis Creek State Recreation Area
Route 1, Box 506
Eustace, TX 75124
214/425-2332

*This large motorhome has an ideal campsite near the
shore of the park's 355-acre lake, known for its superb
fishing.*

Rusk-Palestine State Park

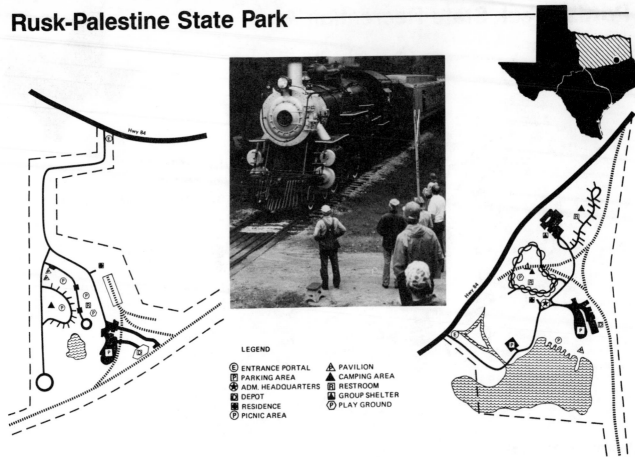

LEGEND

- Ⓔ ENTRANCE PORTAL
- Ⓟ PARKING AREA
- ✪ ADM. HEADQUARTERS
- Ⓓ DEPOT
- Ⓡ RESIDENCE
- Ⓟ PICNIC AREA
- ▲ PAVILION
- ▲ CAMPING AREA
- Ⓡ RESTROOM
- Ⓐ GROUP SHELTER
- Ⓟ PLAY GROUND

Facilities & Activities

Rusk Unit

94 campsites
   16 tent sites with water/electricity
   46 group trailer sites with water/electricity
   32 with water/electricity/sewage
restrooms
showers
trailer dump station
open air gazebo-style pavilion with kitchenette and
   dining area
screened group shelter with kitchen
15 picnic sites
playground
2 tennis courts
swimming
15-acre lake with fishing pier
Rusk depot of the Texas State Railroad

Palestine Unit

12 campsites with water only
restrooms
2 group picnic pavilions
48 picnic sites
playground
Palestine depot of the historic Texas State Railroad

For Information

Rusk-Palestine State Park
Route 4, Box 431
Rusk, TX 75785
214/683-5126

Location

Rusk-Palestine State Park is adjacent to US 84 between Rusk and Palestine in the Piney Woods of East Texas. The park is located at each end of the Texas State Railroad State Historical Park, which offers 50-mile rides on antique coaches pulled by turn-of-the-century steam engines.

About the Texas State Railroad

The railroad was built in 1896 to haul iron ore to a state-owned smelter. The round trip, from either Rusk or Palestine, takes about four hours, including an hour-long stop for lunch. Separate trains are operated from each depot. Advance reservations are recommended. Contact: Texas State Railroad State Historical Park, P.O. Box 39, Rusk, TX 75785. Phone 1-800-442-8951 (in-Texas reservations) or 214/683-2561 (Information and out-of-Texas calls).

Tyler State Park

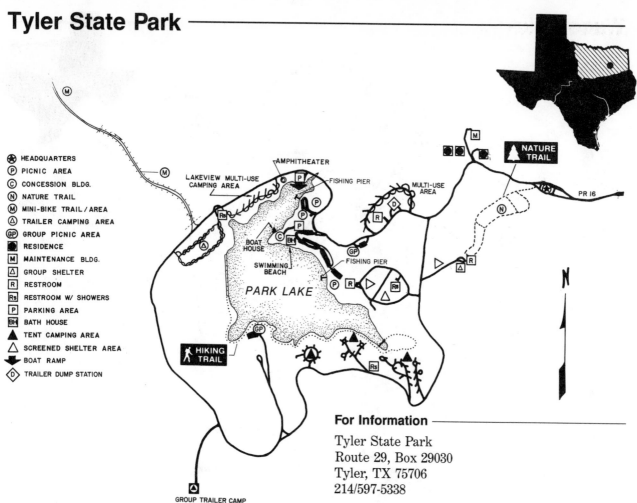

Facilities & Activities

117 campsites
  40 with water only
  38 with water/electricity
  39 with water/electricity/sewage
35 screened shelters
restrooms
showers
trailer dump station
group picnic area
screened group camp (max. 100) with kitchen
group trailer area with 30 sites
amphitheater
picnicking
swimming beach & bathhouse
fishing piers
boat ramp
boats, canoes & pedal boats for rent (seasonal)
¾-mile nature trail
2½-mile hiking trail
mini-bike trail
concessions

For Information

Tyler State Park
Route 29, Box 29030
Tyler, TX 75706
214/597-5338

Location

Tyler State Park is located on Park Road 16 off of FM 14 approximately 8 miles north of Tyler. This 985-acre park has a 64-acre lake.

The 400-foot beach at Tyler State Park provides an excellent area for swimming.

Waco Lake

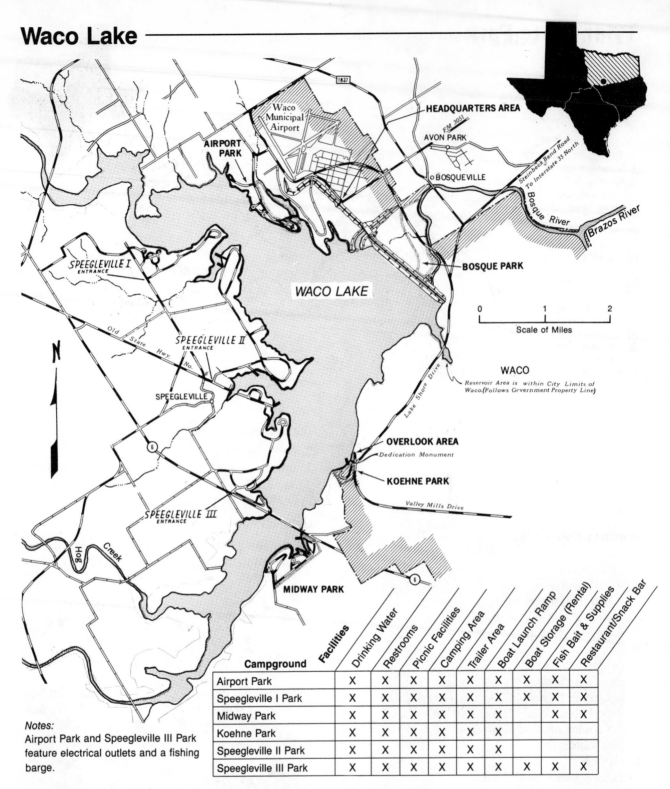

Facilities / Campground	Drinking Water	Restrooms	Picnic Facilities	Camping Area	Trailer Area	Boat Launch Ramp	Boat Storage (Rental)	Fish Bait & Supplies	Restaurant/Snack Bar
Airport Park	X	X	X	X	X	X	X	X	X
Speegleville I Park	X	X	X	X	X	X	X	X	X
Midway Park	X	X	X	X	X	X		X	X
Koehne Park	X	X	X	X	X	X			
Speegleville II Park	X	X	X	X	X	X			
Speegleville III Park	X	X	X	X	X	X	X	X	X

Notes:
Airport Park and Speegleville III Park feature electrical outlets and a fishing barge.

Statistics

Elevation, conservation pool .... 455 feet
Elevation, spillway crest .... 465 feet
Area, conservation pool .... 7,270 acres
Shoreline, conservation pool .... 60 miles

For Information

Reservoir Manager
Waco Lake
Route 10, Box 173-G
Waco, TX 76708-9602
817/756-5359

Whitney Lake

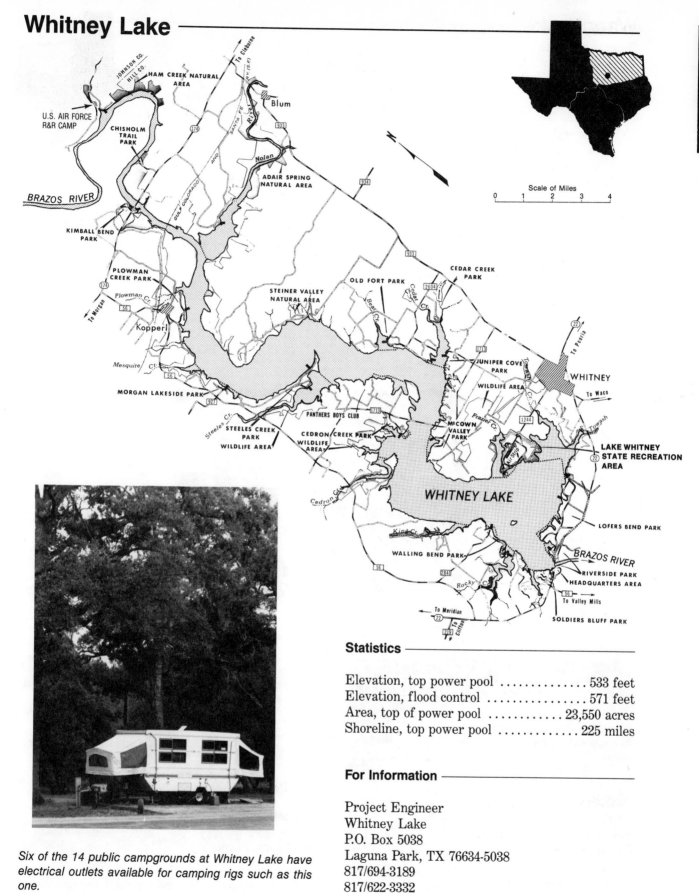

Six of the 14 public campgrounds at Whitney Lake have electrical outlets available for camping rigs such as this one.

Statistics

Elevation, top power pool .... 533 feet
Elevation, flood control .... 571 feet
Area, top of power pool .... 23,550 acres
Shoreline, top power pool .... 225 miles

For Information

Project Engineer
Whitney Lake
P.O. Box 5038
Laguna Park, TX 76634-5038
817/694-3189
817/622-3332

Campground	Drinking Water	Sanitary Facilities	Picnic Facilities	Camping Area	Trailer Area	Electrical Outlets	Boat Launching Ramp	Group Picnic Shelter	Shower Facilities	Boat Storage (Rental)	Fishing Bait & Supplies	Fishing Barge	Boat & Motor Rental	Trailer Dump Station	Fee
Riverside Park	X	X					X								
Lofers Bend Park	X	X	X	X	X	X	X	X	X		X		X	X	X
* Lake Whitney State Recreation Area	X	X	X	X	X	X	X	X	X		X			X	X
McCown Valley Park	X	X	X	X	X	X	X	X	X					X	X
* Juniper Cove Park	X	X	X	X	X	X	X		X	X	X	X	X	X	X
Cedar Creek Park	X	X	X	X	X		X	X							
* Old Fort Park	X	X	X	X			X								
Nolan River Park (closed)															
* Chisholm Trail Park	X	X	X	X	X		X								X
Kimball Bend Park	X	X	X	X	X		X								
Plowman Creek Park	X	X	X	X	X		X	X	X				X		
* Morgan Lakeside Park	X	X	X	X	X	X	X			X	X	X	X	X	
Steeles Creek Park	X	X	X	X	X		X								
Cedron Creek Park	X	X	X	X	X	X	X		X					X	X
Walling Bend Park	X	X	X	X	X		X								
Soldiers Bluff Park	X	X	X	X											

Notes:

Rental cabins are available at Lake Whitney State Park.

Juniper Cove Park provides a restaurant or snack bar.

* Operated by concessionaires.

Whitney Lake is quite large; it has 225 miles of shoreline and a surface area of 23,550 acres.

The baby stroller left near the door indicates that this roomy family-style tent really houses a family.

Whitney Lake has been attracting fishermen for years.

Wright-Patman Lake

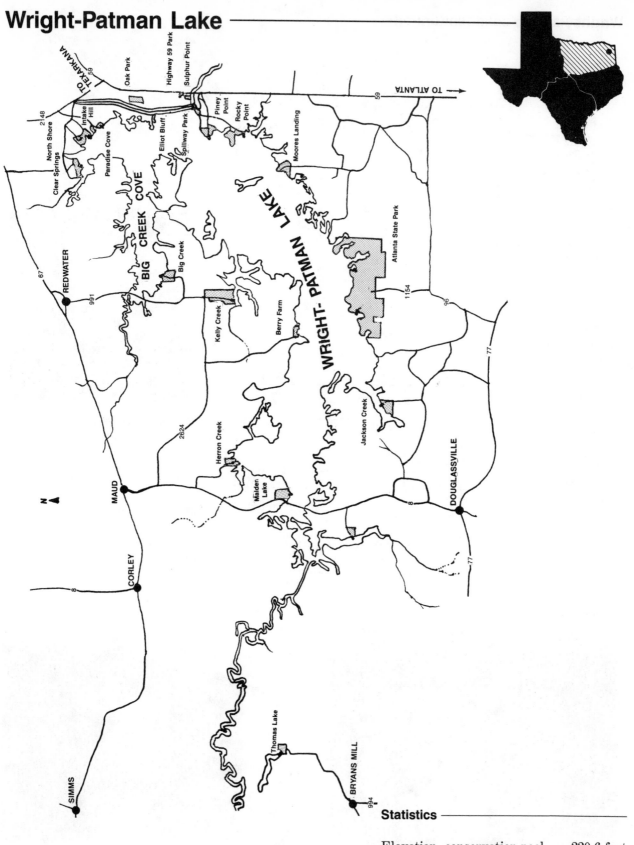

Statistics

Elevation, conservation pool ... 220.6 feet
Elevation, spillway crest ...... 259.5 feet
Area, conservation pool ..... 20,300 acres

Wright-Patman Lake (continued)

Campground	Facilities	Picnic Facilities	Camping Area	Trailer Area	Electrical Outlets	Sanitary Facilities	Drinking Water	Trailer Dump Station	Group Shelter (Picnic)	Boat Launching Ramp
Atlanta State Park	X	X	X	X	X	X	X	X	X	X
Berry Farm Park		X				X				X
Big Creek		X	X	X	X	X				X
Clear Springs	X	X	X	X	X	X	X	X	X	X
Elliott Bluff										X
Herron Creek		X				X	X			X
Highway 59 Park										X
Intake Hill	X	X	X	X	X	X	X	X	X	X
Jackson Creek		X				X	X			X
Kelly Creek	X	X	X	X	X	X	X	X	X	X
Malden Lake		X				X				X
Moores Landing Park	X	X	X	X	X	X	X	X	X	X
North Shore	X					X	X			X
Oak Park	X	X				X	X	X	X	
Overcup		X				X				X
Piney Point	X	X				X	X		X	X
Rocky Point		X	X	X	X	X	X	X	X	X
Spillway Park	X					X				
Sulphur Point		X	X	X		X				
Thomas Lake Park		X				X				X
Paradise Cove	X	X	X	X	X	X				X

Notes:
Sanitary hookups are available at Atlanta State Park, Big Creek, Kelly Creek, and Paradise Cove.

Atlanta State Park, Clear Springs, Kelly Creek, and Rocky Point all offer shower facilities.

A swimming site is available at Atlanta State Park, Clear Springs, North Shore, Rocky Point, and Spillway Park.

This should prove that you're never too young to fish.

For Information

Reservoir Manager
Wright-Patman Lake
P.O. Box 1817
Texarkana, TX 75504-1817
214/838-8781

Happiness is finding a campsite in the shade of some beautiful tall trees.

This fish cleaning facility is typical of those provided at numerous campgrounds located adjacent to lakes.

BONHAM **Lake Bonham Recreation Area**
From Bonham US 82: N on SH 78; E on FM 898; E on FM 3. On *Lake Bonham*. Camper sites w/elec., 82; tent area, fee; fl. toilets, showers, dump sta.; picnic, playground, boat ramp, swim-lake, min-golf course, 9-hole par-3 golf course; concession. (City of Bonham Water Authority, P.O. Box 305, Bonham 75418, tel. 214/583-7555)

BOWIE **Selma Park**
From US 287/81: Tex 59 SW 3.5 mi; FM 2583 S 3.6 mi. On *Lake Amon G. Carter*. Camp area 40 acres; shelters 5. Dump sta. fl. toilets. No drinking water. Swim-lake; picnic shelters, boat ramp. (304 Lindsay, Bowie 76230, tel. 817/872-1114.)

BRIDGEPORT **Wise County Park**
From Tex 101: FM 1810 (in Chico) W 1.2 mi; FM 2952 S & W 2.5 mi. On *Lake Bridgeport*. Wheeled camper sites w/elec. 14; w/elec., water & sewage 8, fee; other camp area 83 acres, fee. Fl. toilets, bait, grills. Swim-lake; bike trails, fish, boat ramp, scenic views, tables. (Co. Pk., Box 565, Bridgeport 76026, tel. 817/627-6655.)

DECATUR **Black Creek Lake Park**
From US 380: FM 730 N 7 mi; local rd W 1.9 mi. On *Black Creek Lake, LBJ Natl Grasslands*. Camp area 2 acres, limit 14 days. Pit toilets, no drinking water. Fish, boat ramp, no swimming or shooting. (US For Serv, Box 507, Decatur 76234, tel 817/627-5475.)

GRAHAM **City Park**
From Tex 16: FM 61 W 3.5 mi; FM 3003 N 1.8 mi. On *Lake Graham*. Camp area 2 acres, tent sites 6, limit 15 days. Fl toilets. Swim-lake; fish. (Box 1449, Graham 76046, tel. 817/549-3324.)

GRAHAM **Firemen's Park**
From Tex 16: Fifth St W 4 blks. On *Salt Creek*. Wheeled back-in camper sites 50 w/elec & water, fee, limit 5 days. Dump sta., picnic shelters, grills. Bike trails, fish, playground, nature & hiking trails. (Box 1449, Graham 76046, tel. 817/549-3324.)

GRAHAM **Kindley Park**
From Tex 16: US 380 NW 7 mi, at E end of bridge. On *Lake Graham*. Wheeled backin camper sites 16, tent sites 11, limit 5 days. Fl toilets. Swim-lake; fish, boat ramp. (Box 1449, Graham 76046, tel. 817/549-3324.)

GRAHAM **Lake Eddleman Park**
From Tex 16: US 380 N 1.6 mi. On *Lake Eddleman*. Wheeled backin camper site 1, tent sites 10, limit 5 days. No drinking water. Fish. (Box 1449, Graham 76046, tel. 817/549-3324.)

GRAHAM **Lake Graham Campgrounds**
Two areas, from Tex 16: FM 61 W 2.7 mi; FM 3003 N 5 mi; local rd N. Also from Tex 16: US 380 N 3.7 mi; Lakeside Rd W .7 mi; City Lake Rd N. On *Lake Graham*. Camp area 160 acres. No drinking water. Swim-lake; fish, boat ramp. (Box 1449, Graham 76046, tel 817/549-3324.)

HAWKINS **Fish Hawk Marina**
From FM 14: US 80 W 4.1 mi; Lake Hawkins Rd N 3 mi. On *Lake Hawkins*. Concessionaire;

wheeled camper sites 18 w/elec & water, fee; other tent area 4 acres. Bait, restaurant, ice, groc. Swim-lake; fish, boat ramp, scenic views. (Rt 1, Box 102, Hawkins 75765, tel 214/769-2134.)

HOLLIDAY **Stonewall Jackson Camp**
From US 82/277: FM 368 S 3 mi; local rd E .8 mi. On *Holliday Creek*. Camp area 81 acres. No toilets, no drinking water. Playground, bicycle trails. (Box 508, Holliday 76366, tel 817/586-1313.)

HONEY GROVE **Coffee Mill Lake Park**
From US 82: FM 100 N 10.5 mi; local rd W 3.5 mi. On 700-acre *Coffee Mill Lake, Caddo National Grassland*. Camp area 2 acres, limit 14 days. Pit toilets, drinking water. Fish, boat ramp, waterfowl hunting, no swimming. (US For Serv, Box 507, Decatur 76234, tel 817/627-5475.)

HONEY GROVE **Lake Crockett**
From US 82: FM 100 N 10.5 mi; local rd W 3.5 mi. At 450-acre *Lake Crockett, Caddo National Grassland*. Camping area 1 acre, limit 14 days. Pit toilets, drinking water, boat ramp, fishing, waterfowl hunting, no swimming. (US For Serv, Box 507, Decatur 76234, tel 817/627-5475.)

JACKSONVILLE **Lake Jacksonville Campground**
From Jct. US 69 & 79: US 79 SW .5 mi, College Ave S 3 mi. On *Lake Jacksonville*. Wheeled camper sites 10 w/elec & water, fee. Screened shelters 10, fee. Dump sta, fl toilets, cold showers, picnic tables. Swim-lake, fish, ski, boat ramp, boat rentals. (Municipal Park, P.O. Box 1837, Jacksonville, 75766, tel 214/586-4160.)

LEWISVILLE **Conner Trailer Park**
From I-35E: FM 407 E .7 mi; Lake Park Rd E .5 mi. On *Lake. Lewisville*. Wheeled backin camper sites w/elec & water 150, fee, limit 14 days. Other tent sites, 10, fee, limit 14 days. Dump sta, fl & pit toilets, cold showers, shelters, tables, grills. Pavilion, fee, resvn; snack bar, ice, groc. Swim-lake; boat rental, fish, playground, softball field, horsehoe pits, nature trails, fishing barge, 18-hole golf, miniature golf, boat ramp. (City Pk, 151 W. Church, Lewisville 75067, tel 214/221-5754.)

MINEOLA **Lake Holbrook Park**
From Tex 37: US 80 W 3.6 mi; Old US 80 W 1 mi; local rd N .3 mi. On *Lake Holbrook*. Wheeled backin camper sites 10; other camp area 40 acres, limit 15 days. Dump sta, pit toilets, no drinking water, snack bar (summer). Swim-lake; fish, boat ramp, playground, scenic views. (Pct 2, County Courthouse, Quitman 75783, tel 214/763-2716.)

MOUNT PLEASANT **Monticello Park**
From I-30: US 271 SW 1.3 mi; FM 172 SW 8 mi; local road SE 1.4 mi. On *Monticello Reservoir*. Wheeled camper sites w/elec, 27, fee, limit 14 days. Primitive tent sites. Dump sta, drinking water nearby, fl toilets, showers, tables, grills. No swimming. Fishing, boat ramp, bathhouse (handicapped accessible), scenic views. Bait, fishing tackle rental, ice and groc nearby. (Titus Co Courthouse, Pct 2, Mount Pleasant 75455, tel 214/572-3991.)

NEWCASTLE **Fort Belknap County Park**
From US 380: Tex 251 S 1.9 mi. Camp area 10 acres, no fee (donations). Water & elec hookups, 8, limit 3 days. Fl toilets. Playground, tennis court, volleyball court, ball field, historic site, 2 museums. (Rt 1, Box 28, Newcastle 76372, tel 817/846-3222.)

NOCONA **Joe Benton Park**
From FM 103: FM 2634 E 3 mi; FM 2953 NE 1.2 mi. On *Lake Nocona*. Tent camping. Fl toilets, sheltered tables, grills. Swim-lake; fish, pier, boat ramp. (Chamber of Commerce, Box 27, Nocona 76255, tel. 817/825-3526.)

NOCONA **Weldon Rob Memorial Park**
From FM 103: FM 2634 E 3 mi, SE .7 mi. On *Lake Nocona*. Tent camping. Pit toilets, sheltered tables, grills. Swim-lake; fish, pier, boat ramp, playground. (Chamber of Commerce, Box 27, Nocona 76255, tel. 817/825-3526.)

OVERTON **City Park Camp**
Within city, from Tex 135: West Henderson St W; Meadowbrook Dr S; local rd W. On *Overton City Lakes*. Wheeled backin camper sites, 24; w/elec, water & sewage, 10, fee; w/elec & water, 10, fee; limit 7 days. Fl toilets, dump sta. Swim-pool (no swimming in lake), fish, boating, playground, 9-hole golf, volleyball, tennis, ball field. Community center, fee, rsvns reqd. (Box 277, Overton 75684, tel 214/834-3171.)

QUITMAN **Lake Quitman Park**
From Tex 37: Tex 154 W .4 mi; FM 2966 N 4.8 mi; Lake Quitman Rd E .9 mi. On *Lake Quitman*. Wheeled backin camper sites, 12; w/ elec., 8, fee, limit 15 days; other camp area 25 acres. Fl toilets, boat rental, bait, grills, ice, groc. Swim-lake; fish, boat ramps, scenic views. (Chamber of Commerce, Box 426, Quitman 75783, tel 214/763-4411.)

STEPHENVILLE **City Park**
From US 377/67/281 (South Loop): Graham St (Tex 108) N .1 mi, across *Bosque River*. Wheeled camper sites, 50 w/elec & water, fee; temporary sites, 50, fee, limit 7 days. Dump sta, fl toilets, 2 group pavilions, grills. Swim-pool; bicycle trails, trail bike area, fish-river, playground, tennis, horseshoes, volleyball, softball, shuffleboard, nature trails. No rsvns acptd. (378 W. Long, Stephenville 76401, tel 817/965-3866.)

WICHITA FALLS **Wichita Bend RV Park**
From I-44: Access rd S of Texas Tourist Bureau .1 mi. Wheeled camper sites, 28 w/elec & water, fee, limit 72 hrs. Dump sta, tables, grills. On *Big Wichita River* adjacent to Lucy Park, nature trails. (1300 7th St, Wichita Falls 76301, tel 817/761-7490.)

WINNSBORO **Lake Winnsboro North Park**
From Tex 11: FM 515 W 4 mi; local rd S .5 mi & E .5 mi. On *Lake Winnsboro*. Wheeled backin camper sites 15, 2 w/elec, fee. Other primitive camp area 4 acres, limit 15 days. Fl toilets, snack bar, ice, groc, boat rental. Swim-lake; boat ramp, fish, marina. (Box 451, Quitman 75783, tel 214/878-2879.)

* Source: *Texas Public Campgrounds*, State Dept. of Highways and Public Transportation, Travel and Information Div., P.O. Box 5064, Austin, TX 78763.

Region 2

1—Angelina National Forest, 51
2—B. A. Steinhagen Lake, 53
3—Bastrop State Park, 54
4—Belton Lake, 55
5—Brazos Bend State Park, 56
6—Buescher State Park, 57
7—Davy Crockett National Forest, 58
   Ratcliff Lake Recreation Area, 59
8—Fort Fisher Park, 60
9—Fort Parker State Recreation Area, 61
10—Galveston Island State Park, 62
11—Granger Lake, 63
12—Huntsville State Park, 64
13—Lake Bastrop, 65
14—Lake Georgetown, 66
15—Lake Livingston State Recreation Area, 67
16—Lake Somerville State Recreation Area (Birch Creek Unit), 68
17—Lake Somerville State Recreation Area (Nails Creek Unit), 69
18—Martin Dies, Jr. State Park, 70
19—Mission Tejas State Historical Park, 71
20—Mother Neff State Park, 72
21—Sabine National Forest, 73
22—Sam Houston National Forest, 75
   Double Lake Recreation Area, 77
23—Sam Rayburn Reservoir, 78
24—Sea Rim State Park, 79
25—Somerville Lake, 80
26—Stephen F. Austin State Historical Park, 81
27—Stillhouse Hollow Lake, 82
28—Toledo Bend Reservoir, 83
29—Wolf Creek Park, 85
   Other Parks in Region 2, 86

More than 30 state parks/recreation areas have fishing piers such as this one at Brazos Bend State Park.

Angelina National Forest

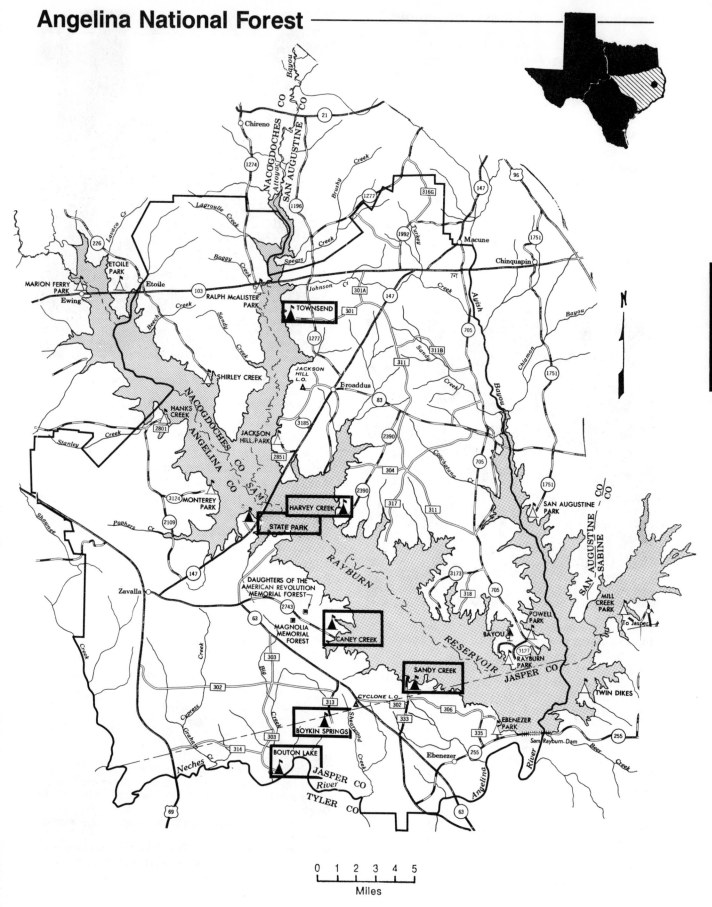

Angelina National Forest *(continued)*

Angelina National Forest, located in Angelina, Jasper, Nacogdoches and San Augustine counties, is the smallest of the four national forests in Texas and contains 154,308 acres.

Location

Bouton Lake Recreation Area is located about 15 miles southeast of Zavalla on FSR 303 via SH 63.

Boykin Springs Recreation Area is located about 14 miles southeast of Zavalla on FSR 313 via SH 63.

Caney Creek Recreation Area is located on Sam Rayburn Reservoir about 14 miles southeast of Zavalla on FM 2743 via SH 63.

Sunset over Sam Rayburn Reservoir, in the middle of Angelina National Forest, 20 miles east of Lufkin, Tx.

Hikers in Angelina National Forest near Zavalla, Tx.

Cassells-Boykin State Recreation Area is located on Sam Rayburn Lake, about 7 miles northeast of Zavalla on FM 3123 via SH 147.

Harvey Creek Recreation Area is located on Sam Rayburn Reservoir about 9 miles east and south of Broaddus on FM 2390 via FM 83.

Sandy Creek Recreation Area is located on Sam Rayburn Reservoir about 21 miles southeast of Zavalla on FSR 333 via SH 63. Subject to seasonal closing.

Townsend Recreation Area is located on Sam Rayburn Reservoir about 5 miles northwest of Broaddus on FM 2923 via SH 147 and FM 1277. Subject to seasonal closing.

For Information

Ranger, Angelina District
P.O. Box 756
(1907 Atkinson Drive)
Lufkin, TX 75902
409/634-7709

Facilities / Campground	Fee Area	No. of Campsites	Boating	Picnicking	Skiing	Swimming
Bouton Lake		7	E			
Boykin Springs	X	36	E	X		X
Caney Creek	X	128	L	X	X	X
Cassels-Boykin State Rec. Area	X	30	L	X	X	X
Harvey Creek	X	42	L	X	X	
Sandy Creek	X	27	L	X	X	X
Townsend	X	67	L	X		

Notes:

E = Electric Motors Only   L = Boat Launch

All parks have drinking water and sanitary facilities and fishing.

Showers are available at Caney Creek, Harvey Creek, and Sandy Creek.

Hiking trails are offered in Bouton Lake, Boykin Springs, and Caney Creek.

Trailer space is available at all parks except Bouton Lake, and trailer dump stations are available at Caney Creek and Cassels-Boykin State Recreation Area.

B. A. Steinhagen Lake

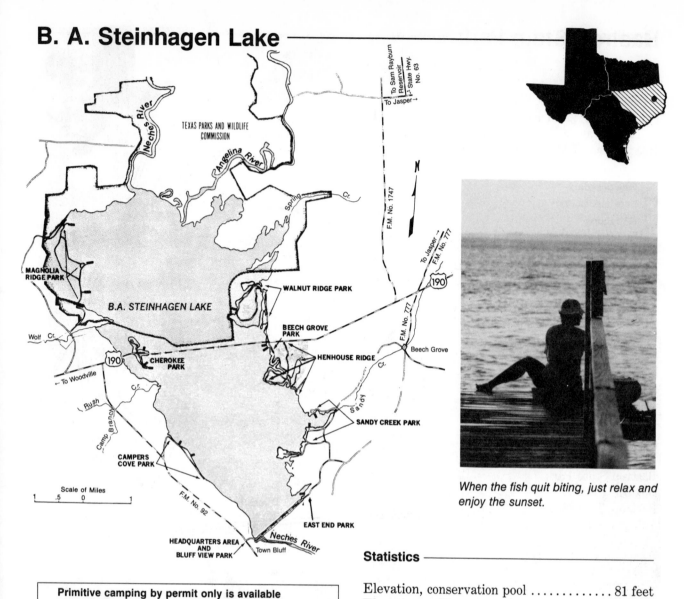

When the fish quit biting, just relax and enjoy the sunset.

Statistics

Elevation, conservation pool . . . . 81 feet
Elevation, spillway crest . . . . 85 feet
Area, conservation pool . . . . 10,950 acres

Primitive camping by permit only is available at specific areas on the Angelina and Neches rivers. Details may be obtained by writing or calling the project office.

For Information

Reservoir Manager
B. A. Steinhagen Lake
890 FM 92
Woodville, TX 75979-9631
409/429-3491

Facilities Campground	Camping Area	Trailer Area	Drinking Water	Electrical Outlets	Picnic Facilities	Boat Launching Ramp
East End Park	X	X	X		X	X
Bluff View Park			X		X	
Campers Cove Park	X	X			X	X
Magnolia Ridge Park	X	X	X	X	X	X
Beech Grove Park	X	X	X	X		X
Sandy Creek Park	X	X	X	X	X	X
* Cherokee Unit	X	X	X	X	X	X
* Hen House Ridge Unit	X	X	X	X	X	X
* Walnut Ridge Unit	X	X	X	X	X	X

Notes:
* These three units comprise Martin Dies, Jr., State Park.
  Sanitary facilities are available at all campsites.
  Showers are available at the Hen House Ridge Unit and
    Walnut Ridge Unit.
  Fishing piers are available at Beech Grove Park, Sandy
    Creek Park, Hen House Ridge Unit, and Walnut Ridge Unit.

Bastrop State Park

Location

Bastrop State Park is located 1 mile east of Bastrop on SH 21; also accessible from the east on SH 71 or by way of Buescher State Park along Park Road 1. The 3,503-acre park includes a 10-acre lake.

\ Park boundary
Park headquarters
Golf course
Swimming pool
Picnic/day use area
Dining hall
Hiking trail
Tent camping (water only)
Multi-use camping
   (water & electricity)
Trailer/RV camping
Group camp
Cabins
Residence

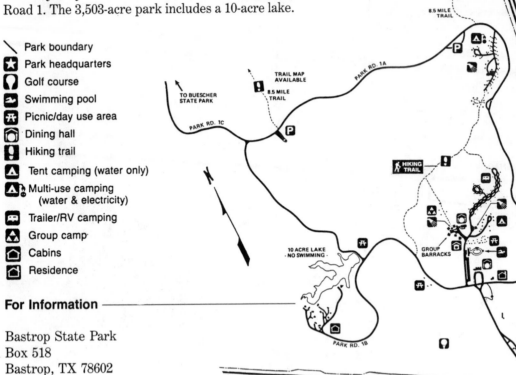

For Information

Bastrop State Park
Box 518
Bastrop, TX 78602
512/321-2101

Facilities & Activities

72 campsites
   18 with water only
   54 with water/electricity
primitive camping area for backpackers
12 cabins
4-bedroom lodge
restrooms
showers
trailer dump station
dining hall with kitchen (day-use only)
group camp: 4 dorms; dining/recreation hall with
   kitchen
picnicking
playground
swimming pool & beachhouse
fishing
8½ miles of hiking trails
9-hole golf course
park store (seasonal)
scenic drive

Eight and one-half miles of backpacking trails are located in Bastrop State Park.

Belton Lake

For Information

Reservoir Manager
Belton Lake
99 FM 2271
Belton, TX 76513-9717
817/939-1829

Statistics

Elevation, conservation pool .... 594 feet
Elevation, flood control pool .... 631 feet
Area, conservation pool .... 12,300 acres
Shoreline, conservation pool .... 136 miles

A favorite fishing spot in the Belton Lake area is below the dam along the banks of the Leon River.

LOCATIONS	FACILITIES	Boat Launching Ramp	Drinking Water	Restrooms	Picnic Area	Camping Area	Nature Trail	Electrical Outlets
BELTON LAKEVIEW PARK		X	X	X	X	X	X	
MILLER SPRING PARK				X	X			
LIVE OAK RIDGE PARK		X	X	X	X	X		X
TEMPLE'S LAKE PARK		X	X	X	X	X		
ROGERS PARK		X	X	X	X	X		
CEDAR RIDGE PARK		X	X	X	X	X	X	X
McGREGOR PARK		X						
LEONA PARK		X	X	X	X	X		
IRON BRIDGE PARK		X	X	X	X	X		
WINKLER PARK		X	X	X	X	X		
WHITE FLINT PARK		X	X	X	X	X		
OWL CREEK PARK		X	X	X	X	X		
WESTCLIFF PARK		X	X	X	X	X		X

Brazos Bend State Park

THOUSAND FEET

0 1 2 3 4 5 6

0 1/2 1 MILE

SCALE

N

BIG CREEK

HORSESHOE LAKE

HALE LAKE

PILANT LAKE

ELM LAKE

40 ACRE LAKE

FM 762

BRAZOS RIVER

🅰 MULTI-USE CAMPING	Ⓞ OBSERVATION TOWER	Ⓘ INTERPRETIVE CENTER
🏢 HEADQUARTERS	Ⓞ OBSERVATION PLATFORM	△ SCREENED SHELTER
🏠 RESIDENCE	P🅰 PRIMITIVE CAMPING	ROAD
🎁 PICNICKING/DAY USE	🎣 FISHING PIER	⋯⋯ HIKING TRAIL
🚻 RESTROOM	🚮 TRAILER DUMP STATION	HIKING/BIKING TRAIL
🔧 MAINTENANCE AREA	Ⓓ GROUP DINING HALL	PARK BOUNDARY
🅰 CAMPING		

For Information

Brazos Bend State Park
21901 FM 762
Needville, TX 77461
409/553-3243

Facilities & Activities

77 campsites
  35 with water only
  42 with water/electricity
20 primitive walk-in sites
14 screened shelters
restrooms
showers
trailer dump station
group picnic area
group dining hall
picnicking
playgrounds
lighted fishing pier
fish cleaning facility
15 miles of nature & hike/bike trails
interpretive center
observation tower/platforms

IH 10   KATY

HOUSTON

RICHMOND

ROSENBERG

U.S. 90

U.S. 59

St. HWY 36

FM 762

PARK SITE

NEEDVILLE

DAMON

FM 1462

St. HWY 288

U.S. 59 BRAZOS RIVER

St. HWY 6

St. HWY 35

ALVIN

ROSHARON

0 5 10 miles

N

Location

Brazos Bend State Park is on FM 762 about 18 miles south of the Rosenberg/Richmond area, and about 11 miles west of Rosharon via FM 1462.

CAUTION - ALLIGATORS
DO NOT FEED OR APPROACH
STAY AT A DISTANCE

Visitors at Brazos Bend State Park are cautioned to pay due respect to alligators; this fishing pier is a safe haven from which to view them.

Buescher State Park

HEADQUARTERS

TRAILER CAMPING

GROUP DAY USE AREA

PICNIC/DAY USE AREA

TRAIL HEAD

PLAYGROUND

SCREENED SHELTERS

TENT CAMPING AREA

MULTI-USE CAMPING

RESTROOM W/SHOWERS

RESTROOM

TRAILER DUMP

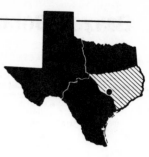

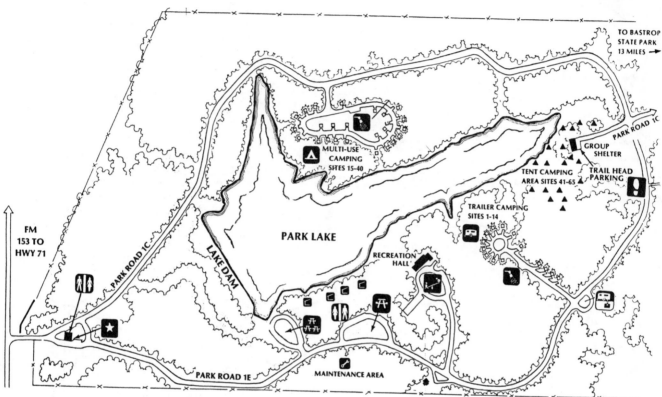

TO BASTROP
STATE PARK
13 MILES

PARK ROAD 1C

GROUP
SHELTER

TRAIL HEAD
PARKING

TENT CAMPING
AREA SITES 41-65

MULTI-USE
CAMPING
SITES 15-40

TRAILER CAMPING
SITES 1-14

PARK LAKE

LAKE DAM

RECREATION
HALL

FM
153 TO
HWY 71

PARK ROAD 1C

PARK ROAD 1E

MAINTENANCE AREA

Facilities & Activities

65 campsites
  25 with water only
  40 with water/electricity
4 screened shelters
restrooms
showers
trailer dump station
group picnic area
group trailer area available
open group shelter
recreation hall with kitchen
picnicking
playground
swimming
fishing
7.7-mile hiking trail
scenic drive on Park Road 1-C

For Information

Buescher State Park
P.O. Box 75
Smithville, TX 78957
512/237-2241

Location

Buescher State Park is located 2 miles north of Smithville. Off of SH 71, travel ½ mile north on FM 153 to Park Road 1. The 1,730-acre park includes a 25-acre lake.

Davy Crockett National Forest

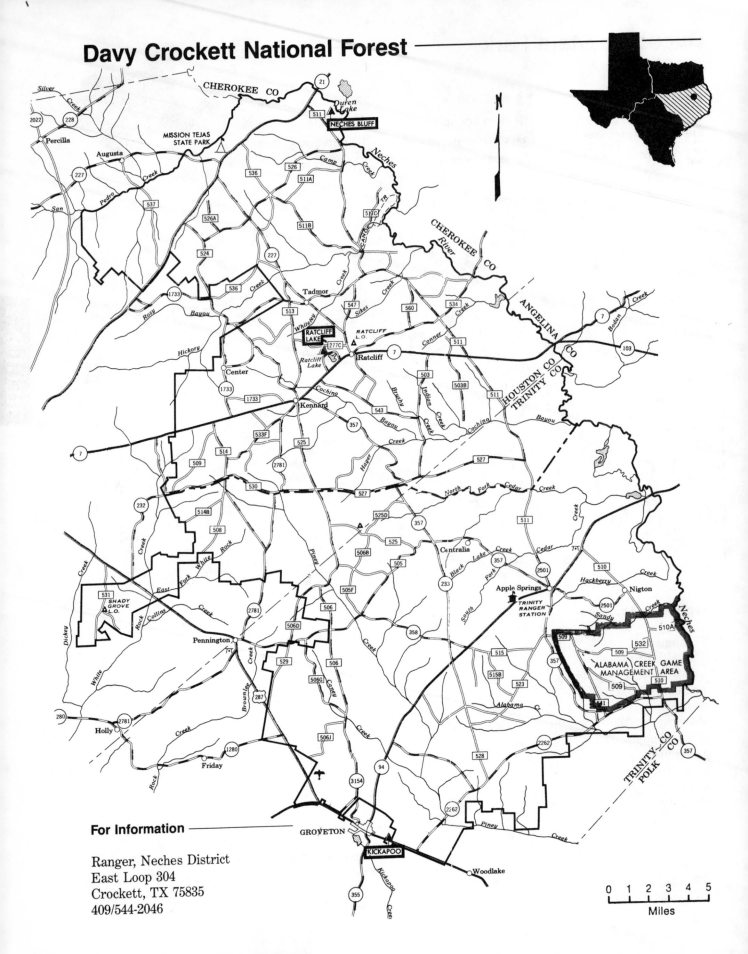

CHEROKEE CO

MISSION TEJAS
STATE PARK

NECHES BLUFF

CHEROKEE CO

ANGELINA CO

Tadmor

RATCLIFF
LAKE

Ratcliff

HOUSTON CO
TRINITY CO

Center

Kennard

Centralia

Apple Springs

TRINITY
RANGER
STATION

SHADY
GROVE
L.O.

Pennington

ALABAMA CREEK GAME
MANAGEMENT AREA

Nigton

Holly

Friday

Woodlake

TRINITY CO
POLK CO

GROVETON

KICKAPOO

For Information

Ranger, Neches District
East Loop 304
Crockett, TX 75835
409/544-2046

0 1 2 3 4 5
Miles

Davy Crockett National Forest (continued)

Davy Crockett National Forest is located in Houston and Trinity counties and has 161,478 acres.

Ratcliff Lake Recreation Area ____

Location ────────

Ratcliff Lake Recreation Area, in the Davy Crockett National Forest, is located one mile west of Ratcliff (approximately 25 miles west of Lufkin) on SH 7.

Paddling down the "Big Slough" canoe trail in Davy Crockett National Forest.

Facilities & Activities ────────

75 campsites
flush toilets/cold showers
trailer dump station
group camping area
group picnic shelter
picnicking
amphitheater
swimming beach & bathhouse
canoe/paddle boat rentals
fishing
boat launch (electric motors only)
concession
nature/hiking trails
*south trailhead to the 20-mile 4-C Hiking Trail
  that ends at Neches Bluff

──────

* Note: For information and detailed maps of the 4-C Hiking Trail, see page 124 of *Hiking and Backpacking Trails of Texas*, 3rd Edition, by Mickey Little, Lone Star Books, 1990.

Enjoying the quiet beauty of the deep woods on a nature trail in Ratcliff Lake Recreation Area, Davy Crockett National Forest.

DAVY CROCKETT NATIONAL FOREST TEXAS

RATCLIFF RECREATION AREA

CAMPING

TALL PINE TRAIL

MEMORIAL TRAIL

LOG TRAM TRAIL

AMPHITHEATER

BOATS, PADDLE BOATS, AND CANOE RENTAL

SWIMMING AREA

GROUP CAMPING

RATCLIFF LAKE

DAM

FEE STATION

HISTORIC (OLD MILL SITE)

7

0 100 200 300 400 500
SCALE IN FEET

RATCLIFF 1.0 MILES

KENNARD 12.0 MILES

P PARKING	C CONCESSIONAIRE
PICNIC AREA	SHELTER
TRAILS	FISHING
RESTROOMS	CAMPING
SHOWER	BOAT LAUNCH

Campground	Camping	Drinking Water	Hiking Trails	Picnicking	Sanitary Facilities
Kickapoo		X		X	X
Neches Bluff			X	X	X
Ratcliff	X	X	X	X	X

Fort Fisher Park

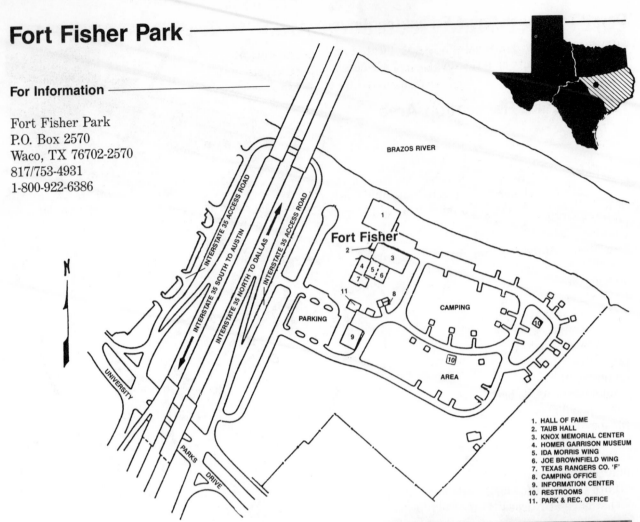

For Information

Fort Fisher Park
P.O. Box 2570
Waco, TX 76702-2570
817/753-4931
1-800-922-6386

Fort Fisher

BRAZOS RIVER

INTERSTATE 35 ACCESS ROAD
INTERSTATE 35 SOUTH TO AUSTIN
INTERSTATE 35 NORTH TO DALLAS
INTERSTATE 35 ACCESS ROAD

UNIVERSITY

PARKS DRIVE

N

PARKING

CAMPING

AREA

1. HALL OF FAME
2. TAUB HALL
3. KNOX MEMORIAL CENTER
4. HOMER GARRISON MUSEUM
5. IDA MORRIS WING
6. JOE BROWNFIELD WING
7. TEXAS RANGERS CO. 'F'
8. CAMPING OFFICE
9. INFORMATION CENTER
10. RESTROOMS
11. PARK & REC. OFFICE

Location

Fort Fisher is located in Waco on IH 35 between the Brazos River and University Parks Drive. The park gets its name from the old Texas Ranger outpost located near the site in the 1830s. The 35-acre Fort Fisher complex is owned and operated by the city of Waco, Parks and Recreation Department.

Facilities & Activities

110 campsites
  20 tent sites
  65 with water/electricity
  10 with water/electricity/sewage
  15 screened shelters
restrooms
showers
dump station
fishing
river walk
Texas Ranger Hall of Fame & Museum

The trees at Fort Fisher Park are not only old, they are tremendous in size. Owned and operated by the city of Waco, the campground is conveniently located on I-35 between the Brazos River and Baylor University.

Fort Parker State Recreation Area

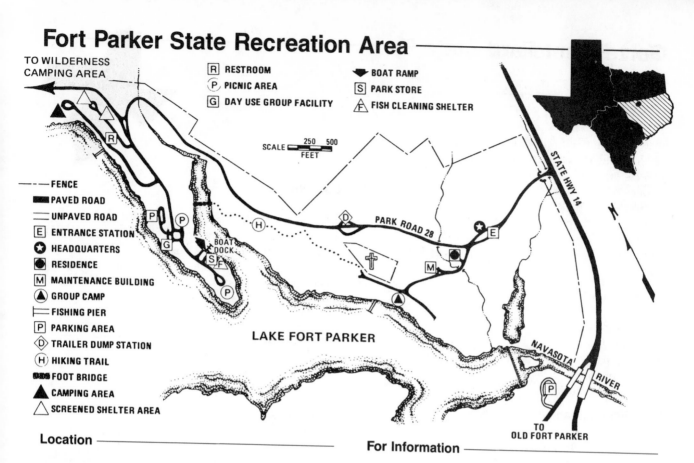

R RESTROOM
P PICNIC AREA
G DAY USE GROUP FACILITY

◄ BOAT RAMP
S PARK STORE
F FISH CLEANING SHELTER

TO WILDERNESS
CAMPING AREA

SCALE 250 500 FEET

- - - FENCE
■■ PAVED ROAD
= UNPAVED ROAD
E ENTRANCE STATION
★ HEADQUARTERS
● RESIDENCE
M MAINTENANCE BUILDING
▲ GROUP CAMP
├─┤ FISHING PIER
P PARKING AREA
D TRAILER DUMP STATION
H HIKING TRAIL
▦ FOOT BRIDGE
▲ CAMPING AREA
△ SCREENED SHELTER AREA

PARK ROAD 28

STATE HWY 14

BOAT DOCK

LAKE FORT PARKER

NAVASOTA RIVER

TO OLD FORT PARKER

Location

Fort Parker State Recreation Area is located 55 miles east of Waco and 6 miles southeast of Mexia, off SH 14 in Limestone County. The park consists of 735 acres of timberland surrounding a 750-acre lake.

Facilities & Activities

25 campsites with water/electricity
wilderness camping area for organized groups
12 screened shelters
restrooms
showers
trailer dump station
group picnic area
open pavilion
group camp: 4 dorms; staff bldg.; recreation hall;
  dining hall with kitchen; 2 modern restrooms
picnicking
playground
swimming
water skiing
fishing piers
fish cleaning facility
boat ramp
canoe & paddle boat rentals
1-mile hiking trail
park store (seasonal)

For Information

Fort Parker State Recreation Area
Route 3, Box 95
Mexia, TX 76667
817/562-5751

Park visitors who swim at Fort Parker State Recreation Area come in many shapes and sizes.

Galveston Island State Park

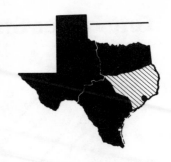

Activities

swimming (1.6 miles of Gulf beach)
water skiing (Gulf & Galveston Bay)
fishing (salt water & fresh water)
fish cleaning facility
4 miles of nature trails with boardwalks &
 observation platforms
summer drama productions at outdoor amphitheatre (*The Lone Star* alternates with a selected
 Broadway musical). For information, call 409/737-
 3442

Facilities on Bayside of Park

10 screened shelters
restrooms/showers
20-site group trailer area with water/electricity
group pavilion
trailer dump station

Facilities on Beachside of Park

150 campsites with water/electricity/shade shelters
60 picnic sites with shade shelters
group picnic area
bathhouses
trailer dump station

Location

Galveston Island State Park is located 6 miles
southwest of the Galveston City Seawall on FM
3005. The 2,000-acre park, also accessible from Bra-
zosport via the toll bridge at San Louis Pass, spans
the width of Galveston Island from the Gulf of Mexico to West Galveston Bay.

For Information

Galveston Island State Park
Route 1, Box 156A
Galveston, TX 77554
409/737-1222

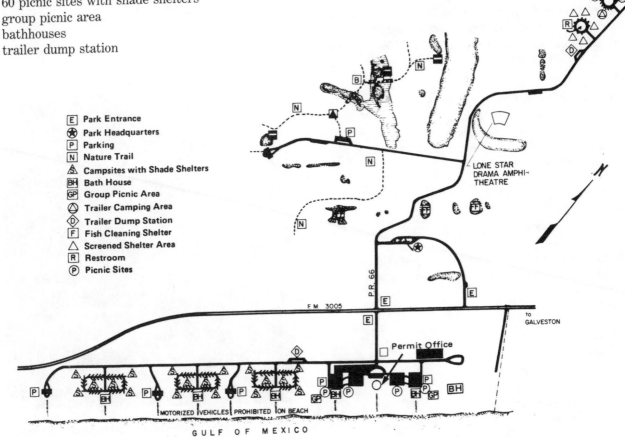

E	Park Entrance
✪	Park Headquarters
P	Parking
N	Nature Trail
⚠	Campsites with Shade Shelters
BH	Bath House
GP	Group Picnic Area
◬	Trailer Camping Area
◈	Trailer Dump Station
F	Fish Cleaning Shelter
△	Screened Shelter Area
R	Restroom
P	Picnic Sites

Granger Lake

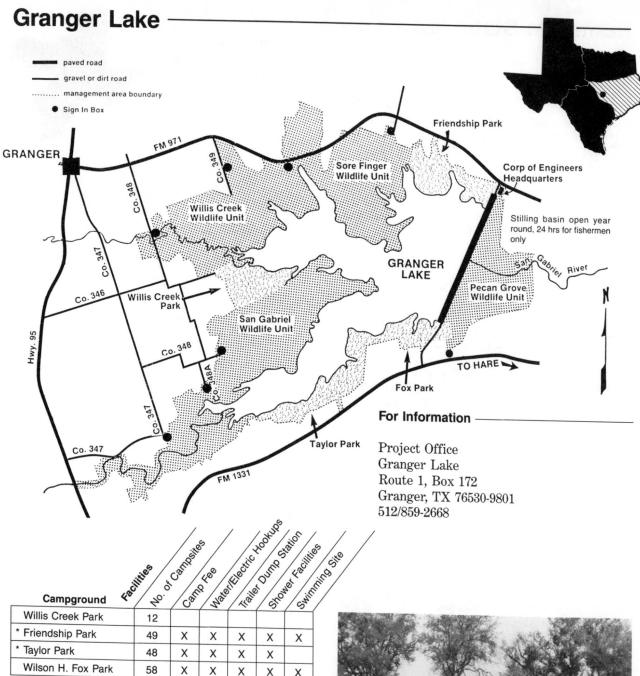

paved road
gravel or dirt road
management area boundary
● Sign In Box

GRANGER

FM 971

Co. 348
Co. 349
Co. 347
Co. 346
Hwy. 95
Co. 347
Co. 347
Co. 348
Co. 48A

Willis Creek Wildlife Unit

Willis Creek Park

San Gabriel Wildlife Unit

Sore Finger Wildlife Unit

Friendship Park

Corp of Engineers Headquarters

Stilling basin open year round, 24 hrs for fishermen only

San Gabriel River

GRANGER LAKE

Pecan Grove Wildlife Unit

Fox Park

TO HARE

Taylor Park

FM 1331

N

For Information

Project Office
Granger Lake
Route 1, Box 172
Granger, TX 76530-9801
512/859-2668

REGION 2

Campground	No. of Campsites	Camp Fee	Water/Electric Hookups	Trailer Dump Station	Shower Facilities	Swimming Site
Willis Creek Park	12					
* Friendship Park	49	X	X	X	X	X
* Taylor Park	48	X	X	X	X	
Wilson H. Fox Park	58	X	X	X	X	X

Notes:
* Season: April–Oct.
All parks have camping areas, sanitary facilities, drinking water, picnic facilities, and boat launching ramps.
Taylor Park has hiking trails available.

Statistics

Elevation, conservation pool .... 504 feet
Elevation, spillway crest .... 528 feet
Area, conservation pool .... 4,400 acres
Shoreline, conservation pool .... 40 miles

Granger Lake's Wilson H. Fox Park stays open year round; the season for Friendship Park and Taylor Park is April through October.

Huntsville State Park

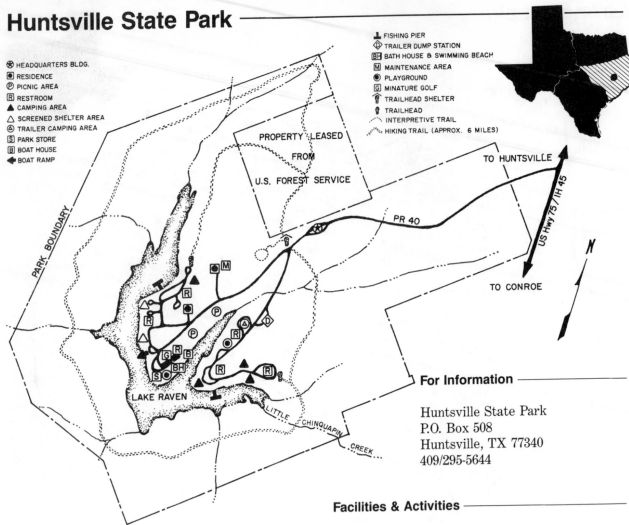

HEADQUARTERS BLDG.
RESIDENCE
PICNIC AREA
RESTROOM
CAMPING AREA
SCREENED SHELTER AREA
TRAILER CAMPING AREA
PARK STORE
BOAT HOUSE
BOAT RAMP

FISHING PIER
TRAILER DUMP STATION
BATH HOUSE & SWIMMING BEACH
MAINTENANCE AREA
PLAYGROUND
MINATURE GOLF
TRAILHEAD SHELTER
TRAILHEAD
INTERPRETIVE TRAIL
HIKING TRAIL (APPROX. 6 MILES)

PROPERTY LEASED FROM U.S. FOREST SERVICE

TO HUNTSVILLE

PR 40

US Hwy 75 / IH 45

TO CONROE

N

PARK BOUNDARY

LAKE RAVEN

LITTLE CHINQUAPIN CREEK

For Information

Huntsville State Park
P.O. Box 508
Huntsville, TX 77340
409/295-5644

Location

Huntsville State Park is located 8 miles south of Huntsville on IH 45, Exit 109, and southwest on Park Road 40. The 2,083-acre park includes the 210-acre man-made lake, Lake Raven.

Lake Raven, at Hunsville State Park, almost needs a traffic director when all the canoes and paddleboats take to the water.

Facilities & Activities

191 campsites
  127 with water only
  64 with water/electricity
30 screened shelters
restrooms
showers
trailer dump station
group picnic shelter
picnicking
playgrounds
swimming beach & bathhouse
lighted fishing piers
fish cleaning facility
boat ramp & dock
canoes, flat bottom & paddle boats for rent
  (seasonal)
½-mile interpretive trail
8 miles of hiking trails
3.2-mile bicycle trail
miniature golf (seasonal)
park store
Interpretive Center

Lake Bastrop

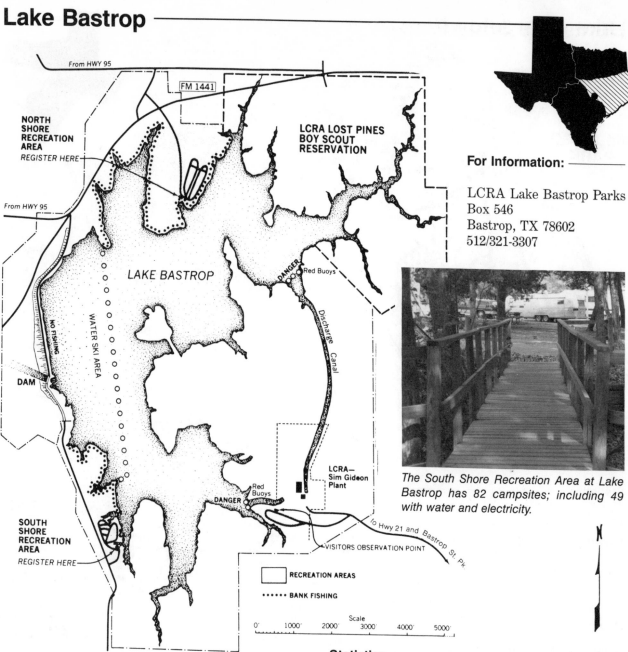

From HWY 95

FM 1441

NORTH SHORE RECREATION AREA
REGISTER HERE

From HWY 95

LCRA LOST PINES BOY SCOUT RESERVATION

LAKE BASTROP

WATER SKI AREA

NO FISHING

DAM

DANGER   Red Buoys

Discharge Canal

Red Buoys

DANGER

SOUTH SHORE RECREATION AREA
REGISTER HERE

LCRA— Sim Gideon Plant

to Hwy 21 and Bastrop St. Pk.

VISITORS OBSERVATION POINT

RECREATION AREAS
•••••• BANK FISHING

Scale
0'   1000'   2000'   3000'   4000'   5000'

N

For Information:

LCRA Lake Bastrop Parks
Box 546
Bastrop, TX 78602
512/321-3307

The South Shore Recreation Area at Lake Bastrop has 82 campsites; including 49 with water and electricity.

REGION 2

South Shore and North Shore Recreation Areas

66 North Shore campsites, including 44 with
  water/electricity and 8 screened shelters
82 South Shore campsites, including 49 with
  water/electricity and 3 screened shelters
flush toilets/showers
dump station
group picnic area (South Shore)
swimming
fishing
boat ramp
(Note: Closed occasionally Sept. 2–April 1)

Statistics

Surface area . . . . 906 acres
Normal elevation . . . . 450.0 feet
Storage capacity . . . . 16,600 acre-feet

Locations

South Shore Recreation Area: From Loop 150, SH 21 northeast 1.1 miles; north 1.9 miles on Lake Bastrop.

North Shore Recreation Area: From SH 71, SH 95 north 3.8 miles; FM 1441 east 2.4 miles; LCRA Road south ½ mile, on Lake Bastrop.

Lake Georgetown

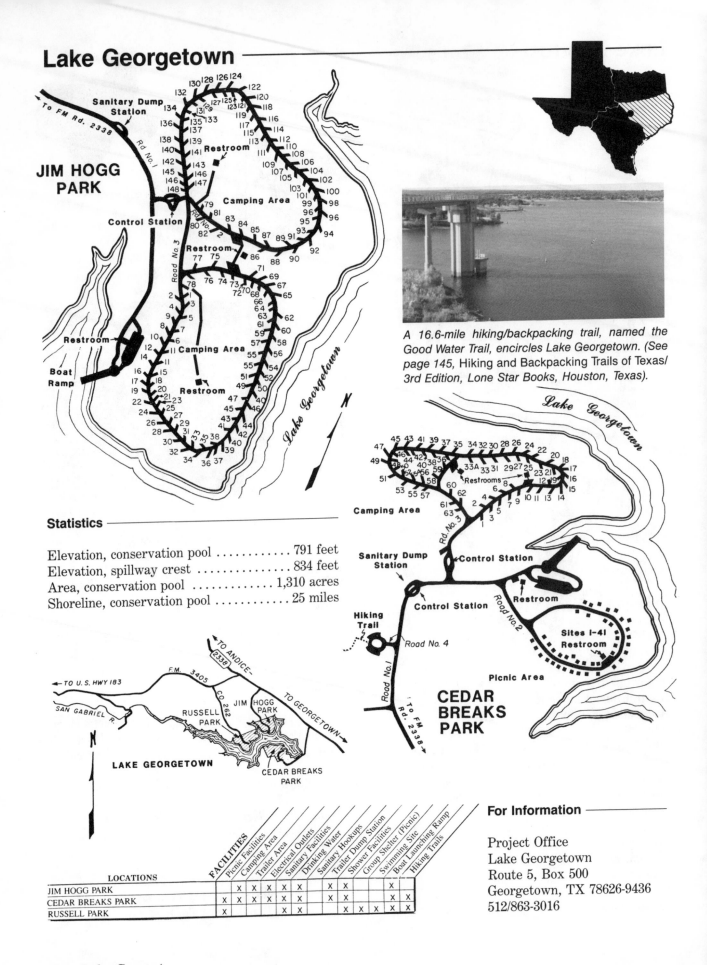

A 16.6-mile hiking/backpacking trail, named the Good Water Trail, encircles Lake Georgetown. (See page 145, Hiking and Backpacking Trails of Texas/ 3rd Edition, Lone Star Books, Houston, Texas).

Statistics

Elevation, conservation pool . . . . 791 feet
Elevation, spillway crest . . . . 834 feet
Area, conservation pool . . . . 1,310 acres
Shoreline, conservation pool . . . . 25 miles

LOCATIONS	FACILITIES	Picnic Facilities	Camping Area	Trailer Area	Electrical Outlets	Sanitary Facilities	Drinking Water	Sanitary Hookups	Trailer Dump Station	Shower Facilities	Group Shelter (Picnic)	Swimming Site	Boat Launching Ramp	Hiking Trails
JIM HOGG PARK			x	x	x	x	x		x	x		x		
CEDAR BREAKS PARK		x	x	x	x	x	x		x	x			x	x
RUSSELL PARK		x				x	x				x	x	x	x

For Information

Project Office
Lake Georgetown
Route 5, Box 500
Georgetown, TX 78626-9436
512/863-3016

Lake Livingston State Recreation Area

Location

Lake Livingston State Recreation Area is located on the east shore of Lake Livingston with a total acreage of 635.5. The park is 1 mile south of Livingston on US 59, 4 miles west on FM 1988, and ½ mile north on FM 3126.

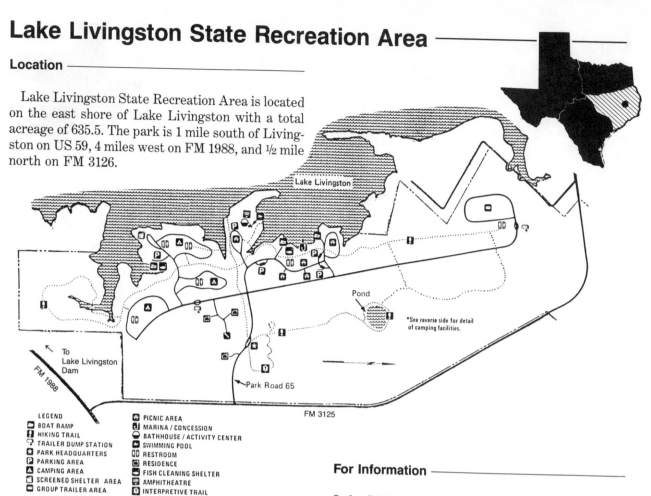

*See reverse side for detail of camping facilities.

LEGEND
- 🚤 BOAT RAMP
- 🚶 HIKING TRAIL
- ⛽ TRAILER DUMP STATION
- 🏛 PARK HEADQUARTERS
- 🅿 PARKING AREA
- ⛺ CAMPING AREA
- SCREENED SHELTER AREA
- GROUP TRAILER AREA
- 🏕 PICNIC AREA
- MARINA / CONCESSION
- BATHHOUSE / ACTIVITY CENTER
- SWIMMING POOL
- 🚻 RESTROOM
- RESIDENCE
- FISH CLEANING SHELTER
- AMPHITHEATRE
- INTERPRETIVE TRAIL

Facilities & Activities

163 campsites
  16 with water only
  97 with water/electricity
  50 in group trailer area with water/electricity
10 screened shelters
restrooms
showers
trailer dump station
group picnic area
group shelter in group trailer area
amphitheater
picnicking
playgrounds
swimming pool
bathhouse/activity center
water skiing
lighted fishing pier
fish cleaning facility
boat ramps
interpretive trail
4 miles of hiking trails
marina/concession

For Information

Lake Livingston State Recreation Area
Route 9, Box 1300
Livingston, TX 77351
409/365-2201

Canoeing on Lake Livingston.

REGION 2

Lake Somerville State Recreation Area— Birch Creek Unit

✪	HEADQUARTERS	▲	MULTIUSE CAMPSITES	Ⓟ	PICNIC AREA
☗	RESIDENCE	⛺	GROUP TRAILER AREA	⬔	GROUP SHELTER
Ⓜ	MAINTENANCE	⬓	GROUP DINING HALL	Ⓕ	FISH CLEANING SHELTER
Ⓡ	RESTROOM	⬕	PAVILION	☐	INTERPRETIVE SHELTER
Ⓡ﹆	RESTROOM WITH SHOWER	Ⓟ	PARKING AREA	■	SCENIC OVERLOOK
Ⓓ	TRAILER DUMP STATION	⬖	GROUP CAMPING		

Facilities & Activities

123 campsites
  20 with water only
  103 with water/electricity
equestrian camping area
primitive campsites in the backcountry for
  equestrians/backpackers
restrooms
showers
trailer dump stations
group picnic shelters
30-site group trailer area with water/electricity
group shelter with kitchen
picnicking
swimming
water skiing
fishing pier
fish cleaning facility
boat ramps & docks
boat mooring slips
boat dump station
5 miles of hiking trails
14-mile hiking/horseback trail (21.6 miles, including
  loops) connecting the Birch and Nails Units
Interpretive Shelter

For Information

Lake Somerville State Recreation Area
Birch Creek Unit
Route 1, Box 499
Somerville, TX 77879
409/535-7763

The marina at Overlook Park at Somerville Lake.

Location

The Birch Creek Unit of Lake Somerville State Recreation Area is located on the north shore of Somerville Lake and contains 640 acres. From SH 36 travel 7.6 miles west on FM 60 to Park Road 57, then south for 4.3 miles.

Lake Somerville State Recreation Area— Nails Creek Unit

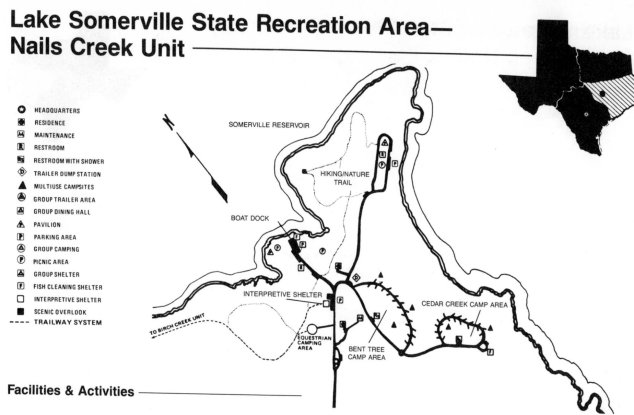

HEADQUARTERS
RESIDENCE
MAINTENANCE
RESTROOM
RESTROOM WITH SHOWER
TRAILER DUMP STATION
MULTIUSE CAMPSITES
GROUP TRAILER AREA
GROUP DINING HALL
PAVILION
PARKING AREA
GROUP CAMPING
PICNIC AREA
GROUP SHELTER
FISH CLEANING SHELTER
INTERPRETIVE SHELTER
SCENIC OVERLOOK
TRAILWAY SYSTEM

Facilities & Activities

70 campsites
  20 with water only
  40 with water/electricity
  10 walk-in tent sites
10-site equestrian camping area
primitive campsites in backcountry for
  equestrians/backpackers
restrooms
showers
trailer dump station
group picnic shelters
picnicking
swimming
water skiing
fishing
fish cleaning facility
boat ramp & dock
3 miles of hiking trails
14-mile hiking/horseback trail (21.6 miles, including
  loops) connecting the Birch and Nails Units
Interpretive Shelter

Location

The Nails Creek Unit of Lake Somerville State
Recreation Area is located on the south shore of Somerville Lake. From US 290 in Burton travel FM
1697 northwest, then FM 180 to park (see detailed
map of Somerville Lake, page 80).

For Information

Lake Somerville State Recreation Area
Nails Creek Unit
Route 1, Box 61C
Ledbetter, TX 78946
409/289-2392

*Enjoying a quiet moment on the lake as evening comes
to Texas. The two state recreation areas at Somerville
Lake have excellent camping and recreational facilities.*

Martin Dies, Jr. State Park

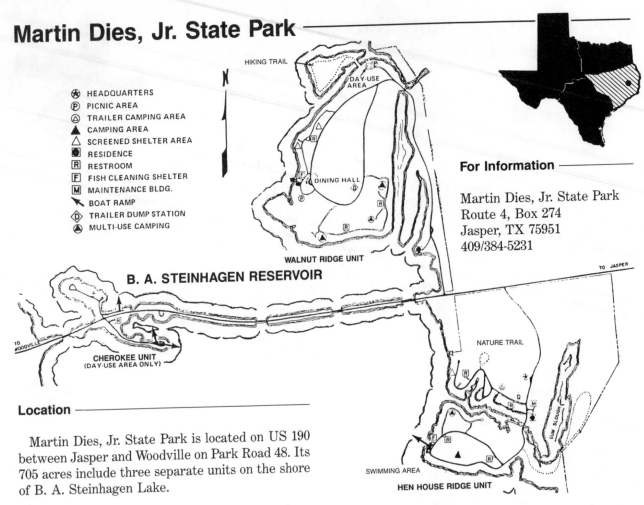

HIKING TRAIL

- ⊛ HEADQUARTERS
- Ⓟ PICNIC AREA
- △ TRAILER CAMPING AREA
- ▲ CAMPING AREA
- △ SCREENED SHELTER AREA
- Ⓑ RESIDENCE
- Ⓡ RESTROOM
- Ⓕ FISH CLEANING SHELTER
- Ⓜ MAINTENANCE BLDG.
- ↖ BOAT RAMP
- Ⓓ TRAILER DUMP STATION
- ⊿ MULTI-USE CAMPING

DAY-USE AREA

DINING HALL

WALNUT RIDGE UNIT

B. A. STEINHAGEN RESERVOIR

For Information

Martin Dies, Jr. State Park
Route 4, Box 274
Jasper, TX 75951
409/384-5231

TO JASPER

TO WOODVILLE

NATURE TRAIL

GUM SLOUGH

CHEROKEE UNIT
(DAY-USE AREA ONLY)

SWIMMING AREA

HEN HOUSE RIDGE UNIT

Location

Martin Dies, Jr. State Park is located on US 190 between Jasper and Woodville on Park Road 48. Its 705 acres include three separate units on the shore of B. A. Steinhagen Lake.

About the Park

A waterfowl refuge, operated by the Texas Parks and Wildlife Department, is adjacent to the park, which is itself a nature sanctuary abundant with wildlife. This park is also a delight for birdwatchers—it is the home of a wide variety of bird species.

This scenic slough on the B.A. Steinhagen Lake is accessible from the Walnut Ridge Unit of Martin Dies, Jr. State Park.

Facilities & Activities

182 campsites
  24 with water only (Walnut Ridge)
  44 with water only (Hen House Ridge)
  58 with water/electricity (Walnut Ridge)
  46 with water/electricity (Hen House Ridge)
  10 with water/electricity/sewage (Hen House Ridge)
25 screened shelters (Walnut Ridge)
21 screened shelters (Hen House Ridge)
restrooms
showers
trailer dump stations
dining hall
picnicking
playgrounds
swimming
water skiing
lighted fishing piers
fish cleaning facilities
boat ramps
boats for rent
3 nature/hiking trails

Mission Tejas State Historical Park

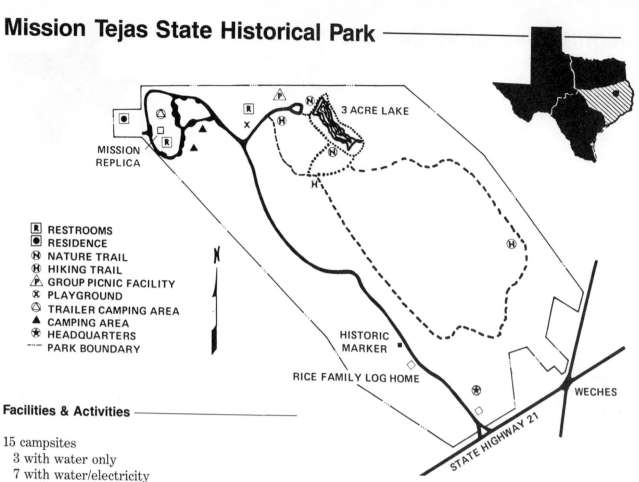

R RESTROOMS
⊙ RESIDENCE
Ⓝ NATURE TRAIL
Ⓗ HIKING TRAIL
Ⓟ GROUP PICNIC FACILITY
⊗ PLAYGROUND
⌂ TRAILER CAMPING AREA
▲ CAMPING AREA
✹ HEADQUARTERS
- - - PARK BOUNDARY

3 ACRE LAKE

MISSION REPLICA

HISTORIC MARKER

RICE FAMILY LOG HOME

WECHES

STATE HIGHWAY 21

Facilities & Activities

15 campsites
  3 with water only
  7 with water/electricity
  5 with water/electricity/sewage
restrooms
showers
trailer dump station
group picnic pavilion
group camp
picnicking
playground
fishing
¼-mile interpretive trail
1½ miles of hiking trails
historic structures: Rice family log home & Mission
  replica

Location

Mission Tejas State Historical Park is located
southwest of Weches off SH 21 to Park Road 44.
The 118-acre park includes a 2-acre lake.

For Information

Mission Tejas State Historical Park
Route 2, Box 108
Grapeland, TX 75844
409/687-2394

*Mission San Francisco De Los Tejas, Mission Tejas
State Park, Weches, Tx.*

Mother Neff State Park

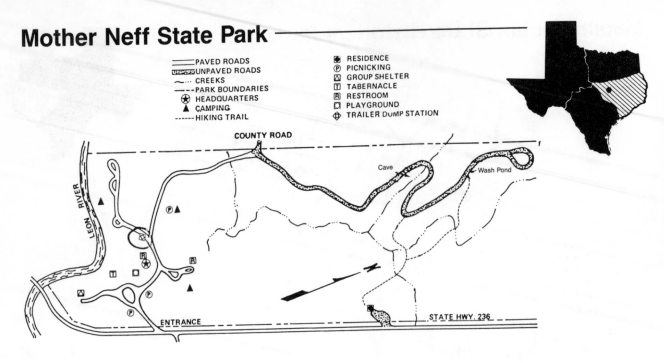

PAVED ROADS
UNPAVED ROADS
~ CREEKS
PARK BOUNDARIES
★ HEADQUARTERS
▲ CAMPING
HIKING TRAIL

RESIDENCE
P PICNICKING
GROUP SHELTER
T TABERNACLE
R RESTROOM
PLAYGROUND
TRAILER DUMP STATION

COUNTY ROAD

Cave

Wash Pond

LEON RIVER

ENTRANCE

STATE HWY. 236

Location

Mother Neff State Park is located 15 miles northwest of Temple on SH 36, then 5 miles north on SH 236. It may also be reached off of SH 317 by traveling 6.4 miles west of Moody on FM 107, then 1.8 miles south on SH 236. The 259-acre park is by the Leon River.

Facilities & Activities

21 campsites
  15 with water only
  6 with water/electricity
restrooms
showers
trailer dump station
group shelters
picnicking
playground
fishing (on nearby Leon River)
1½ miles of hiking trails
National Champion Texas Oak
Tonkawa Indian Cave

For Information

Mother Neff State Park
Route 1, Box 58
Moody, TX 76557
817/853-2389

About the Park

The park's 259 acres embrace every soil type known to Coryell County, from rich alluvial soils along the Leon River to the semibarren lands atop the limestone hills that reach into the prairie. Recreational facilities, with emphasis on picnicking and camping, are concentrated in the river bottom area. A natural environment prevails throughout the remainder of the park, where wooded areas provide recreational opportunities for hikers, birdwatchers and nature study.

One outstanding feature of Mother Neff State Park is its beautiful trees; among them is the National Champion Texas Oak.

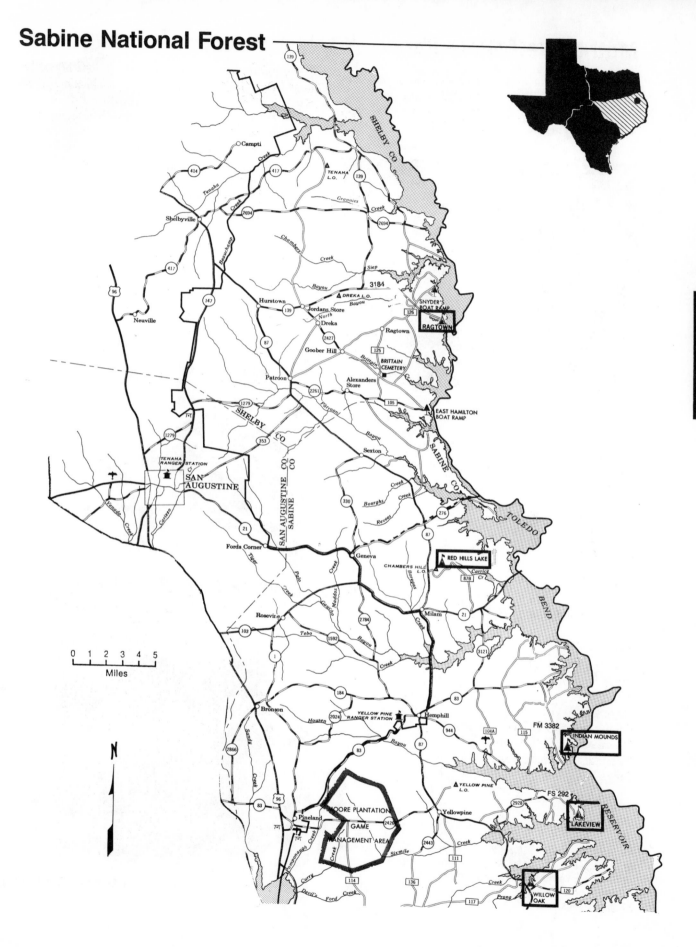

Sabine National Forest (continued)

Sabine National Forest is located in Jasper, Sabine, San Augustine, Newton and Shelby counties and is the largest of the national forests in Texas, with 158,450 acres.

Camping at Redhills Lake, Sabine National Forest in East Texas.

For Information

East Hamilton, Ragtown, Snyders:
Ranger, Tenaha District
101 S. Bolivar
San Augustine, TX 75972
409/275-2632

Indian Mounds, Lakeview, Red Hills Lake,
and Willow Oak:
Ranger, Yellowpine District
P.O. Box F
(201 S. Palm)
Hemphill, TX 75948
409/787-3870

Campground	Facilities	Fee Area	No. of Campsites	Showers	Boating	Trailer Dump Station	Trailer Space
Indian Mounds		X	56		L		X
Lake View		X	10		A		X
Ragtown		X	25	X	L	X	X
Red Hills Lake		X	28	X	E	X	X
Willow Oak		X	10		L		X

Notes:
A = Boat Access   E = Electric Motors Only   L = Boat Launch
All campsites have drinking water and sanitary facilities.
Camping and fishing is available at all campsites.
Red Hills Lake also offers some campsites with electricity, picnicking, swimming and a hiking trail.

Locations

Indian Mounds Recreation Area is located on Toledo Bend Reservoir, east of Hemphill via FM 83 about 8 miles, then 4 miles south on FM 3382.

Red Hills Lake Recreation Area is located about 3 miles north of Milam off of SH 87.

Willow Oak Lake Recreation Area is located on Toledo Bend Reservoir about 15 miles southeast of Hemphill off of SH 87.

Lakeview Recreation Area is located about 14 miles southeast of Hemphill on FM 2928 off of SH 87.

Ragtown Recreation Area is located on Toledo Bend Reservoir about 15 miles southeast of Shelbyville via SH 87, FM 139, FM 3184, and Forest Service roads.

State Highway 87 two miles north of Milam in Sabine National Forest.

An unoccupied picnic table by any river or lake is an open invitation to fun.

Sam Houston National Forest

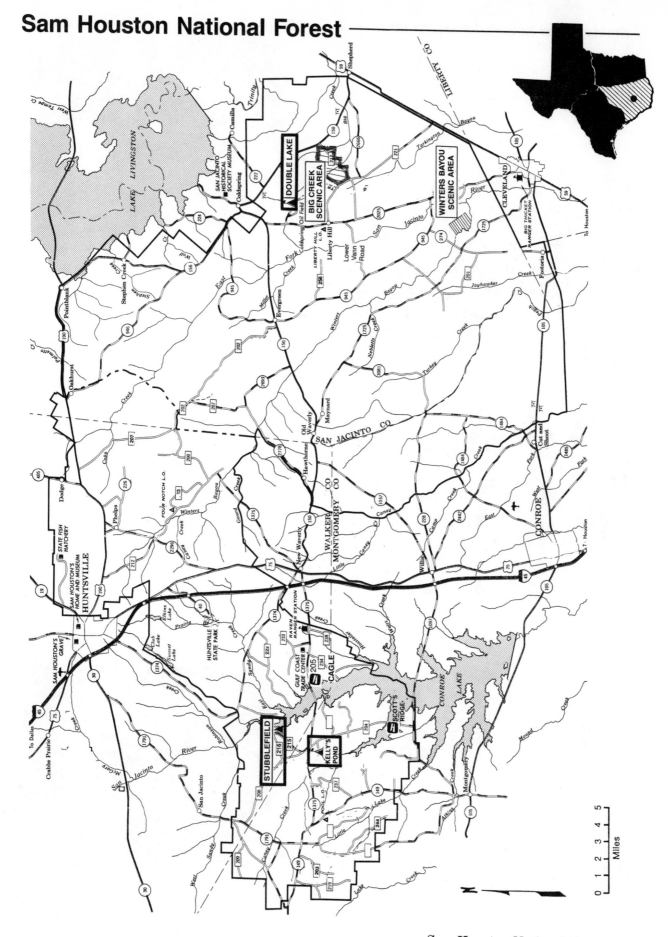

Sam Houston National Forest (continued)

Sam Houston National Forest is located in Montgomery, San Jacinto and Walker counties and contains 158,647 acres.

Fishing from the bridge on Forest Road 215. . .

. . .where the San Jacinto River feeds into Lake Conroe.

This pavillion at Stubblefield Lake Recreation Area is designated as a group picnic area.

Locations

Stubblefield Lake Recreation Area is located on the west fork of the San Jacinto River on FSR 215 off of FM 1375, approximately 8 miles west of New Waverly from IH 45.

Kelly's Pond Recreation Area is located off of FSR 204 south of FM 1375 approximately 8 miles west of New Waverly from IH 45.

For Information

Kelly's Pond and Stubblefield
Ranger, Raven District
P.O. Drawer 1000
(FM 1375)
New Waverly, TX 77358
409/344-6205

Campground \ Facilities	# of Campsites	Fee Area	Boating	Fishing	Hiking Trails	Trailer Space
Double Lake	49	X	E	X	X	X
Kelly Pond	Pr				X	
Stubblefield	28	X	A	X	X	X

Notes:
A = Boat Access   E = Electric Motors Only
Pr = Primitive
All campgrounds are equipped for camping and provide sanitary facilities.
Picnicking is available at all campsites.
Kelly Pond is not equipped with drinking water.

Sam Houston National Forest (continued)
Double Lake Recreation Area

Location

Double Lake Recreation Area is located 4 miles south of Coldspring just off of FM 2025 via SH 150. The 310-acre recreation area located in the Sam Houston National Forest surrounds a beautiful 20-acre lake.

For Information

Ranger, San Jacinto District
308 N. Belcher
(FM 2025)
Cleveland, TX 77327
713/592-6461

Swimmers and boaters alike enjoy the beauty of the lake at Double Lake Recreation Area.

This fisherman appears to be tranquilized by his surroundings. . . I wonder if he even has bait on his hook?

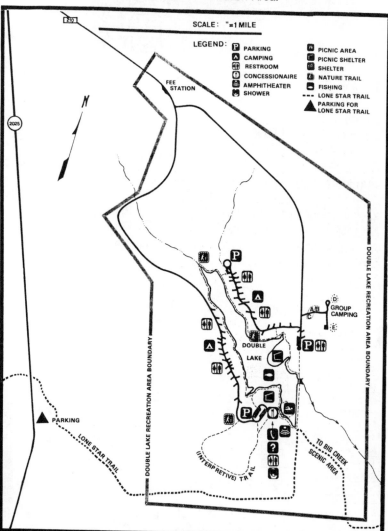

Facilities & Activities

49 campsites
6 group camping units
flush toilets/showers
group picnic shelter
amphitheater
picnicking
swimming beach & beachhouse
canoe/paddle boat rentals
fishing
boat launch (electric motors only)
concession
¾-mile self-guided nature trail
1.4-mile Lakeshore Hiking Trail
* 5-mile trail leading to the Big Creek Scenic Area; access to the 140-mile Lone Star Hiking Trail that traverses the Sam Houston National Forest

* Note: For information and detailed maps of the Big Creek Scenic Area and the Lone Star Trail, see page 154 of *Hiking and Backpacking Trails of Texas*, 3rd Edition, by Mickey Little, Lone Star Books, 1990.

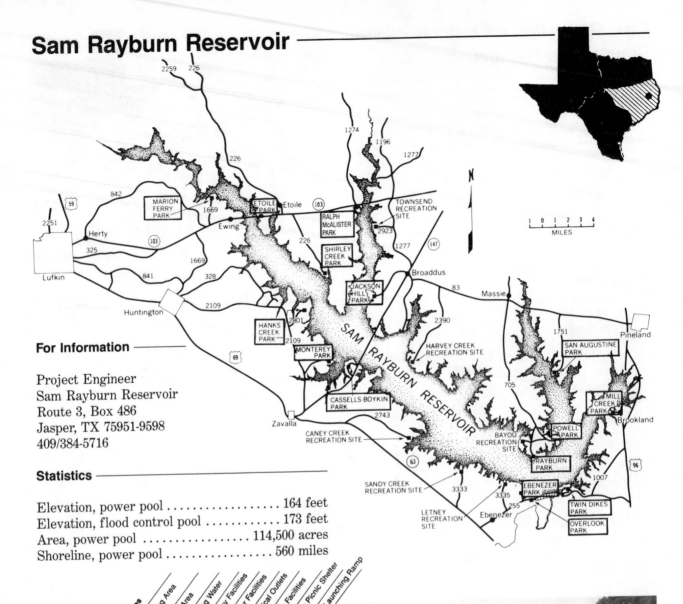

For Information

Project Engineer
Sam Rayburn Reservoir
Route 3, Box 486
Jasper, TX 75951-9598
409/384-5716

Statistics

Elevation, power pool . . . . 164 feet
Elevation, flood control pool . . . . 173 feet
Area, power pool . . . . 114,500 acres
Shoreline, power pool . . . . 560 miles

Facilities Campground	Camping Area	Trailer Area	Drinking Water	Sanitary Facilities	Shower Facilities	Electrical Outlets	Picnic Facilities	Group Picnic Shelter	Boat Launching Ramp
Overlook Park			X	X			X		
Ebenezer Park	X		X	X			X		
Cassells-Boykin Park	X	X	X	X			X		X
Monterey Park				X					X
Hanks Creek Park	X	X	X	X	X	X	X	X	X
Marion Ferry Park				X					X
Etoile Park	X		X	X			X		X
Shirley Creek Park	X	X	X	X	X	X	X		X
Ralph McAlister Park				X					X
Jackson Hill Park	X	X	X	X	X	X	X	X	X
Rayburn Park	X		X	X			X		X
Powell Park	X	X	X	X	X	X	X	X	X
San Augustine Park	X		X	X	X	X	X	X	X
Mill Creek Park	X	X	X	X	X	X	X	X	X
Twin Dikes Park	X	X	X	X	X	X	X	X	X

Notes:
These parks are all operated by the Corps of Engineers with the following exceptions:
—Cassells-Boykin State Park is operated by the state of Texas.
—Shirley Creek Park is operated by Nacogdoches County.
—The locations of 6 other recreation sites are shown on the map. They are operated by Angelina National Forest. See page 51.

Boat ramps and trailer parking areas at Sam Rayburn Reservoir are quite spacious to take care of the many fishing enthusiasts, particularly on weekends.

Sea Rim State Park

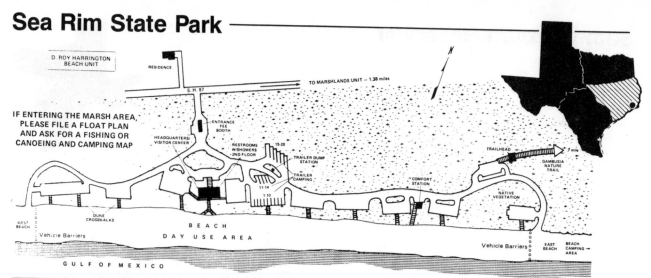

IF ENTERING THE MARSH AREA, PLEASE FILE A FLOAT PLAN AND ASK FOR A FISHING OR CANOEING AND CAMPING MAP

The 7/10-mile interpretive marsh trail at Sea Rim State Park is a boardwalk trail.

About the Park

The park is named for that portion of the Gulf shoreline where the marsh grasses extend into the surf in a zone termed sea rim marsh. Of the park's 5.2 miles of coastline, 2.2 miles contain a biologically important zone wherein salt tidal marshlands meet the Gulf waters. The three remaining miles of shoreline are sandy beach with small, picturesque sand dunes that separate the beach from the marshlands. Behind the dunes lies the headquarters complex with interpretive exhibits, overnight camping facilities and an interpretive marsh trail.

Location

Sea Rim State Park is located 10 miles west of Sabine Pass and consists of 15,019 acres of Gulf coast beach and marshland. State Highway 87 separates the park into 2 distinct areas. South of the highway lies the D. Roy Harrington Beach Unit and north of SH 87 is the Marshlands Unit, which comprises the greater portion of the park.

Facilities & Activities

20 campsites with water/electricity
primitive camping on 2 miles of open beach
6 camping platforms (Marshlands Unit)
restrooms
showers
trailer dump station
picnicking
swimming beach
Visitor Center with interpretive exhibits
observation deck
concessions
7/10-mile boardwalk interpretive marsh trail
fishing (marsh/lake system & coastal surf)
boat ramp (Marshlands Unit)
boat channel and pirogue/canoe trails
  (Marshlands Unit)
4 wildlife observation blinds (Marshlands Unit)

The unique Visitor Center at Sea Rim affords a good view of the beach and Gulf of Mexico.

For Information

Sea Rim State Park
P.O. Box 1066
Sabine Pass, TX 77655
409/971-2559

Somerville Lake

For Information

Somerville Lake
P.O. Box 549
Somerville, TX 77879-0549
409/596-1622

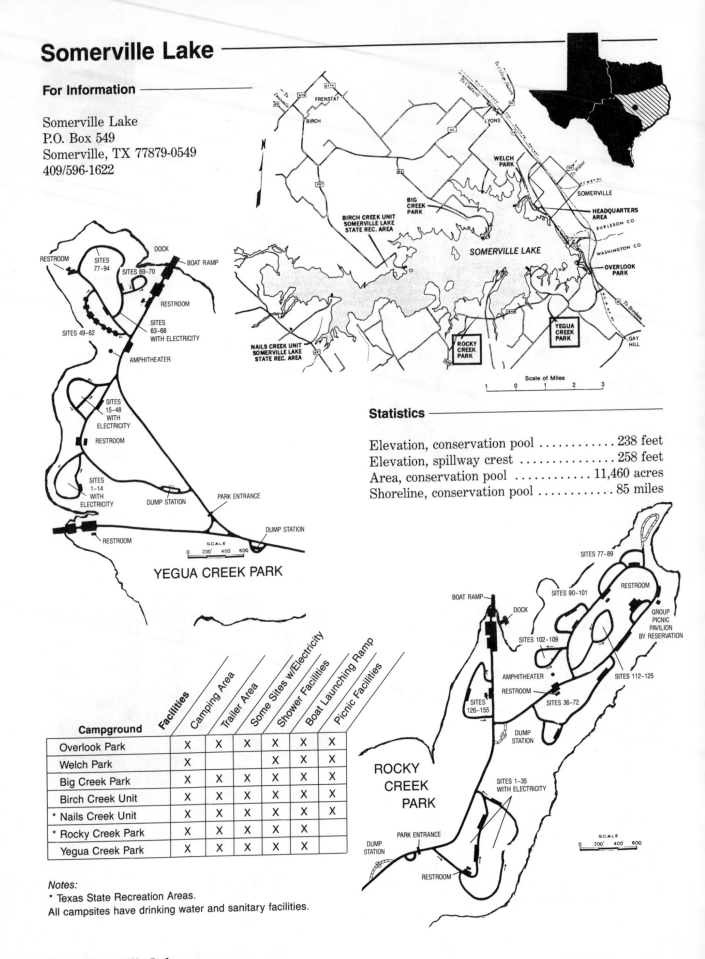

YEGUA CREEK PARK

Statistics

Elevation, conservation pool . . . . 238 feet
Elevation, spillway crest . . . . 258 feet
Area, conservation pool . . . . 11,460 acres
Shoreline, conservation pool . . . . 85 miles

ROCKY CREEK PARK

Campground	Facilities / Camping Area	Trailer Area	Some Sites w/Electricity	Shower Facilities	Boat Launching Ramp	Picnic Facilities
Overlook Park	X	X	X	X	X	X
Welch Park	X			X	X	X
Big Creek Park	X	X	X	X	X	X
Birch Creek Unit	X	X	X	X	X	X
* Nails Creek Unit	X	X	X	X	X	X
* Rocky Creek Park	X	X	X	X	X	
Yegua Creek Park	X	X	X	X	X	

Notes:
* Texas State Recreation Areas.
All campsites have drinking water and sanitary facilities.

Stephen F. Austin State Historical Park

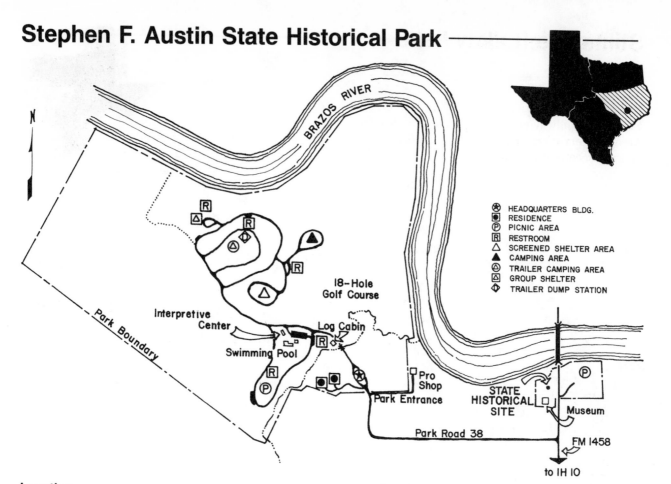

HEADQUARTERS BLDG.
RESIDENCE
PICNIC AREA
RESTROOM
SCREENED SHELTER AREA
CAMPING AREA
TRAILER CAMPING AREA
GROUP SHELTER
TRAILER DUMP STATION

Location

Stephen F. Austin State Historical Park is located 2.2 miles north of San Felipe off of FM 1458 from IH 10. The 664-acre park is on the Brazos River.

For Information

Stephen F. Austin State Historical Park
P.O. Box 125
San Felipe, TX 77473
409/885-3613

Facilities & Activities

80 campsites
   40 with water only
   40 with water/electricity/sewage
20 screened shelters
restrooms
showers
trailer dump station
group screened shelter with kitchen
picnicking
playground
swimming pool
fishing
1-mile hiking trail
18-hole golf course
park store
historic structure: log cabin
State Historical Site/Museum

*Stephen F. Austin State Historical Park has 20 screened shelters (see page **148** for a list of other state parks/recreation areas with screened shelters).*

Stillhouse Hollow Lake

Statistics

Elevation, conservation pool .... 622 feet
Elevation, spillway crest .... 666 feet
Area, conservation pool .... 6,430 acres
Shoreline, conservation pool .... 58 miles

(Map of Stillhouse Hollow Lake showing: FM 2410, TO NOLANVILLE, US HWY 190, TO BELTON, STILLHOUSE PARK, MARINA, FM 1670, HEADQUARTERS AREA, OVERLOOK PARK, Lampasas, DANA PEAK PARK, COMMANCHE GAP ROAD, CEDAR KNOB ROAD, Shallow, STILLHOUSE HOLLOW LAKE, CEDAR GAP PARK, Union Grove, UNION GROVE PARK, YOUNGSPORT–BELTON ROAD, BLUFF PARK, FM 2484, FM 1670, To U.S. Hwy 81, Scale of Miles 0 .5 1 2 3, N)

Stillhouse Hollow Lake, created by impoundment of the Lampasas River, has 58 miles of shoreline.

For Information

Reservoir Manager
Stillhouse Hollow Lake
Route 3, Box 3407
Belton, TX 76513
817/939-1829

LOCATIONS	Drinking Water	Restrooms	Picnic Facilities	Camping Area	Boat Launching Ramp	Boat Storage (Rental)	Boat & Motor Rental	Fishing Bait & Supplies	Restaurant or Snack Bar	Fishing Barge	Electrical Outlets
CEDAR GAP PARK		X		X	X				X		X
DANA PEAK PARK	X	X	X	X	X				X		X
OVERLOOK PARK	X	X	X								
STILLHOUSE PARK	X	X	X	X	X	X	X	X	X	X	
UNION GROVE PARK	X	X	X	X	X				X		X

Toledo Bend Reservoir

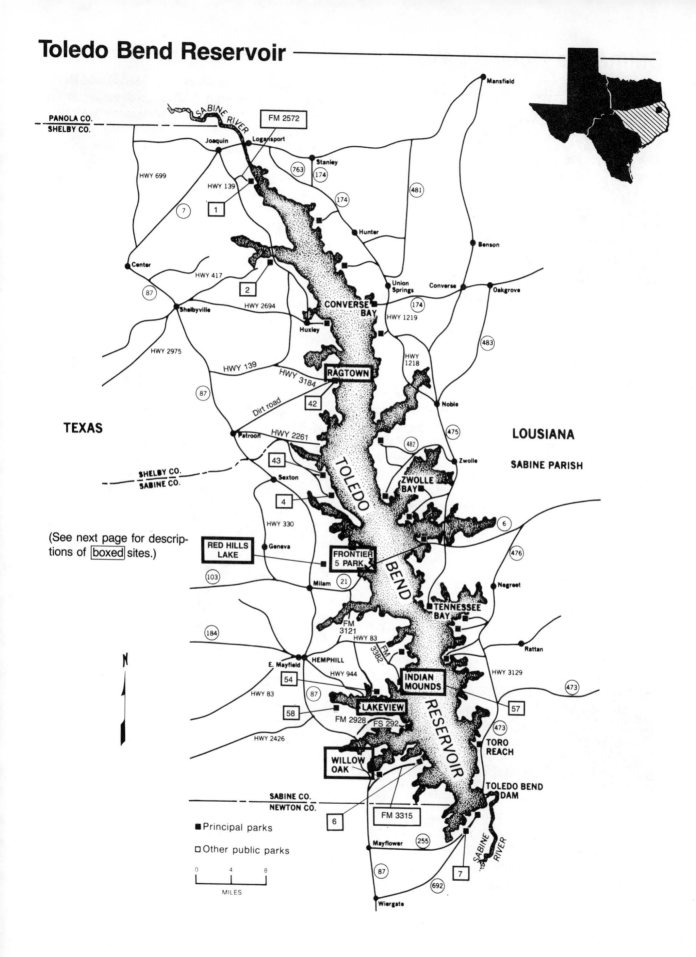

FM 2572

PANOLA CO.
SHELBY CO.

Joaquin
Logansport

HWY 699
HWY 139

1

763
174
Stanley

174

481

Hunter

Benson

Center

HWY 417

2

Union
Springs
Converse
Oakgrove

87

Shelbyville

HWY 2694

CONVERSE
BAY

174

HWY 1219

Huxley

HWY 2975

RAGTOWN

HWY 1218

483

HWY 139
HWY 3184

42

TEXAS

87

Dirt road

HWY 2261

Patroon

Noble

482

475

LOUSIANA

SABINE PARISH

Zwolle

SHELBY CO.
SABINE CO.

43

Sexton

ZWOLLE
BAY

4

HWY 330

TOLEDO

6

(See next page for descriptions of boxed sites.)

RED HILLS
LAKE

Geneva

FRONTIER
5 PARK

476

103

Milam

21

BEND

Negreet

FM
3121
HWY 83

TENNESSEE
BAY

184

FM
3382

Rattan

E. Mayfield
HEMPHILL

HWY 944

HWY 3129

473

54

INDIAN
MOUNDS

HWY 83

87

LAKEVIEW

57

58

FM 2928
FS 292

473

N

HWY 2426

TORO
REACH

WILLOW
OAK

RESERVOIR

TOLEDO BEND
DAM

SABINE CO.
NEWTON CO.

6

FM 3315

■ Principal parks

□ Other public parks

Mayflower

255

87

7

0   4   8
MILES

692

Wiergate

Toledo Bend Reservoir   83

Toledo Bend Reservoir (continued)

Toledo Bend Reservoir, a sportsman's paradise bordering Sabine National Forest, in East Texas.

Facilities

The Toledo Bend Reservoir map distributed by the Sabine River Authority of Texas locates the various recreation areas by site numbers. The recreation areas maintained by the Sabine National Forest are also located on their map (see pages 73–74 for details on facilities) and are thus displayed here. The eight recreation sites in Texas provided by the Sabine River Authority have only primitive facilities, whereas, the five recreation sites maintained by the U.S. Forest Service are more developed. Facilities at each site are listed below in the order that they appear on the map, reading from north to south.

Site 1—Picnic tables, toilet facilities & boat ramp

Site 2—Boat ramp

Site 42—*Ragtown* (U.S. Forest Service)

Site 43—Undeveloped & suitable for primitive camping

Site 4—Undeveloped & suitable for primitive camping
   —*Red Hills Lake* (U.S. Forest Service)

Site 5—*Frontier Park* (commercial lease); full service marina, tackle shop, swimming pool, restaurant, rental units, RV hookups and campsites.

Site 57—*Indian Mounds* (U.S. Forest Service)

Site 54—Undeveloped & suitable for primitive camping

Site 58—Undeveloped & suitable for primitive camping
   —*Lakeview* (U.S. Forest Service)
   —*Willow Oak* (U.S. Forest Service)

Site 6—Undeveloped & suitable for primitive camping

Site 7—Picnic tables, toilet facilities & boat ramp

About Toledo Bend

With 1,200 miles of shoreline, Toledo Bend Reservoir offers an almost unlimited opportunity for recreation. Public facilities, as well as many private facilities, are available for swimming, boating, picnicking, fishing, camping, hunting, and sightseeing.

Fed by the Sabine River on its route to the Gulf of Mexico, Toledo Bend Reservoir is one of the nation's largest man-made bodies of water, covering an area of 185,000 acres.

Statistics

Elevation, power pool drawdown . . . . . . 162.2 feet
Elevation, power pool . . . . 172 feet
Area, power pool . . . . 185,000 miles
Shoreline . . . . 1,200 miles

A view of Toledo Bend from the observation point near the dam.

For Information

Reservoir Manager
Sabine River Authority of Texas
Toledo Bend Division
Route 1, Box 270
Burkeville, TX 75932
409/565-2273

Wolf Creek Park

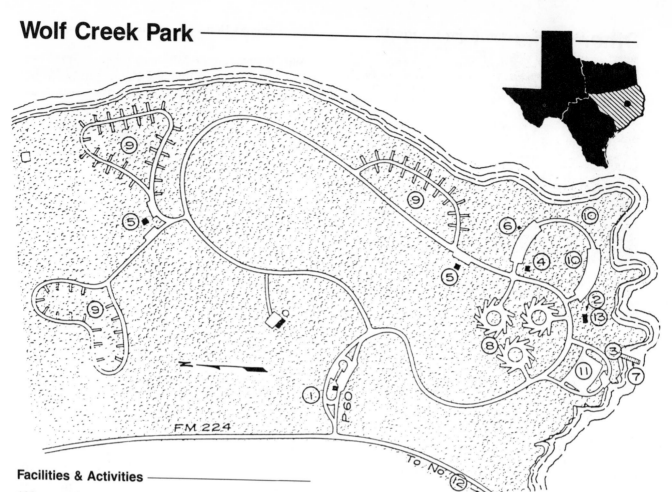

Facilities & Activities

103 campsites
   30 sites with full hook-ups
   54 tent sites with electricity
   19 tent sites without electricity
restrooms/showers/washateria
group shelter
picnicking
playground
swimming (beach)
water skiing/sailing/boating
fishing
fishing pier
fish cleaning facility
boat ramp
marina & store
adjacent lakeside 18-hole golf course

* Park facilities are open March 1–November 30
  each year.
Reservations accepted.

For Information

Wolf Creek Park
P.O. Box 309
Coldspring, TX 77331
409/653-4312

Location

Wolf Creek Park is located off of US 190 east of Huntsville. Take SH 156 at Point Blank, then FM 224. The park is located on the west shore of 90,000-acre Lake Livingston, impounding water of the Trinity River.

The park is as popular with tent campers as it is with those who camp in pop-up tents and RVs.

Other Parks in Region 2*

ANAHUAC — **Double Bayou Park**
From I-10: Tex 61 S 4 mi; FM 562 S 7 mi; Eagle Ferry Rd W .5 mi. On *East Fork of Double Bayou.* Camp area 30 acres; limit 10 days. Fl toilets. Fish, playground, ball field. (County Pk Dept, Box 1206, Anahuac 77514, tel 409/267-3571.)

ANAHUAC — **Fort Anahuac Park**
From I-10: FM 563 S 7 mi; Tex 61 W 1 mi; S. Main St S 1 mi. On *Trinity Bay.* Wheeled camper sites 6 w/elec & water, fee. Other camp area 40 acres. Limit 4 days. Fl toilets. Swim-lake; fish, boat ramp, playground, 2 picnic shelters, historical markers, 3 ball fields. (County Pk Dept, Box 1206, Anahuac 77514, tel 409/267-3571.)

ANAHUAC — **James H. Robbins Memorial Park**
From I-10: Tex 61 S 4 mi; FM 562 S 22 mi; Smith Point Rd S 1 mi; Hawkins Camp Rd NW 1.6 mi. On *Galveston & East Bays.* Camp area 10 acres, limit 14 days. Fl toilets, no drinking water. Fish, boat ramp, scenic views, observation tower. (County Pk Dept, Box 1206, Anahuac 77514, tel 409/267-3571.)

ANAHUAC — **Job Beason Park**
From I-10: FM 563 S 11 mi; Eagle Rd S 4.7 mi; W Bayshore Rd S .5 mi. On *Double Bayou.* Camp area 12 acres, limit 14 days. Fl toilets. Bait, fish, boat ramp, playground. (County Pk Dept, Box 1206, Anahuac 77514, tel 409/267-3571.)

ANAHUAC — **McCollum Park**
From I-10: FM 3180 S 5 mi; FM 2354 S 3 mi; McCollum Park Rd E 1 mi. On *Trinity Bay.* Camp area 10 acres, fee. Fl toilets. Fish, playground. (County Pk Dept, Box 1206, Anahuac 77514, tel 409/267-3571.)

ANAHUAC — **White Memorial Park**
From I-10: Tex 61 S .1 mi. On *White's & Turtle Bayous.* Wheeled camper sites 7; other camp area 83 acres, limit 14 days. Fl toilets, picnic shelters. Swim-lake; fish, boat ramp, historical markers, nature trails. (County Pk Dept, Box 1206, Anahuac 77514, tel 409/267-3571.)

ANAHUAC — **Winnie-Stowell Park**
From I-10: Tex 124 S 1 mi; LeBlanc Rd E .1 mi. Camp area 30 acres, limit 14 days. Fl toilets. Playground, pavilion, ball field. (County Pk Dept, Box 1206, Anahuac 77514, tel 409/267-3571.)

BEAUMONT — **Tyrrell Park**
From I-10 Walden Rd Exit (848): Walden Rd SE .5 mi; Tyrrell Park Rd S .8 mi. Wheeled backin camper sites 94 w/elec & water, fee; limit 7 days. Dump sta. Golf, grills, playground, riding stable, botanical gardens & garden center in nearby park. (City Parks Dept., Box 3827, Beaumont 77704, tel 409/838-0652.)

GATESVILLE — **Faunt LeRoy Park**
Within city: 7th St S, 2 blks S of courthouse. On *Leon River.* Wheeled backin camper sites w/elec, water & sewage, 8, free first day, limit 14 days; primitive tent sites, 3, free first day, limit 14 days. Fl toilets, tables & grills. Playground, volleyball court. (City Park Dept., City Hall, Gatesville 76528, tel 817/865-2226.)

GROESBECK — **Public Use Area #2**
From Tex 164: FM 937 SE 11.3 mi; FM 3371 E & N 3.6 mi to W side of *Lake Limestone.* Primitive camp area 25 acres, no drinking water, limit 14 days. Fish, boat ramp. (Brazos Riv Auth, Rt 3, Box 89-A, Thornton 76687, tel 214/529-2141.)

GROESBECK — **Public Use Area #3**
From Tex 164: FM 937 SE 11.3 mi; FM 3371 E & N 5 mi to E side of *Lake Limestone.* Primitive camp area 17 acres, no drinking water, limit 14 days. Fish, boat ramp. (Brazos Riv Auth, Rt 3, Box 89-A, Thornton 76687, tel 214/529-2141.)

GROESBECK — **Public Use Area #5**
From US 79: FM 1146 N 6.7 mi; local rd W 1.8 mi to E end of dam. On *Lake Limestone.* Primitive camp area 10 acres, no drinking water, limit 14 days. Fish, boat ramp. (Brazos Riv Auth, Rt 3, Box 89-A, Thornton 76687, tel 214/529-2141.)

HOUSTON — **Alexander Deussen County Park**
From I-10/US 59: I-10 E 7.9 mi; Federal Rd & C.E. King Pkwy N & E 11.9 mi (12303 Sonnier Dr). On *Lake Houston.* Tent camping permitted on weekends only; RVs any time, limit 14 days. Wheeled backin camper sites 14 w/elec & water, fee. Dump sta, fl toilets, shelters, grills, snack bar, ice, groc. Swim-lake; bicycle trails, fish, boat & sailboat ramps, playgrounds (one for handicapped). (Rt 5, Box 1151, Houston 77044, tel 713/454-7057.)

HOUSTON — **Spring Creek Park**
From FM 1960: FM 149 NW 11.5 mi; Brown Rd W 1 mi. On *Spring Creek.* Wheeled backin camper sites w/elec & water 8, tent sites 75; other camp area 114 acres, limit 2 days; 7 days advance rsvns needed. Dump sta, fl toilets, grills. Fish, playground. (11901 W. Hardy, Houston 77076, tel 713/447-3619.)

LIVINGSTON — **Tombigbee Lake Campground**
From US 59: US 190 E 17 mi; local rd S 2 mi. Alabama-Coushatta Indian Reservation. On *Tombigbee Lake.* Wheeled camper sites 137; w/elec, water & sewage 49, w/elec & water 45, fee; tent sites 43, fee. Cabin by rsvn, fee. Dump sta, fl toilets, showers, grills. Swim-lake; fish, scenic views. (Rt 3, Box 640, Livingston 77351, tel 409/563-4391, or in TX, 1-800-392-4794.)

MARLIN — **Falls on the Brazos Park**
From Tex 7: Tex 6 S 2.1 mi; FM 712 SW 2.6 mi; local rd SW .3 mi. On *Brazos River.* Wheeled camper sites w/elec & water 13, fee; tent sites 15, fee; other camp area 5 acres. Dump sta, fl toilets, grills, snack bar, ice, groc. Swim-river; fish, playground. (Co Pk, Box 312-A, Marlin 76661, tel 817/883-3203.)

MEXIA — **Lake Mexia Marina**
From Tex 14: US 84 W 6.4 mi; FM 2681 S 1.3 mi. On *Lake Mexia.* Wheeled camper sites 25 w/elec & water, fee; other camp area 12 acres, fee; screened shelters 9, fee. Dump sta, fl toilets, showers, bait, tables, ice, groc, bathhouse. Swim-lake; fish, boat ramp, game room, playground. (Rt 1, Box 471-A, Mexia 76667, tel 817/562-5483.)

VIDOR — **Claiborne West Park**
From I-10: Exit 864 to north access rd, E 2 mi. On *Cow Bayou.* Prepared tent sites 20, fee. Fl toilets, showers; pavilions, deposit fee. Shelters, grills, fish, playground, softball, amphitheater, 5-mile nature trail. (Co Pk, 4105 North St, Vidor 77662, tel 409/745-2255. Rsvns acptd.)

ZAVALLA — **Cassells-Boykin State Park**
From Tex 69: Tex 147 E 6.1 mi; FM 3123 N .8 mi. On *Sam Rayburn Lake.* Wheeled camper sites 30, fee, limit 14 days. Dump sta, pit toilets, grills. Fish, boat ramp, tables, scenic views. Gas, bait, groc, ice nearby. (Rt 4, Box 274, Jasper 75951, tel 409/384-5231.)

The boat ramp at Cassells-Boykin State Park, is heavily used by fishermen to gain access to Sam Rayburn Reservoir; the campground is small and rustic, but quite scenic.

* Source: *Texas Public Campgrounds*, State Dept. of Highways and Public Transportation, Travel and Information Div., P.O. Box 5064, Austin, TX 78763.

Region 3

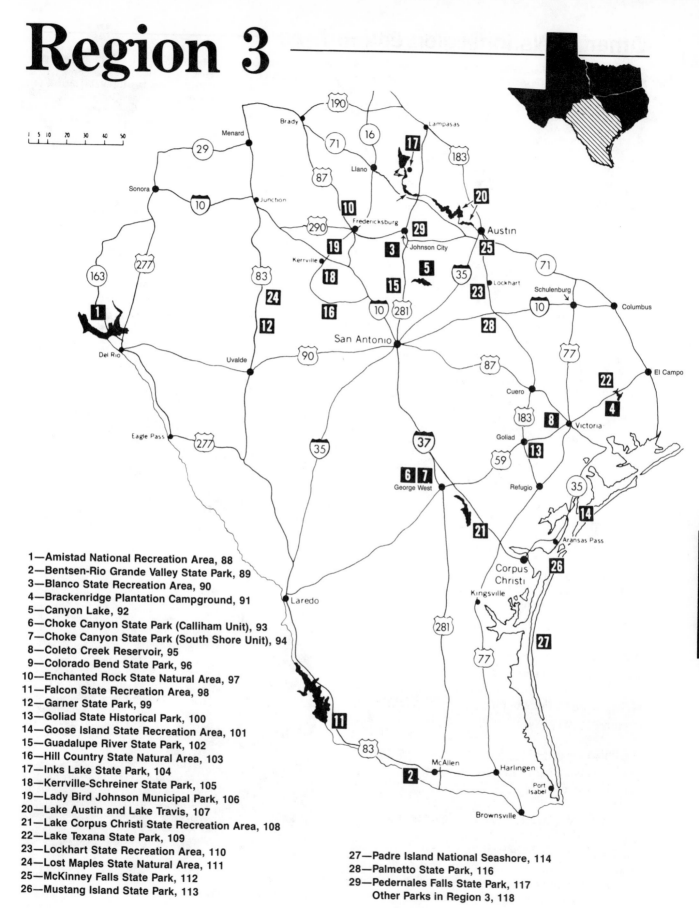

1—Amistad National Recreation Area, 88
2—Bentsen-Rio Grande Valley State Park, 89
3—Blanco State Recreation Area, 90
4—Brackenridge Plantation Campground, 91
5—Canyon Lake, 92
6—Choke Canyon State Park (Calliham Unit), 93
7—Choke Canyon State Park (South Shore Unit), 94
8—Coleto Creek Reservoir, 95
9—Colorado Bend State Park, 96
10—Enchanted Rock State Natural Area, 97
11—Falcon State Recreation Area, 98
12—Garner State Park, 99
13—Goliad State Historical Park, 100
14—Goose Island State Recreation Area, 101
15—Guadalupe River State Park, 102
16—Hill Country State Natural Area, 103
17—Inks Lake State Park, 104
18—Kerrville-Schreiner State Park, 105
19—Lady Bird Johnson Municipal Park, 106
20—Lake Austin and Lake Travis, 107
21—Lake Corpus Christi State Recreation Area, 108
22—Lake Texana State Park, 109
23—Lockhart State Recreation Area, 110
24—Lost Maples State Natural Area, 111
25—McKinney Falls State Park, 112
26—Mustang Island State Park, 113

27—Padre Island National Seashore, 114
28—Palmetto State Park, 116
29—Pedernales Falls State Park, 117
Other Parks in Region 3, 118

Amistad National Recreation Area

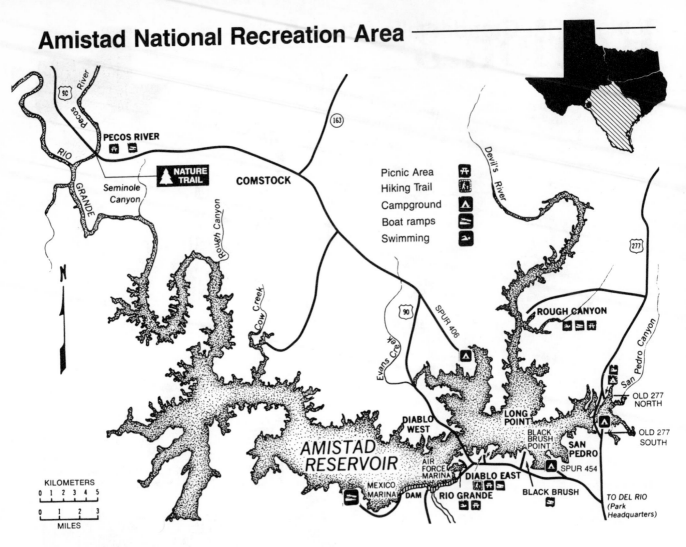

PECOS RIVER

COMSTOCK

NATURE TRAIL

Seminole Canyon

Rough Canyon

Cow Creek

Pecos River

RIO GRANDE

Devil's River

Picnic Area
Hiking Trail
Campground
Boat ramps
Swimming

SPUR 406

Evans Creek

ROUGH CANYON

San Pedro Canyon

DIABLO WEST

LONG POINT

BLACK BRUSH POINT

SAN PEDRO

OLD 277 NORTH

OLD 277 SOUTH

SPUR 454

AMISTAD RESERVOIR

AIR FORCE MARINA

MEXICO MARINA

DAM

DIABLO EAST

RIO GRANDE

BLACK BRUSH

TO DEL RIO (Park Headquarters)

KILOMETERS
0 1 2 3 4 5

0 1 2 3
MILES

For Information

Amistad Recreation Area
P.O. Box 420367
Del Rio, TX 77842-0367
512/775-7491

Statistics

Elevation, conservation pool .... 1,117 feet
Elevation, flood control pool .... 1,144.3 feet
Area, conservation pool .... 67,000 acres
Shoreline, conservation pool .... 850 miles

Facilities

primitive camping at designated sites
chemical toilets
trash cans
drinking water available at Headquarters &
   Diablo East
camping from boats permitted on the shore below
   contour 1,144.3 feet except in restricted areas
   such as the immediate vicinity of marinas and designated swim beaches

Impoundment water of Amistad Reservoir extends some 25 miles up the Devils River.

Bentsen-Rio Grande Valley State Park

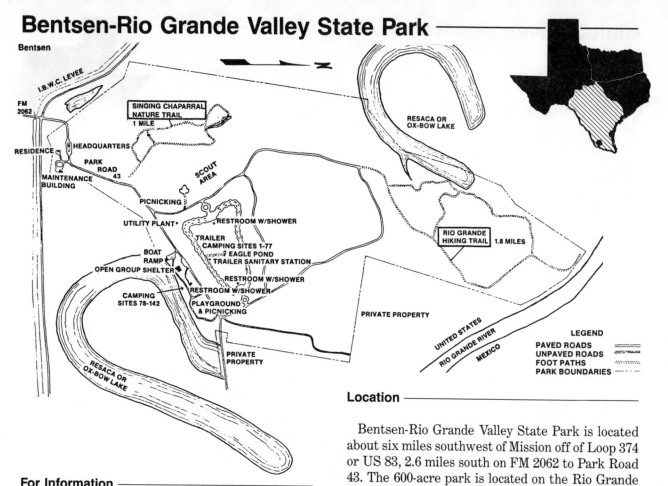

Bentsen

I.B.W.C. LEVEE

FM 2062

RESIDENCE

HEADQUARTERS

PARK ROAD 43

MAINTENANCE BUILDING

SCOUT AREA

PICNICKING

UTILITY PLANT

BOAT RAMP

OPEN GROUP SHELTER

CAMPING SITES 78-142

PRIVATE PROPERTY

SINGING CHAPARRAL NATURE TRAIL 1 MILE

RESTROOM W/SHOWER

TRAILER CAMPING SITES 1-77

EAGLE POND

TRAILER SANITARY STATION

RESTROOM W/SHOWER

RESTROOM W/SHOWER

PLAYGROUND & PICNICKING

PRIVATE PROPERTY

RESACA OR OX-BOW LAKE

RESACA OR OX-BOW LAKE

RIO GRANDE HIKING TRAIL 1.8 MILES

UNITED STATES

RIO GRANDE RIVER

MEXICO

LEGEND

PAVED ROADS
UNPAVED ROADS
FOOT PATHS
PARK BOUNDARIES

For Information

Bentsen-Rio Grande Valley State Park
P.O. Box 988
Mission, TX 78572
512/585-1107

Facilities & Activities

142 campsites
  64 with water only
  77 with water/electricity/sewage
restrooms
showers
trailer dump station
group picnic area
open group shelter
youth group camp
picnicking
playground
fishing
fish cleaning facility
boat ramp
1-mile nature trail
1.8-mile hiking trail
scenic drive

Location

Bentsen-Rio Grande Valley State Park is located about six miles southwest of Mission off of Loop 374 or US 83, 2.6 miles south on FM 2062 to Park Road 43. The 600-acre park is located on the Rio Grande River.

This park is widely known as one of the birding "hot spots" of Texas; a bird checklist is available at park head-quarters. (Also see Birder's Guide to Texas *by Ed Kutac, Lone Star Books, Houston, Texas.)*

Blanco State Recreation Area

⊛ HEADQUARTERS
ⓖ CLUBHOUSE PAVILION
ⓐ CAMPSITES W/ WATER, ELECTRICITY, SEWAGE
⦿ CAMPSITES W/ WATER, ELECTRICITY
△ SCREENED SHELTER AREA
Ⓡ RESTROOMS

Ⓓ SANITARY DUMP STATION
Ⓧ PLAYGROUND
⊡ RESIDENCE
Ⓜ MAINTENANCE BUILDING
Ⓟ PICNIC AREA
🚿 RESTROOM W/ SHOWERS

Location

Blanco State Recreation Area is located at the south city limits of Blanco from US 281 on Park Road 23. The 110-acre park is on the banks of the Blanco River.

TO JOHNSON CITY

PARK ENTRANCE

RIVER

SHORT HIKING TRAIL

TO SAN ANTONIO

BLANCO

For Information

Blanco State Recreation Area
Box 493
Blanco, TX 78606
512/833-4333

Facilities & Activities

31 campsites
    21 with water/electricity
    10 with water/electricity/sewage
7 screened shelters
restrooms
showers
trailer dump station
group picnic area
picnic shelter with kitchen for day-use
picnicking
playgrounds
swimming
fishing
boats for rent (seasonal)
¾-mile hiking trail

One mile of the Blanco River lies within the park boundaries, providing a fun place to swim, fish, and boat.

Boquillas Canyon in
Big Bend National Park
(pages 123–124) can
be a humbling experience.

The Chisos Mountain Range of the Big Bend area offers
splendid scenes of rugged mountains rising abruptly above
the flatlands.

The rugged terrain and scarcity of water in areas such as Big Bend National
Park and Guadalupe Mountains National Park demand that campers and
hikers know where they are and where they are going.

Campers at Palmetto State Park
(page 116) are treated to an abundant
array of lush vegetation and palmetto
palm along the hiking and nature trails.

It may be hard to believe, but this oak tree and beautiful black-eyed susans are growing atop a 400-foot high, 1,600-acre solid granite dome, better known as Enchanted Rock (page 97).

MICKEY LITTLE

MICKEY LITTLE

Beginning a hike in the morning haze of the Texas Hill Country is an inspiring way to start the day.

Expanses like this near the Davis Mountains (page 127) are what make Texas seem as wide as the sky.

MICKEY LITTLE

RICHARD REYNOLDS/TEXAS TOURIST DEVELOPMENT AGENCY

Vistas like this make Palo Duro Canyon State Park (page 141) one of camper's favorites.

Hamilton Pool has been cooling University of Texas students and local Austin residents for many years.

Brackenridge Plantation Campground

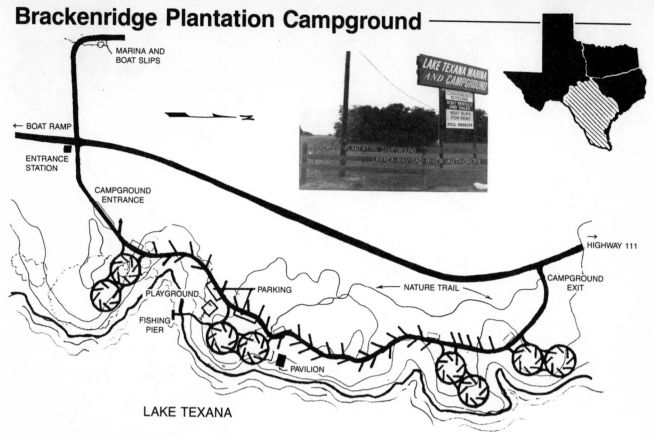

MARINA AND BOAT SLIPS

← BOAT RAMP

ENTRANCE STATION

CAMPGROUND ENTRANCE

PLAYGROUND

FISHING PIER

PARKING

PAVILION

NATURE TRAIL

HIGHWAY 111 →

CAMPGROUND EXIT

LAKE TEXANA

For Information

Brackenridge Plantation Campground
Lavaca-Navidad River Authority
P.O. Box 429
Edna, TX 77957
512/782-5249

Facilities & Activities

100 campsites
  18 with water/electricity
  82 with water/electricity/sewage
restrooms
showers
trailer dump station
covered pavilion
picnicking
playground
swimming
water skiing
fishing
lighted fishing pier
boat ramp
marina with covered & open slips
nature/historic trails
baseball diamond
volleyball courts
snack bar/groceries

Location

Brackenridge Plantation Campground may be reached by taking the SH 111 exit south from US 59 in Edna. Travel east on SH 111 for 7.5 miles; the campground is to the right before reaching the Lake Texana bridge and is located on the western shore of Lake Texana. The Lavaca-Navidad River Authority owns and manages Brackenridge Plantation Campground and Lake Texana Marina.

Lake Texana Marina is adjacent to the Brackenridge Plantation Campground.

REGION 3

Canyon Lake

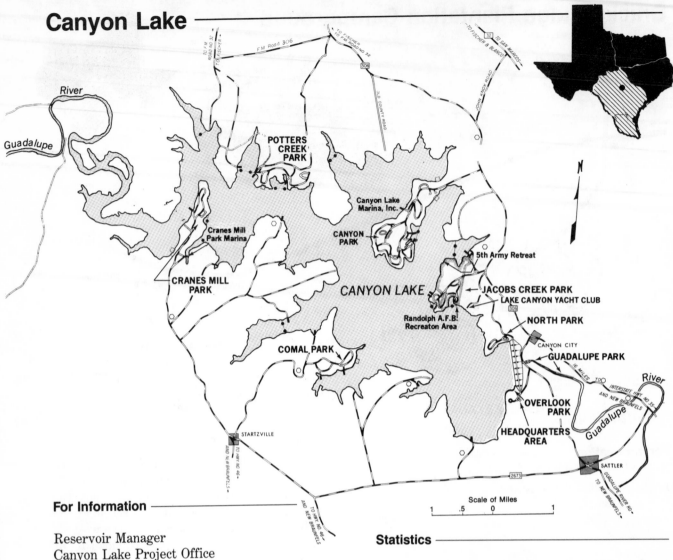

For Information

Reservoir Manager
Canyon Lake Project Office
HC Rt. 4, Box 400
Canyon Lake, TX 78133
512/964-3341

Notes:
Drinking water and restrooms are available at all campsites.
Canyon Park provides a group picnic shelter.

Statistics

Elevation, conservation pool .... 909 feet
Elevation, spillway crest .... 943 feet
Area, conservation pool .... 8,240 acres
Shoreline, conservation pool .... 80 miles

Sailing is extremely popular at Canyon Lake.

Campground	Showers (cold)	Picnic Facilities	Camping Area	Trailer Areas	Boat Launching Ramp	Sanitary Dump
North Park		X	X	X		
Jacobs Creek Park	X	X	X	X	X	X
Canyon Park		X	X	X	X	X
Potters Creek Park	X	X	X	X	X	X
Cranes Mills Park	X	X	X	X	X	X
Comal Park		X	X	X	X	X
Overlook Park						

Choke Canyon

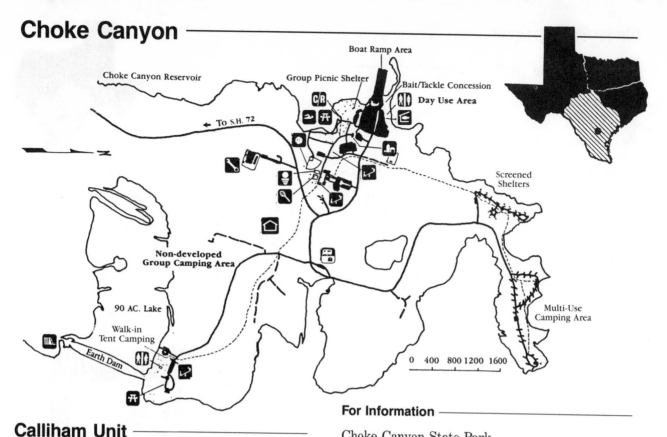

Choke Canyon Reservoir

← To S.H. 72

Boat Ramp Area

Group Picnic Shelter

Bait/Tackle Concession

Day Use Area

Screened Shelters

Non-developed Group Camping Area

90 AC. Lake

Walk-in Tent Camping

Earth Dam

Multi-Use Camping Area

0   400   800 1200 1600

Calliham Unit

Facilities & Activities

59 campsites
   19 with water only
   40 with water/electricity
20 screened shelters
restrooms
showers
trailer dump station
6 group picnic shelters
non-developed group camping area
group dining hall
auditorium/gym
picnicking
playgrounds
swimming beach
swimming pool & bathhouse
water skiing
fishing
fish cleaning facility
boat ramp
bait/tackle shop
boats for rent (seasonal)
hiking trail
tennis & basketball courts
baseball diamond
park store

For Information

Choke Canyon State Park
Calliham Unit
P.O. Box 2
Calliham, TX 78007
512/786-3868

Location

The Calliham Unit of Choke Canyon State Park is located north of SH 72 between Three Rivers and Tilden on a 1,100-acre peninsula on Choke Canyon Reservoir. The reservoir consists of 26,000 surface acres and is on the Frio River. Choke Canyon was most likely named for steep banks of resistant rocks near the dam site that "choked" the Frio River during floods.

Clearing was limited when Choke Canyon Reservoir was constructed on the Frio River; thus, fish habitat remains.

Choke Canyon (continued)

South Shore Unit

For Information

Choke Canyon State Park
South Shore Unit
Box 1548
Three Rivers, TX 78071
512/786-3538

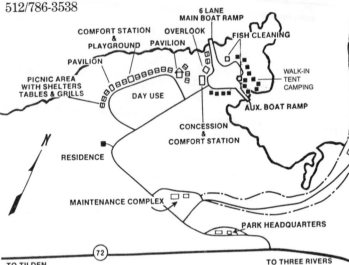

Surprised? Choke Canyon is the western-most common occurrence of the American alligator.

Location

The South Shore Unit of Choke Canyon State Park is located 4.2 miles west of Three Rivers off of SH 72 on Choke Canyon Reservoir. The 385-acre park provides access to the reservoir and the Frio River below the dam. Two recreational areas are available: Near headquarters is a large day-use area and below the dam is the camping area.

Fishing piers are convenient even if you own a boat.

Facilities & Activities

54 campsites
    20 walk-in tent sites (below dam)
    14 walk-in tent sites (day-use area)
    20 with water/electricity
restrooms
showers
trailer dump station
2 group picnic pavilions
group shelter
picnicking
playgrounds
swimming
water skiing
fishing
fish cleaning facility
boat ramp to lake
canoe/small boat launch to river
concession

Coleto Creek Reservoir

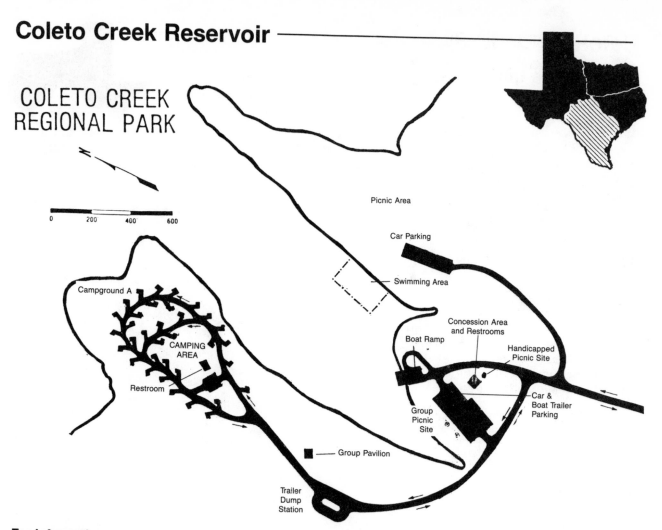

COLETO CREEK REGIONAL PARK

0   200   400   600

Picnic Area

Car Parking

Swimming Area

Campground A

CAMPING AREA

Restroom

Concession Area and Restrooms

Boat Ramp

Handicapped Picnic Site

Car & Boat Trailer Parking

Group Picnic Site

Group Pavilion

Trailer Dump Station

For Information

Coleto Creek Reservoir & Regional Park
P.O. Drawer 68
Fannin, TX 77960
512/575-6366

About the Reservoir & Park

Coleto Creek Reservoir, located 12 miles southwest of Victoria on US 59, is operated by the Guadalupe-Blanco River Authority and serves as cooling water for an electric generating plant. Access to the reservoir is through the 190-acre Regional Park, located on the southwest shore. The average lake depth is 11 feet; depths up to 45 feet occur in former stream beds of Coleto and Perdido Creeks. Typical lake bed soils are sandy to sandy loam; aquatic habitat range from submerged rock escarpments to inundated timber. Visitors to this 3,100-acre freshwater reservoir may enjoy boating, sailing, skiing, swimming, fishing, picnicking, and camping.

Facilities & Activities

33 campsites with electricity/water
flush toilets/showers
dump station
group pavilion
picnicking

swimming
skiing
fishing
boat ramp
concession

Coleto Creek Regional Park is located on the shores of a beautiful tree-lined reservoir.

Colorado Bend State Park

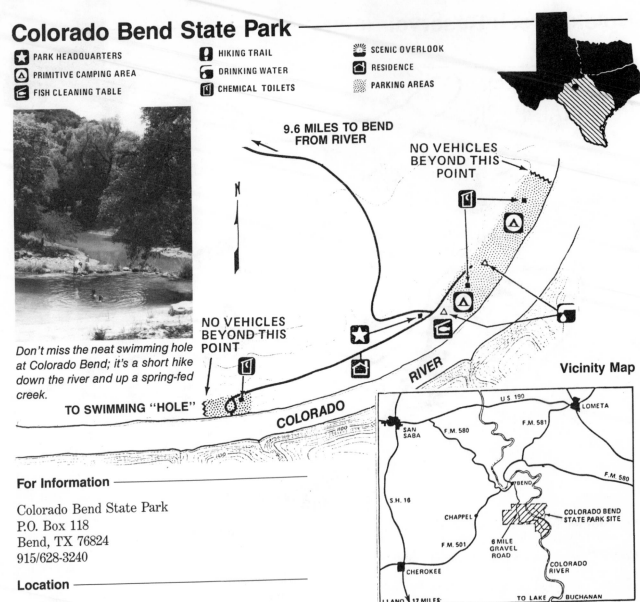

★ PARK HEADQUARTERS
△ PRIMITIVE CAMPING AREA
🖾 FISH CLEANING TABLE

🚹 HIKING TRAIL
🚰 DRINKING WATER
🚽 CHEMICAL TOILETS

🏞 SCENIC OVERLOOK
🏠 RESIDENCE
🅿 PARKING AREAS

9.6 MILES TO BEND FROM RIVER

NO VEHICLES BEYOND THIS POINT

NO VEHICLES BEYOND THIS POINT

TO SWIMMING "HOLE"

COLORADO RIVER

Don't miss the neat swimming hole at Colorado Bend; it's a short hike down the river and up a spring-fed creek.

Vicinity Map

US 190
LOMETA
F.M. 580
F.M. 581
SAN SABA
F.M. 580
S.H. 16
BEND
CHAPPEL
COLORADO BEND STATE PARK SITE
F.M. 501
6 MILE GRAVEL ROAD
COLORADO RIVER
CHEROKEE
LLANO 17 MILES
TO LAKE BUCHANAN

For Information

Colorado Bend State Park
P.O. Box 118
Bend, TX 76824
915/628-3240

Location

Colorado Bend State Park is on the Colorado River approximately 10 miles above Lake Buchanan. Paved access is available to the small community of Bend from US 281 and US 183 at Lampasas via FM 580. From Bend there is approximately 3.6 miles of unpaved road to the entrance of the park, then 6 miles of *rough* unpaved road to the Park Headquarters near the river.

Caution: The Colorado River and other low-lying areas such as the Cherokee Creek crossing on the unimproved park entrance road near Bend are subject to flooding. After rain, these and several other locations on the unpaved road may be difficult for standard two-wheel drive vehicles to negotiate. It is advisable to leave the park if heavy rain is expected. Many caves exist within the park, and some contain hazardous conditions. Therefore, all caves are closed to the public at this time.

Facilities & Activities

no reservations
limit 300 vehicles
primitive camping only
drinking water
garbage containers
chemical toilets
picnicking
swimming
fishing
fish cleaning facility
boat ramp
5¼ miles of backpacking trails
primitive camping area for backpackers
Note: The area known as Gorman Falls is closed pending future development.

Enchanted Rock State Natural Area

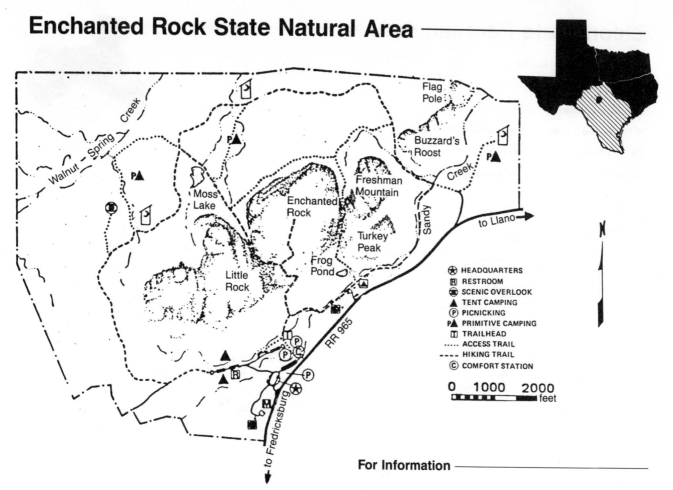

HEADQUARTERS
RESTROOM
SCENIC OVERLOOK
TENT CAMPING
PICNICKING
PRIMITIVE CAMPING
TRAILHEAD
..... **ACCESS TRAIL**
- - - **HIKING TRAIL**
Ⓒ **COMFORT STATION**

0   1000   2000 feet

Location

The Enchanted Rock State Natural Area may be reached by traveling 18 miles north of Fredericksburg on RR 965 or by traveling south from Llano on SH 16 for 14 miles and then west on RR 965 for 8 miles. The 1,643 acres are dominated by massive dome-shaped hills of pinkish granite that rise more than 400 feet above the surrounding terrain. Enchanted Rock was designated as a National Natural Landmark in 1971.

Facilities & Activities

46 walk-in tent sites (no vehicle or RV camping allowed)
60 tent sites at 3 primitive camping areas for backpackers
restrooms
showers
group picnic shelter
picnicking in day-use area
playground
rock climbing areas (use of bolts or pitons prohibited)
7 miles of hiking/backpacking trails

For Information

Enchanted Rock State Natural Area
Route 4, Box 170
Fredericksburg, TX 78624
915/247-3903

Enchanted Rock State Natural Area is dominated by massive dome-shaped hills of pinkish granite.

REGION 3

Falcon State Recreation Area

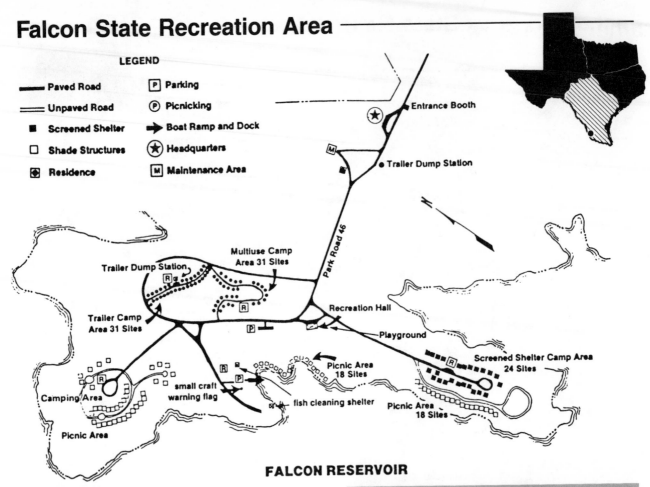

LEGEND

— Paved Road
= Unpaved Road
■ Screened Shelter
□ Shade Structures
⊡ Residence

P Parking
P Picnicking
➤ Boat Ramp and Dock
★ Headquarters
M Maintenance Area

FALCON RESERVOIR

For Information

Falcon State Recreation Area
P.O. Box 2
Falcon Heights, TX 78545
512/848-5327

Facilities & Activities

62 campsites in summer
  31 with water/electricity
  31 with water/electricity/sewage
55 shade structure sites are campsites in winter and
  picnic sites in summer
24 screened shelters
restrooms
showers
trailer dump stations
recreation hall
picnicking
playground
swimming
water skiing
fishing
fish cleaning facility
boat ramp and dock

Falcon Lake is a fishing paradise, especially for those seeking black and white bass, catfish, crappie and stripers.

Location

Falcon State Recreation Area, located on the Texas-Mexico border, may be reached by traveling 15 miles northwest of Roma on US 83, FM 2098 and Park Road 46. The 573-acre park is on the eastern shore of the 60-mile long Falcon Reservoir on the Rio Grande River.

Garner State Park

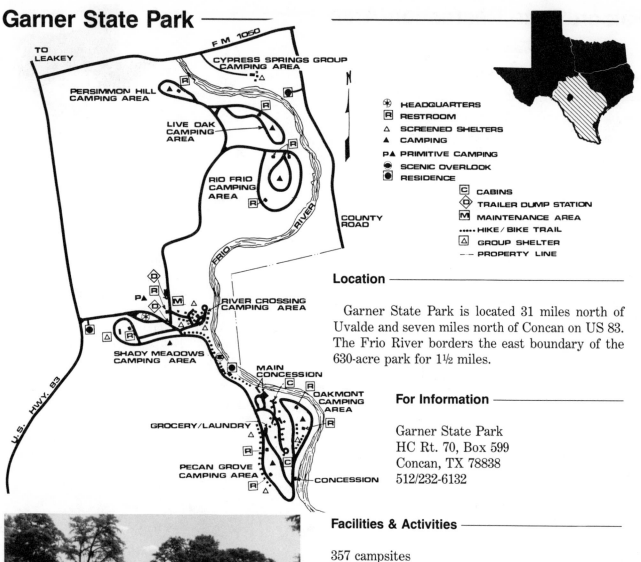

Legend:
- ✺ HEADQUARTERS
- Ⓡ RESTROOM
- △ SCREENED SHELTERS
- ▲ CAMPING
- P▲ PRIMITIVE CAMPING
- ◉ SCENIC OVERLOOK
- ▣ RESIDENCE
- Ⓒ CABINS
- ◈ TRAILER DUMP STATION
- Ⓜ MAINTENANCE AREA
- ••••• HIKE / BIKE TRAIL
- ◿ GROUP SHELTER
- - - PROPERTY LINE

Location

Garner State Park is located 31 miles north of Uvalde and seven miles north of Concan on US 83. The Frio River borders the east boundary of the 630-acre park for 1½ miles.

For Information

Garner State Park
HC Rt. 70, Box 599
Concan, TX 78838
512/232-6132

Facilities & Activities

357 campsites
  211 with water only
  146 with water/electricity
17 cabins
40 screened shelters
restrooms
showers
trailer dump stations
group camp (5 enclosed shelters and dining hall)
dining hall only available
large screened shelter/dining hall with kitchen for day-use only
picnicking
swimming
fishing
pedal boats for rent (seasonal)
hike/bike trail
18-hole miniature golf course (seasonal)
pavilion with nightly dance during summer
grocery store
concession stand (seasonal)

The pure spring water of the Frio River in Garner State Park is perfect for swimming and pedal boats, and also offers good fishing.

Goliad State Historical Park

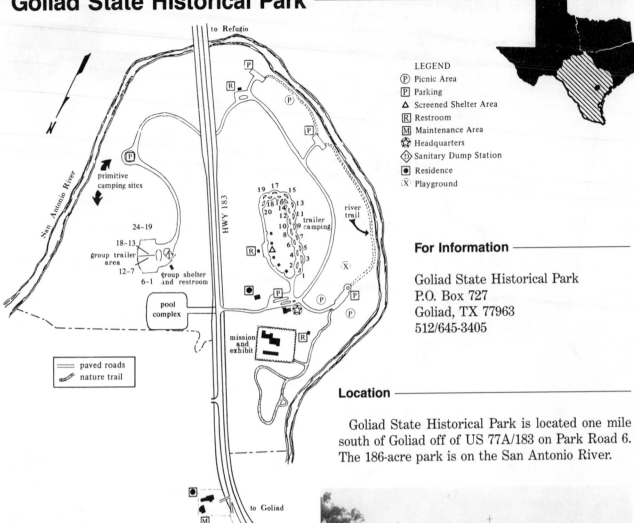

to Refugio

LEGEND
- Ⓟ Picnic Area
- P Parking
- △ Screened Shelter Area
- R Restroom
- M Maintenance Area
- ✪ Headquarters
- ◇ Sanitary Dump Station
- ⊡ Residence
- (X) Playground

San Antonio River

primitive camping sites

HWY 183

24–19
18–13
group trailer area
12–7
6–1
group shelter and restroom

19 17 15
18 16
14 13
20
12 11
10 9 trailer camping
8 7
6 5
4 3
2 1

river trail

pool complex

mission and exhibit

to Goliad

paved roads
nature trail

For Information

Goliad State Historical Park
P.O. Box 727
Goliad, TX 77963
512/645-3405

Location

Goliad State Historical Park is located one mile south of Goliad off of US 77A/183 on Park Road 6. The 186-acre park is on the San Antonio River.

The reconstructed church and numerous interpretive exhibits of Mission Espiritu Santo are located at Goliad State Historical Park.

Facilities & Activities

54 campsites
  24 with water/electricity
  20 with water/electricity/sewage
  10 primitive sites
5 screened shelters
restrooms
showers
trailer dump station
group picnic area
group shelter
group trailer area (24)
picnicking
playground
swimming pool complex
⅓-mile nature trail
1½-mile hiking trail
museum/exhibits
mission

Goose Island State Recreation Area

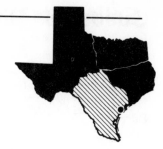

Location

Goose Island State Recreation Area is located approximately 12 miles north of Rockport off of SH 35 on Park Road 13. The 307-acre park is on Aransas Bay between Copano Bay and St. Charles Bay.

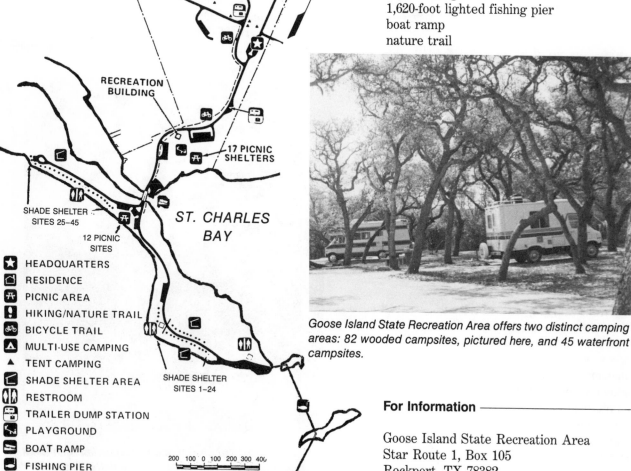

TO I.H. 35

YOUTH GROUP AREA

TO THE BIG TREE

PARK ROAD 13

NATURE TRAIL

N

RECREATION BUILDING

17 PICNIC SHELTERS

ST. CHARLES BAY

SHADE SHELTER SITES 25–45

12 PICNIC SITES

SHADE SHELTER SITES 1–24

⭐ HEADQUARTERS
🏠 RESIDENCE
🎪 PICNIC AREA
❗ HIKING/NATURE TRAIL
🚲 BICYCLE TRAIL
🅰 MULTI-USE CAMPING
▲ TENT CAMPING
◧ SHADE SHELTER AREA
🚻 RESTROOM
🚐 TRAILER DUMP STATION
🎣 PLAYGROUND
🛶 BOAT RAMP
📋 FISHING PIER
〰 PARK BOUNDARY

200 100 0 100 200 300 400
SCALE IN FEET

Facilities & Activities

127 campsites
   25 tent sites with water only
   45 with water/electricity (waterfront)
   57 with water/electricity (wooded)
restrooms
showers
trailer dump station
youth group area
recreation hall
picnicking
playground
swimming
water skiing
1,620-foot lighted fishing pier
boat ramp
nature trail

Goose Island State Recreation Area offers two distinct camping areas: 82 wooded campsites, pictured here, and 45 waterfront campsites.

For Information

Goose Island State Recreation Area
Star Route 1, Box 105
Rockport, TX 78382
512/729-2858

Guadalupe River State Park

For Information

Guadalupe River State Park
HC 54, Box 2087
Bulverde, TX 78163
512/438-2656

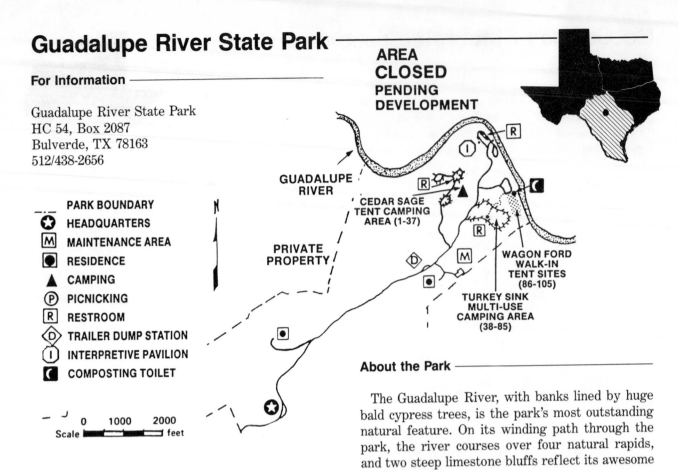

AREA CLOSED PENDING DEVELOPMENT

GUADALUPE RIVER

PRIVATE PROPERTY

CEDAR SAGE TENT CAMPING AREA (1-37)

WAGON FORD WALK-IN TENT SITES (86-105)

TURKEY SINK MULTI-USE CAMPING AREA (38-85)

---- PARK BOUNDARY

⊛ HEADQUARTERS

Ⓜ MAINTENANCE AREA

◉ RESIDENCE

▲ CAMPING

Ⓟ PICNICKING

Ⓡ RESTROOM

◈ TRAILER DUMP STATION

Ⓘ INTERPRETIVE PAVILION

☾ COMPOSTING TOILET

Scale |————| 0 1000 2000 feet

Location

Guadalupe River State Park, bisected by the clear, flowing waters of the Guadalupe River, comprises a 1,900-acre segment of the Texas Hill Country noted for its ruggedness and scenic beauty. The 3-mile road to the park can be reached by traveling 13 miles east of Boerne on SH 46 or 8 miles west of the US 281 intersection with SH 46.

Facilities & Activities

105 campsites
    37 tent camping with water only
    48 with water/electricity
    20 walk-in tent sites with water
restrooms
showers
trailer dump station
amphitheater
picnicking
playground
swimming
fishing
hiking trails

About the Park

The Guadalupe River, with banks lined by huge bald cypress trees, is the park's most outstanding natural feature. On its winding path through the park, the river courses over four natural rapids, and two steep limestone bluffs reflect its awesome erosive power.

Beautiful bald cypress trees line the banks of the Guadalupe River.

Hill Country State Natural Area

Facilities & Activities

1 primitive camping area near headquarters

primitive toilet near headquarters

faucet near trailhead; NO drinking water along trail

2 designated primitive camping areas for backpackers and horseback riders

disposal of human waste should follow standard field disposal practice

all water for drinking, cooking & washing must be carried

all garbage & litter must be packed out

6-mile hiking loop plus numerous other trails

equestrian trails

Note: Park is closed each Tuesday & Wednesday. Park use is by advance registrations only in order to avoid conflicts with the user groups (mainly backpackers and horseback riders)

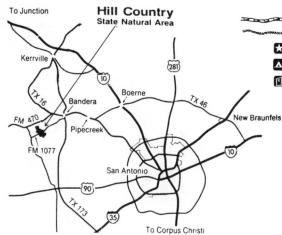

Four state parks offer equestrian camping; Hill Country is one of them.

For Information

Hill Country State Natural Area
Route 1, Box 601, FM 1077
Bandera, TX 78003
512/796-4413

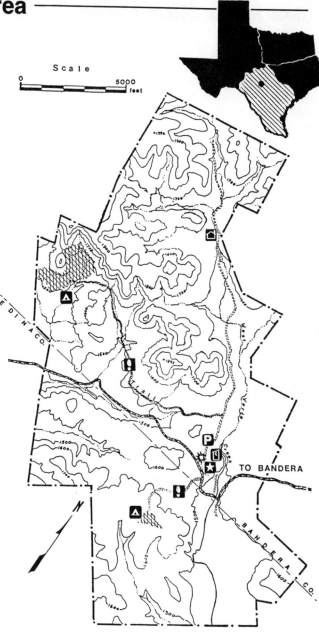

COUNTY ROAD & FM 1077

HILL COUNTRY WILDERNESS TRAIL

★ HEADQUARTERS

▲ CAMPING AREA

🚻 PRIMITIVE TOILET

☼ VEHICLE STAGING AREA

🚶 HIKING TRAIL

P PARKING AREA

⌂ PARK RESIDENCE

Location

Hill Country State Natural Area is located southwest of Bandera on FM 1077. At the present time, this 5,370-acre area is being allowed to revert to its natural condition and is being used as a primitive camping, hiking, and horseback riding area.

Inks Lake State Park

Location

Inks Lake State Park is located between Burnet and Llano off of SH 29 three miles south on Park Road 4. Also accessible from US 281 between Burnet and Marble Falls via Park Road 4 west. The 1,200-acre park borders 803-acre Inks Lake, created by a dam on the Colorado River.

For Information

Inks Lake State Park
Route 2, Box 31
Burnet, TX 78611
512/793-2223

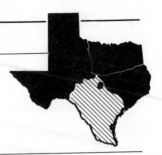

Facilities & Activities

197 campsites
   143 with water only
   54 with water/electricity
9 sites in primitive camping area for backpackers
22 screened shelters
restrooms
showers
trailer dump station
group picnic area
sponsored youth group camping area
amphitheater
picnicking
playgrounds
swimming
water skiing
lighted fishing piers
fish cleaning facilities
boat ramps
canoes, fishing boats, & paddle boats for rent
7½ miles of hiking trails
9-hole golf course
park store

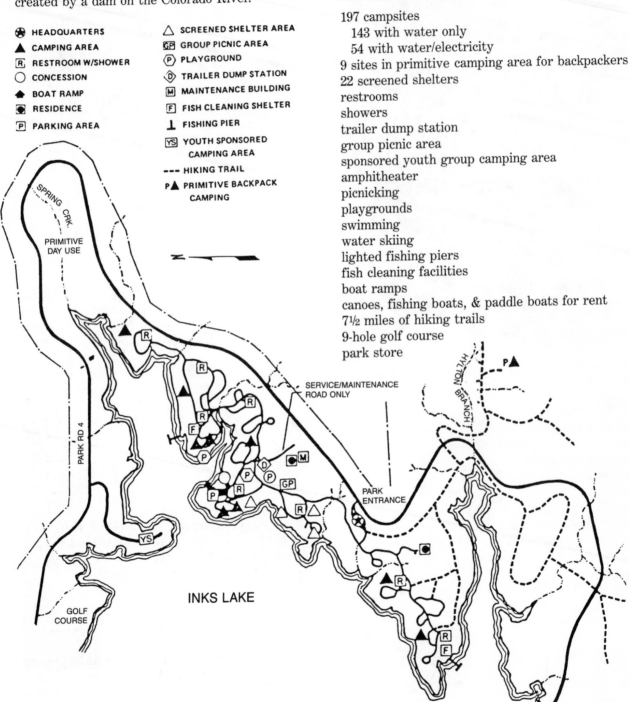

	HEADQUARTERS		SCREENED SHELTER AREA
▲	CAMPING AREA	GP	GROUP PICNIC AREA
R	RESTROOM W/SHOWER	P	PLAYGROUND
○	CONCESSION	D	TRAILER DUMP STATION
♠	BOAT RAMP	M	MAINTENANCE BUILDING
	RESIDENCE	F	FISH CLEANING SHELTER
P	PARKING AREA		FISHING PIER
		YS	YOUTH SPONSORED CAMPING AREA
		- - -	HIKING TRAIL
		P▲	PRIMITIVE BACKPACK CAMPING

Kerrville-Schreiner State Park

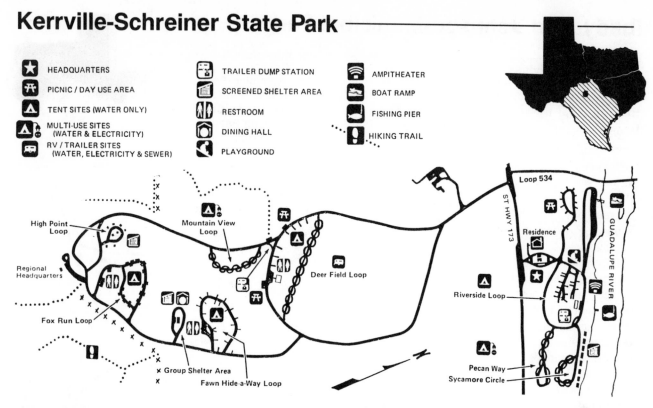

HEADQUARTERS

PICNIC / DAY USE AREA

TENT SITES (WATER ONLY)

MULTI-USE SITES (WATER & ELECTRICITY)

RV / TRAILER SITES (WATER, ELECTRICITY & SEWER)

TRAILER DUMP STATION

SCREENED SHELTER AREA

RESTROOM

DINING HALL

PLAYGROUND

AMPITHEATER

BOAT RAMP

FISHING PIER

HIKING TRAIL

High Point Loop

Mountain View Loop

Regional Headquarters

Deer Field Loop

Fox Run Loop

Group Shelter Area

Fawn Hide-a-Way Loop

Loop 534

ST HWY 173

Residence

Riverside Loop

GUADALUPE RIVER

Pecan Way

Sycamore Circle

For Information

Kerrville-Schreiner State Park
2385 Bandera Highway
Kerrville, TX 78028-9605
512/257-5392

Facilities & Activities

120 campsites
  65 with water only
  35 with water/electricity
  20 with water/electricity/sewage
16 screened shelters
restrooms
showers
trailer dump station
group picnic areas
group camping area with 7 screened shelters
large screened shelter dining hall with kitchen
  (day-use only)
recreation hall with kitchen (day-use or overnight
  use)
amphitheater
picnicking
playground
swimming
lighted fishing pier
boat ramp
7.7 miles of hiking trails

Location

Kerrville-Schreiner State Park, located southeast of Kerrville on SH 173, is reached via SH 16 or from IH 10, via Loop 534 just south of IH 10 off of SH 16. The 517-acre park is on the Guadalupe River.

Campsites at Kerrville-Schreiner State Park are located on both the river side and the Hill Country side of the park.

Lady Bird Johnson Municipal Park

Facilities & Activities

112 campsites
  10 tent sites
  26 with water/electricity
  86 with water/electricity/sewage
restrooms
showers
dump station
3 group pavilions
Pioneer Pavilion/auditorium
picnicking
playground
swimming pool & bathhouse
20-acre lake for boating & fishing
9-hole golf course
2 putting greens
driving range
baseball diamonds
volleyball & badminton courts
tennis courts
dance patio

1. Pavilion No. 1
2. Swimming Pool
3. Tennis Courts
4. Badminton Courts
5. Dancing Patio
6. Rock House
7. Auditorium
8. Pavilion No. 2
9. Pavilion No. 3
10. Golf Clubhouse
11. Maintenance Shop

Ⓐ TRAILER CAMPING AREA
Ⓟ PICNIC AREA
Ⓡ RESTROOM

ENTRANCE FROM HWY. 16

PARK HQ.

BALL PARK

BALL PARK

GILLESPIE COUNTY AIRPORT

DAM

BOAT DOCK

LAKE

DRIVING RANGE

TIVYDALE ROAD

LIVE OAK CREEK

NINE HOLE GOLF COURSE

Location

The Lady Bird Johnson Municipal Park is located on Live Oak Creek three miles southwest of Fredericksburg on SH 16. The park, comprising about 190 acres, is run by the city of Fredericksburg.

. . . as is the trailer camping area.

The 9-hole golf course at Lady Bird Johnson Municipal Park is quite popular . . .

For Information

Lady Bird Johnson Municipal Park
P.O. Box 111
Fredericksburg, TX 78624
512/997-4202

Lake Austin and Lake Travis

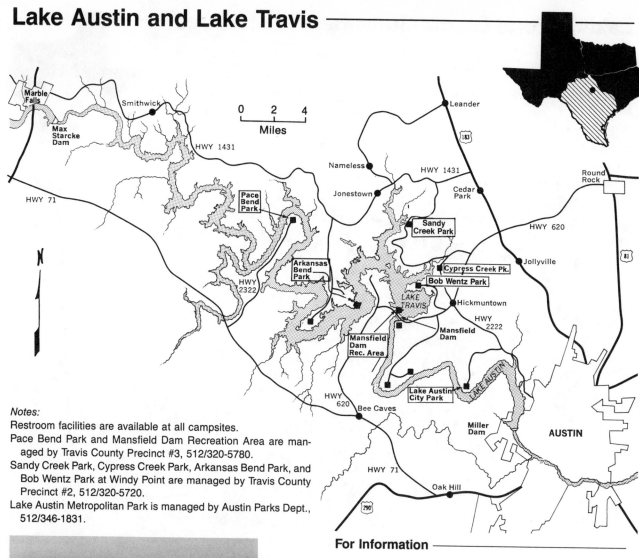

Notes:

Restroom facilities are available at all campsites.

Pace Bend Park and Mansfield Dam Recreation Area are managed by Travis County Precinct #3, 512/320-5780.

Sandy Creek Park, Cypress Creek Park, Arkansas Bend Park, and Bob Wentz Park at Windy Point are managed by Travis County Precinct #2, 512/320-5720.

Lake Austin Metropolitan Park is managed by Austin Parks Dept., 512/346-1831.

View of Lake Austin on the Colorado River from Mt. Bonnell in Austin, Tx.

For Information

Lower Colorado River Authority
P.O. Box 220
Austin, TX 78767
512/473-4083

Campground	No. of Campsites	Tent Camping	Water/Electrical Hookups	Showers	Trailer Dump Station	Boat Ramp
Pace Bend Park	420	400	20	X	X	X
Mansfield Dam Recreation Area	36	X			X	X
Sandy Creek Park	31	X			X	X
Cypress Creek Park	10	X				X
Arkansas Bend Park	12	X				X
Bob Wentz Park at Windy Point		X				
Lake Austin Metropolitan Park	20	X	20	X	X	X

Lake Corpus Christi State Recreation Area

For Information

Lake Corpus Christi State Recreation Area
Box 1167
Mathis, TX 78368
512/547-2635

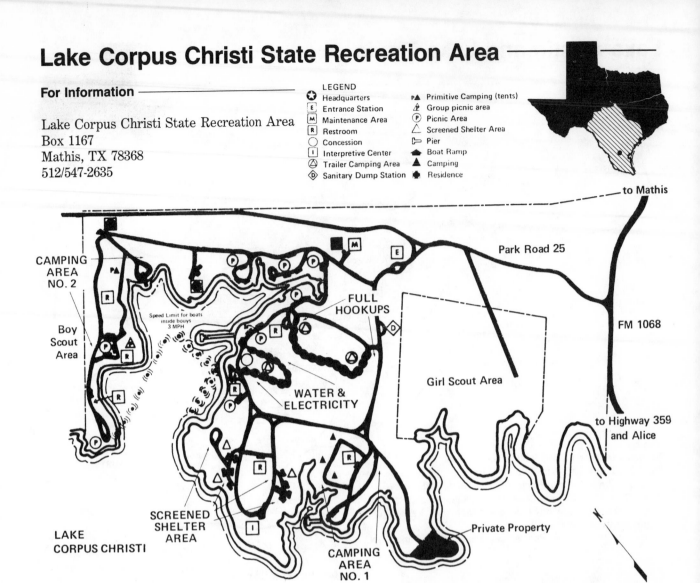

LEGEND

- ⊛ Headquarters
- E Entrance Station
- M Maintenance Area
- R Restroom
- ○ Concession
- I Interpretive Center
- △ Trailer Camping Area
- ◈ Sanitary Dump Station
- ᴘ▲ Primitive Camping (tents)
- 🎪 Group picnic area
- Ⓟ Picnic Area
- △ Screened Shelter Area
- 🏳 Pier
- ⛴ Boat Ramp
- ▲ Camping
- ⛺ Residence

to Mathis

Park Road 25

FM 1068

CAMPING AREA NO. 2

Boy Scout Area

Speed Limit for boats inside bouys 3 MPH

FULL HOOKUPS

Girl Scout Area

to Highway 359 and Alice

WATER & ELECTRICITY

LAKE CORPUS CHRISTI

SCREENED SHELTER AREA

Private Property

CAMPING AREA NO. 1

Facilities & Activities

83 campsites
  35 with water only
  23 with water/electricity
  25 with water/electricity/sewage
primitive tent camping area
25 screened shelters
restrooms
showers
trailer dump station
group picnic area
group pavilion
picnicking
swimming
water skiing
fishing piers
boat ramp
boats for rent (seasonal)
concession
interpretive center

Location

Lake Corpus Christi State Recreation Area is located 6 miles southwest of Mathis off of SH 359 via FM 1068 and Park Road 25. The 350-acre park is located on 27-mile long Lake Corpus Christi.

This campsite has a breezy location overlooking the 24-mile long Lake Corpus Christi.

Lake Texana State Park

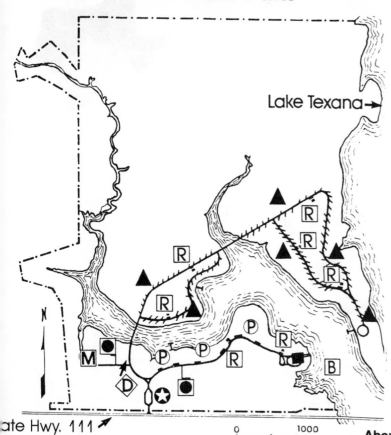

- --- PARK BOUNDARY
- ✪ HEADQUARTERS
- ◉ RESIDENCE
- Ⓡ RESTROOM
- Ⓟ PICNICKING
- ⬦ TRAILER DUMP STATION
- Ⓜ MAINTENANCE AREA
- ▲ CAMPING
- Ⓑ BOAT LAUNCH
- ⊣ FISHING PIER

For Information

Lake Texana State Park
P.O. Box 760
Edna, TX 77957
512/782-5718

Location

Lake Texana State Park is located on Lake Texana in central Jackson County approximately halfway between Houston and Corpus Christi, and comprises 575 acres of coastal prairie and oak woodlands. The park entrance is on SH 111, 6½ miles east of the city of Edna.

Facilities & Activities

141 campsites
  55 with water only
  86 with water/electricity
restrooms
showers
trailer dump station
group picnic area

picnicking
playgrounds
swimming
fishing jetty & pier
2 lighted fishing piers
boat ramp

About the Park

Palmetto Bend Dam, approved by Congress in 1968 and completed in 1979, is a rolled earth-filled structure almost 8 miles long with a maximum crest elevation of 55 feet. It backs up water from the Navidad River for a distance of 18 miles creating a reservoir with about 11,000 surface acres, 125 miles of shoreline and a storage of 170,000-acre feet of water for industrial and municipal supply and recreational use. The water body, called Lake Texana, is named for the historic town of Texana founded in 1832 near the junction of the Navidad and Lavaca rivers downstream from the present damsite.

An abundance of oak, pecan, and elm trees provide a shaded campground at Lake Texana State Park.

Lockhart State Recreation Area

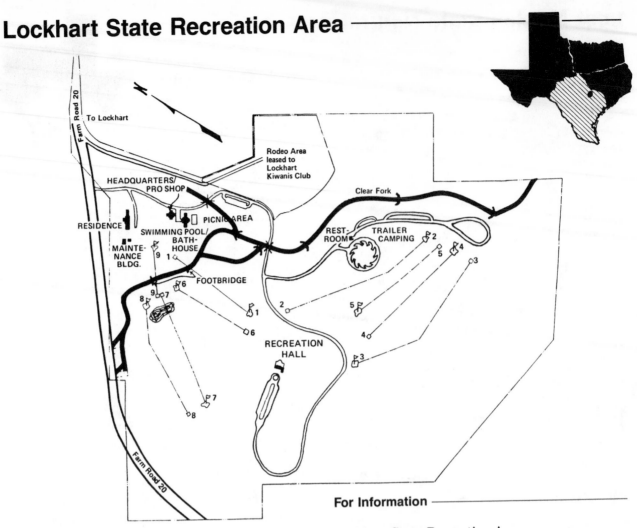

Facilities & Activities

20 campsites
   10 with water/electricity
   10 with water/electricity/sewage
primitive campsites
restrooms
showers
group picnic area
recreation hall with kitchen for day-use
picnicking
playground
fishing
swimming pool & bathhouse
9-hole golf course

Location

Lockhart State Recreation Area is located about 4 miles southwest of Lockhart via US 183 and FM 20 to Park Road 20.

For Information

Lockhart State Recreation Area
Route 3, Box 69
Lockhart, TX 78644
512/398-3479

Four state parks have golf courses: Bastrop, Inks Lake, Lockhart, and Stephen F. Austin.

Lost Maples State Natural Area

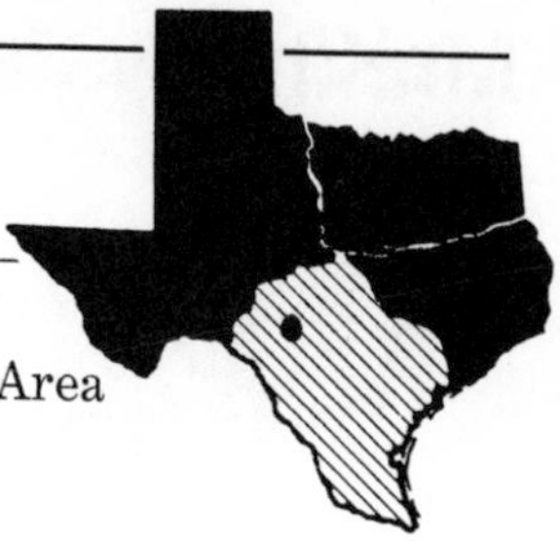

Location

Lost Maples State Natural Area is located in western Bandera County on the Sabinal River, 5 miles north of Vanderpool on RR 187. The 2,208-acre park is named for its relict stands of bigtooth maple trees.

For Information

Lost Maples State Natural Area
HC 01 Box 156
Vanderpool, TX 78885
512/966-3413

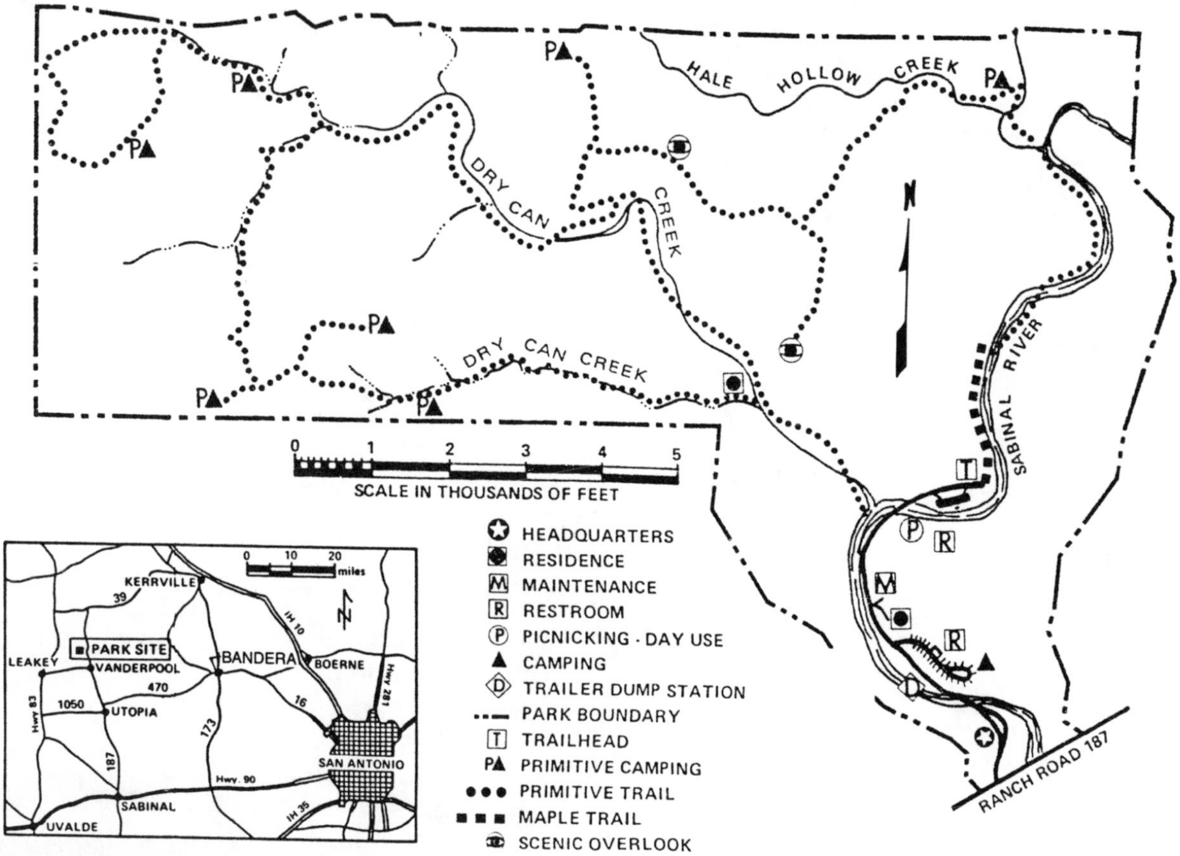

HALE HOLLOW CREEK
DRY CAN CREEK
DRY CAN CREEK
SABINAL RIVER
RANCH ROAD 187
N
0 1 2 3 4 5
SCALE IN THOUSANDS OF FEET
HEADQUARTERS
RESIDENCE
MAINTENANCE
RESTROOM
PICNICKING - DAY USE
CAMPING
TRAILER DUMP STATION
PARK BOUNDARY
TRAILHEAD
PRIMITIVE CAMPING
PRIMITIVE TRAIL
MAPLE TRAIL
SCENIC OVERLOOK
0 10 20 miles
KERRVILLE
PARK SITE
LEAKEY
VANDERPOOL
BANDERA
BOERNE
UTOPIA
SAN ANTONIO
SABINAL
UVALDE
IH 10
IH 35
Hwy 281
Hwy 83
Hwy. 90
1050
470
187
173
39
16

About the Maples

The bigtooth maples or canyon maples are the outstanding feature of Lost Maples State Natural Area. Fall displays of red, yellow, and orange foliage on the maple trees depend on the favorable combination of several factors, and these conditions do not occur every year. Generally, the foliage changes the last two weeks of October through the first two weeks of November. To obtain information on the condition of autumn coloration before planning a visit, call the toll-free number 1-800-792-1112 after the first of October. Parking in the park is limited to 250 spaces. The park is often crowded on weekends during the fall. When possible, visitors are urged to schedule trips during the weekdays.

Facilities & Activities

30 campsites with water/electricity
8 primitive camping areas for backpackers
restrooms
showers
trailer dump station
picnicking
swimming
fishing
interpretive center
4/10-mile nature trail
10 miles of hiking/backpacking trails

McKinney Falls State Park

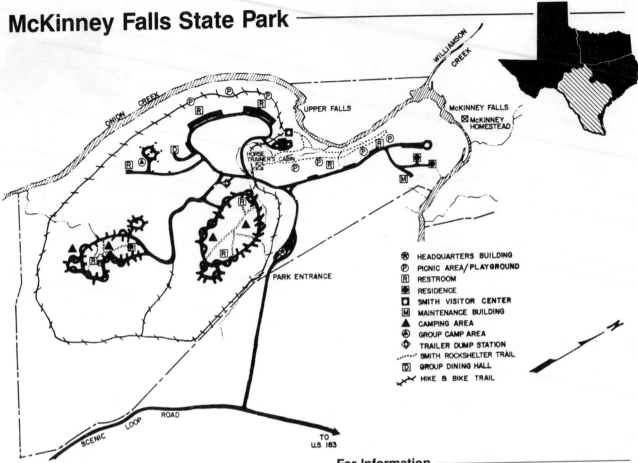

HEADQUARTERS BUILDING
PICNIC AREA/PLAYGROUND
RESTROOM
RESIDENCE
SMITH VISITOR CENTER
MAINTENANCE BUILDING
CAMPING AREA
GROUP CAMP AREA
TRAILER DUMP STATION
SMITH ROCKSHELTER TRAIL
GROUP DINING HALL
HIKE & BIKE TRAIL

Facilities & Activities

84 campsites
    14 with water only
    70 with water/electricity
restrooms
showers
trailer dump station
group camp with 6 screened shelters
group dining hall with kitchen
youth group primitive area
picnicking
playgrounds
fishing
¾-mile interpretive trail
3-mile hike/bike trail
interpretive center with exhibits
historic structures

Location

McKinney Falls State Park is located approximately 13 miles southeast of the State Capitol in Austin. The park may be reached from the east by US 183 (to Lockhart) via Scenic Loop Road, and from the west by IH 35 (take William Cannon exit #228) via North Bluff/Bluff Springs Road.

For Information

McKinney Falls State Park
7102 Scenic Loop Road
Austin, TX 78744
512/243-1643

The ¾-mile Smith Rockshelter interpretive trail provides cool, shady rest stops along the way.

Mustang Island State Park

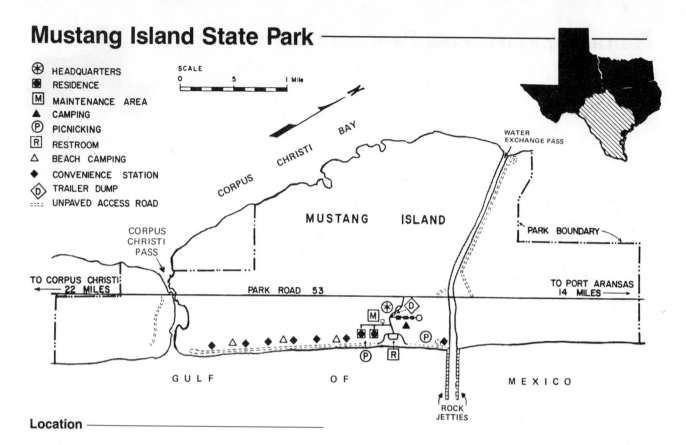

Legend:

- ⊛ HEADQUARTERS
- ▣ RESIDENCE
- Ⓜ MAINTENANCE AREA
- ▲ CAMPING
- Ⓟ PICNICKING
- Ⓡ RESTROOM
- △ BEACH CAMPING
- ◆ CONVENIENCE STATION
- ◇ TRAILER DUMP
- ⋯⋯ UNPAVED ACCESS ROAD

CORPUS CHRISTI BAY

WATER EXCHANGE PASS

MUSTANG ISLAND

PARK BOUNDARY

CORPUS CHRISTI PASS

TO CORPUS CHRISTI 22 MILES ←

PARK ROAD 53

TO PORT ARANSAS 14 MILES →

GULF OF MEXICO

ROCK JETTIES

Location

Mustang Island State Park is located on one of the coastal barrier islands that lie between the mainland and the open waters of the Gulf; it comprises 3,703 acres at the southern end of Mustang Island, including 5½ miles of beach. The park is accessible by traveling southeast from Corpus Christi to Padre Island, then north on Park Road 53 for a total distance of about 22 miles. The park also can be reached by taking the toll-free ferry from Aransas Pass to Port Aransas and traveling south on Park Road 53.

Facilities & Activities

48 campsites with water/electricity/individual shade shelters/restrooms & hot water showers nearby
300 open beach primitive campsites along a 7,000-foot stretch of coastline with chemical toilets, rinsing showers and bulkwater supply
trailer dump station
picnic tables with shade shelters
swimming beach
beach bathhouse with dressing rooms, restrooms & outside rinsing showers
surf fishing
fishing off the jetties
fish cleaning facility on south jetty

For Information

Mustang Island State Park
P.O. Box 326
Port Aransas, TX 78373
512/749-5246

Almost any stretch of beach along the Texas coast can provide a challenge for the surf fisherman.

Padre Island National Seashore

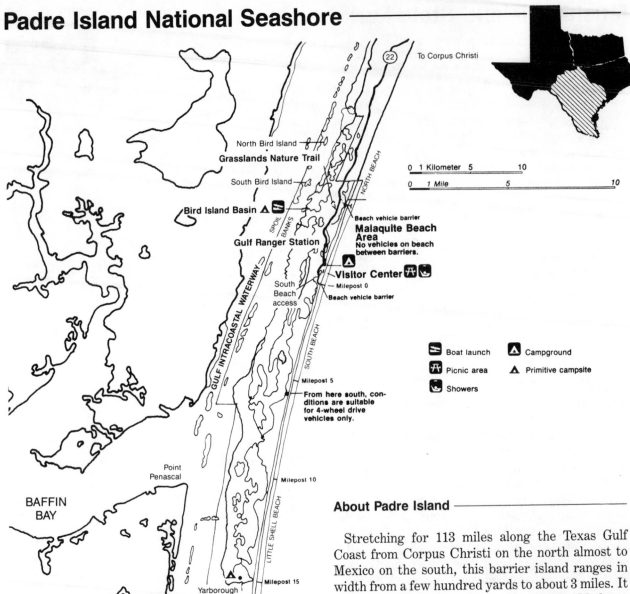

To Corpus Christi

North Bird Island
Grasslands Nature Trail
South Bird Island
Bird Island Basin ▲ 🛥
Gulf Ranger Station

NORTH BEACH

SPOIL BANKS

GULF INTRACOASTAL WATERWAY

SOUTH BEACH

South Beach access

Beach vehicle barrier
Malaquite Beach Area
No vehicles on beach between barriers.

▲ **Visitor Center** 🏕 🚿
— Milepost 0
Beach vehicle barrier

| 0 | 1 Kilometer | 5 | | 10 |
| 0 | 1 Mile | | 5 | 10 |

Milepost 5
From here south, conditions are suitable for 4-wheel drive vehicles only.

Point Penascal

Milepost 10

LITTLE SHELL BEACH

BAFFIN BAY

▲
Yarborough Pass
Milepost 15

🛥 Boat launch   ▲ Campground
🏕 Picnic area   ▲ Primitive campsite
🚿 Showers

Activities

National Park Service interpretive programs
exhibits
self-guiding ¾-mile Grasslands Nature Trail
beach hiking
supervised swimming at Malaquite Beach in
  summer months
beachcombing
boating
fishing
other water sports

About Padre Island

Stretching for 113 miles along the Texas Gulf Coast from Corpus Christi on the north almost to Mexico on the south, this barrier island ranges in width from a few hundred yards to about 3 miles. It is separated from the mainland by Laguna Madre, a shallow body of water with a maximum width of 10 miles. The national seashore boundaries encompass the undeveloped central part of the island, which is 80.5 miles long.

You can drive a conventional car for 14 miles southward from the northern boundary of the national seashore. Beyond this, a 4-wheel-drive vehicle must be used as the soft sand, intermixed with tiny shells will not support an ordinary passenger car. The Mansfield Channel intersects the island and prevents a continuous trip along its entire length.

Private boats cannot be launched in the surf within the national seashore. Bird Island Basin provides a boat launch that leads into Laguna Madre and Intracoastal Waterway. Launching sites are also located underneath the Kennedy Causeway.

Padre Island National Seashore (continued)

The Malaquite Beach complex overlooking the Gulf of Mexico is the center of visitor services for the National Seashore. A new complex, completed in the summer of 1989, includes a visitor center, observation deck, snack bar and gift shop, restrooms, rinse-off showers, and changing rooms. The center, which is open daily, also has books, brochures, maps, and exhibits. Schedules of special activities, such as beach walks and evening campfire programs, are posted. A fee is charged for entry to Padre Island National Seashore.

A beached shrimp boat adds to the mystique of the seashore.

Camping Facilities

The paved campground (50 sites for tents or RVs) is 1 mile south of the ranger station and ½ mile north of Malaquite Beach. Picnic tables, restrooms, cold showers, and a sanitary dump station are provided; fire grills are not. The campground is open all year on a first-come, first-served basis; a fee is charged. No electrical, water, or sewage hookups are available.

A primitive campsite is located at Bird Island Basin, which faces the Laguna Madre and provides the park's only boat launching ramp, which is open all year; chemical toilets and picnic tables are provided. A primitive campsite at Yarborough Pass, overlooking the Laguna Madre, can be reached only by 4-wheel-drive vehicles via a loose shell road. Chemical toilets and tables are available.

Camping is permitted on the beach corridor seaward of any vegetation or dunes. Camping *is not permitted* on or in dunes or grasslands. North Beach is a mile-long stretch of open beach at the north end of the seashore and is provided with dumpsters and chemical toilets. South Beach is a 5-mile stretch of open beach beginning at the end of the paved road and is provided with dumpsters and chemical toilets. Camping *is not permitted* between the barricades of North and South Beaches. Camping *is not permitted* on or at Malaquite Beach. Beyond South Beach there are 55 miles of Gulf beach that are open to 4-wheel-driving and primitive camping. No visitor services are available in this remote portion of the national seashore.

This lonesome gull is probably waiting for a handout!

For Information

Padre Island National Seashore
9405 South Padre Island Drive
Corpus Christi, TX 78418-5597
512/949-8173 (Ranger Station)
512/949-8175 (For recorded informational message on tides, weather, water temperature and conditions, beach conditions, etc.)

Palmetto State Park

Location

Palmetto State Park, located in an area once known as the Ottine Swamp, closely resembles a tropical botanical garden. On the San Marcos River, the 263-acre park of swampy woodlands is located on Park Road 11 off of US 183 between Luling and Gonzales.

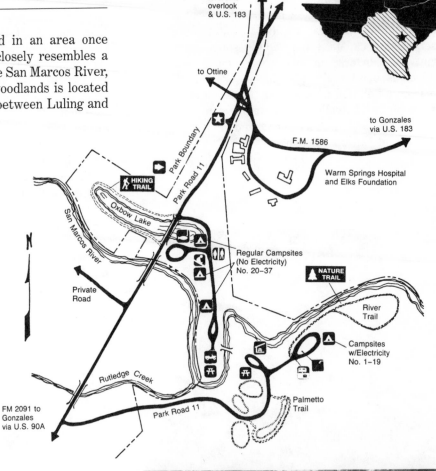

![playground]	PLAYGROUND
![park entrance]	PARK ENTRANCE
![headquarters]	HEADQUARTERS BUILDING
![trailer dump]	TRAILER DUMP STATION
![restroom]	RESTROOM
![restroom showers]	RESTROOM W SHOWERS
![picnic]	PICNIC AREA
![parking]	PARKING
![group picnic]	GROUP PICNIC AREA W. SHELTER
![camping]	CAMPING AREA
![fishing pier]	FISHING PIER

For Information

Palmetto State Park
Route 5, Box 201
Gonzales, TX 78629
512/672-3266

Facilities & Activities

37 campsites
    18 with water only
    19 with water/electricity
restrooms
showers
trailer dump station
group picnic area
group dining hall with kitchen
picnicking
playground
swimming (lake & river)
river & lake fishing
fishing pier at lake
1½ miles of nature trails
1-mile hiking trail
historic structure
Red Hill scenic overlook

Palmetto State Park has 2½ miles of trails; some in areas that closely resemble a tropical botanical garden.

Pedernales Falls State Park

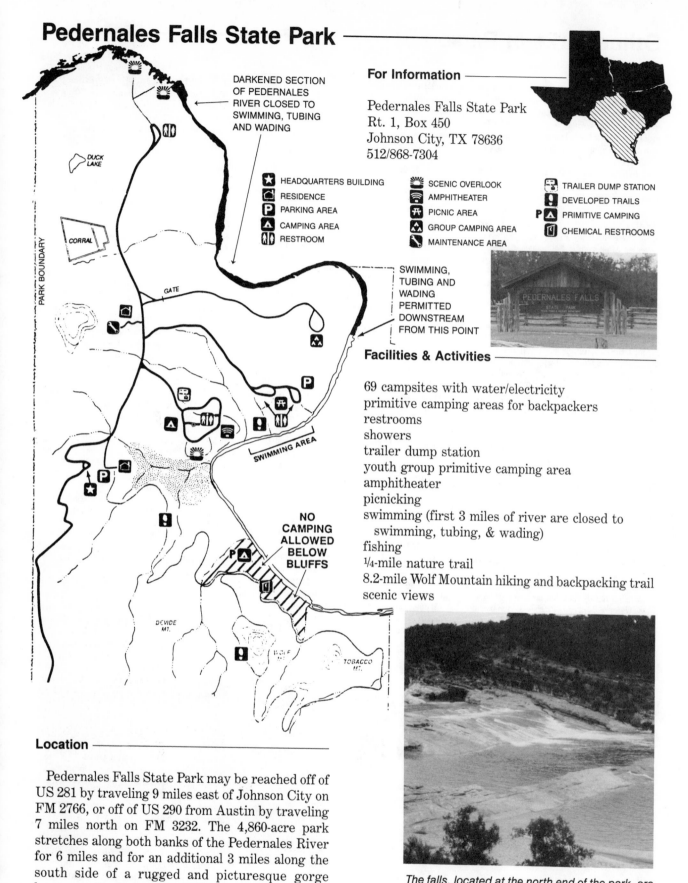

Pedernales Falls State Park
Rt. 1, Box 450
Johnson City, TX 78636
512/868-7304

DARKENED SECTION OF PEDERNALES RIVER CLOSED TO SWIMMING, TUBING AND WADING

⭐ HEADQUARTERS BUILDING
🏠 RESIDENCE
🅿 PARKING AREA
⛺ CAMPING AREA
🚻 RESTROOM

🌅 SCENIC OVERLOOK
🎭 AMPHITHEATER
🎪 PICNIC AREA
⛺ GROUP CAMPING AREA
🔧 MAINTENANCE AREA

🚐 TRAILER DUMP STATION
🥾 DEVELOPED TRAILS
🅿⛺ PRIMITIVE CAMPING
🚽 CHEMICAL RESTROOMS

DUCK LAKE

PARK BOUNDARY

CORRAL

GATE

SWIMMING, TUBING AND WADING PERMITTED DOWNSTREAM FROM THIS POINT

SWIMMING AREA

NO CAMPING ALLOWED BELOW BLUFFS

DEVIDE MT.

WOLF

TOBACCO MT.

Facilities & Activities

69 campsites with water/electricity
primitive camping areas for backpackers
restrooms
showers
trailer dump station
youth group primitive camping area
amphitheater
picnicking
swimming (first 3 miles of river are closed to swimming, tubing, & wading)
fishing
¼-mile nature trail
8.2-mile Wolf Mountain hiking and backpacking trail
scenic views

The falls, located at the north end of the park, are the park's main attraction.

Location

Pedernales Falls State Park may be reached off of US 281 by traveling 9 miles east of Johnson City on FM 2766, or off of US 290 from Austin by traveling 7 miles north on FM 3232. The 4,860-acre park stretches along both banks of the Pedernales River for 6 miles and for an additional 3 miles along the south side of a rugged and picturesque gorge known as the Pedernales Falls.

Other Parks in Region 3*

BRADY   **Brady Lake Park**
From US 87: FM 2028 W 4.5 mi. On *Brady Lake*. Concessionaire: wheeled camper sites 20 w/elec, water & sewage, fee; tent sites 40, fee; other camp area 300 acres, fee. Screened shelters 20, fee. Dump sta, fl toilets, showers, bait, picnic shelters, pavilion, ice, groc. Swim-lake; fish, fishing barge, boat ramp, skiing, playground, scenic views. (Rt 1, Box 75, Brady 76825, tel 915/597-1256.)

BRADY   **Richards Park**
US 87 W to Memory Lane. On *Brady Creek*. Wheeled camper sites 102, w/elec, 65, fee, w/ water, 47; fee; other camp area 15 acres. Dump sta nearby, fl toilets, grills. Playground, ball field, bicycle trails. (City Pk, Box 351, Brady 76825, tel 915/597-2152.)

BROWNSVILLE   **Brazos Island State Park**
From US 77/83: Tex 48 E 1.3 mi; Tex 4 N & NE 23.5 mi. On *Gulf of Mexico*. Public land, no development. Primitive camping only. No drinking water. Swim-beach, fish. (Brownsville Convention & Visitors Bureau, 1600 E. Elizabeth Ln, Brownsville, 78520, tel 512/546-3721.)

CAMP WOOD   **Lake Nueces Park**
From Tex 55: 33.9 mi NW. On *Lake Nueces*. Wheeled camper or tent sites, 25, fee, 6 w/elec, water & sewage, 19 w/elec, water nearby, fee. Fl toilets, cold showers, tables, grills. Swim-lake; fishing, 2 boat ramps. (Uvalde Co. Judge Office, Uvalde 78801, tel 512/278-3216.)

CASTROVILLE   **Castroville Regional Park**
From JCT US 90 in city: Athens St S 5 blks; Lisbon St W 3 blks. On *suburban, grassy hill by Medina River*. Wheeled camper sites 35 w/ elec, water & sewage. Fl toilets, dump sta, showers, grills, pay phone. Swim-pool, river; fishing, playground, picnic areas. (City Pk, Box 479, Castroville 78009, tel 512/538-2224.)

CORPUS CHRISTI   **Nueces County Padre Balli Park**
From Park Rd 53: Park Rd 22 SW 2.8 mi; local rd E .2 mi. On *Gulf of Mexico*. Wheeled camper sites 66 w/elec & water, fee, limit 3 days; tent sites 60, fee, limit 3 days; other camp area 40 acres, fee. Dump sta, fl toilets, showers, bait, tables, snack bar, laundry, bathhouse. Swim-beach; fish, lighted fishing pier, fee; boating. (10901 S. Padre Island Dr, Cluster Box 3G, Corpus Christi 78418, tel 512/949-8121.)

CUERO   **Municipal Park**
Within city, from US 87: Main St E .5 mi. On *10-acre lake in park*. Wheeled camper sites 6 w/elec & water, fee, limit 4 days; other camp area 10 acres, limit 4 days. Fl toilets, picnic shelters, grills, bathhouse. Swim-pool; fish, playground, tennis, ball field, golf. Curfew 11 pm. (201 E. Main, Cuero 77954, tel 512/275-6114.)

GONZALES   **Independence City Park**
Within city: US 183 S at Guadalupe River. Camp area 3 acres (overnight permit req'd), limit 3 days; 20 RV riverfront sites w/elec, water, fee. Fl toilets, dump sta, grills. Swim-pool (summer); fish, playground, tennis, volleyball, quadroplex softball field, rodeo arena & show barn, bicycle trails, golf. Historical tours available. (Drawer 547, Gonzales 78629, tel 512/672-2815.)

GONZALES   **Lake Wood Recreation Area**
From US 183: US 90-A W 3.1 mi; FM 2091 S 3 mi. On *Lake Wood* (Lake 5-H) & Guadalupe River. Day use fee. Concessionaire: wheeled backin camper sites w/elec, water & sewage 15, fee. Dump sta, fl toilets, showers, bait, grills, snack bar, ice, groc, bathhouse. Swim-river & lake; fish, boat ramp (fee). (Rt 2, Box 158-A, Gonzales 78629, tel 512/672-2779.)

HALLETTSVILLE   **City Recreation Park**
Within city, from N limits: US 77 S 1 mi. Wheeled camper and tent sites 23; w/elec 16, w/elec & water 7, fee. Dump sta, fl toilets, cold showers, picnic areas, grills. Playground, walking trail, tennis, golf. (Box 257, Hallettsville 77964, tel 512/798-3681.)

JUNCTION   **Schreiner City Park**
Within city: US 290 at *Lake Junction*. Camp area 15 acres, limit 7 days. Swim-lake & pool; fish, boat ramp, playground, ball field, scenic views. (102 N. 5th St, Junction 76849, tel 915/446-2622.)

KINGSVILLE   **Kaufer-Hubert Memorial Park & SeaWind RV Resort**
From FM 771: US 77 N 3.7 mi; FM 628 E 11.4 mi. On *Baffin Bay*. Wheeled camper sites 134 w/elec, water, sewer, & telephone hookups available, fee. Fl toilets, showers, rec room, PO boxes available, laundromat, restaurant, groc, bait/tackle stands, pets allowed. Park has picnic shelters, grills, boat ramp, 2 fresh water lakes, fl toilets, bird observation tower, lighted fishing pier, sandy beach w/shower, playground, horseshoe pits, soccer/softball fields, 1-mile walking/jogging trail w/12-station "senior" fitness course. (County Pct 3, Rt 1, Box 67-D, Riviera 78379, tel 512/297-5738.)

LLANO   **Black Rock Park**
From Tex 16: Tex 29 E 16.1 mi; Tex 261 N 4 mi. On *Lake Buchanan*. Wheeled backin camper sites 20, fee, limit 14 days. Fl toilets, grills. Fish, boat ramp, dump sta, playground, scenic views. (LCRA, Box 220, Austin 78767, tel 512/473-4083.)

LLANO   **Llano County Community Center**
From Tex 16: RM 152 W 1.2 mi, adjacent to city park, swimming pool, rodeo arena & 9-hole golf. Wheeled backin camper sites w/elec, water & sewage 150, fee. Group bldg w/ kitchen & rest rooms, fee. rp rsvns acptd. (Chamber of Commerce, 700 Bessemer, Llano 78643, tel 915/247-5354.)

LLANO   **Robinson City Park**
From Tex 16: RM 152 W 2 mi. On *Llano River*. Camp area 5 acres, limit 14 days. Dump sta, fl toilets, picnic tables. Swim-river & pool; fish, boat ramp (limit 5 hp), 9-hole golf, playground, volleyball, hiking trails, scenic views. (301 W. Main, Llano 78643, tel 915/246-4158.)

* Source: *Texas Public Campgrounds*, State Dept. of Highways and Public Transportation, Travel and Information Div., P.O. Box 5064, Austin, TX 78763.

Backpacking isn't just for the mountains; the open beach presents a different type of challenge.

PORT ARANSAS

Port Aransas County Park

From Tex 361 ferry landing in Port Aransas: Cotter St to park. On *Gulf of Mexico*. Wheeled camper sites 5 w/elec & water, fee; other camp area 10 acres, fee, limit 14 days. Dump sta, fl toilets, showers, snack bar, ice, groc, bathhouse. Swim-beach; fish, lighted fishing pier, fee. Pk Rangers on duty 24 hrs. (Port Aransas Co Pk, Port Aransas 78373, tel 512/749-6117.)

PORT LAVACA

Port Lavaca State Fishing Pier

E city limits at Lavaca Bay Causeway (Tex 35). On *Lavaca Bay*, fishing fee. Campground & concessions operated by City of Port Lavaca. Wheeled camper or tent sites 52 w/ elec & water, fee; 19 have adjacent covered picnic shelters and TV hookups, fee. Limit 14 days. Dump sta, fl toilets, showers, tackle rental, bait, shelters, tables, snack bar, ice, bathhouse. Swim-pool (fee); fish, boat ramp and dock, playground, scenic views. (Box 434, Point Comfort 77979, tel 512/552-4402.)

PORT O'CONNOR

Matagorda Island State Park & Wildlife Management Area

From Port O'Connor S 7 mi; separated from mainland by Espiritu Santo & San Antonio Bays; accessible only by chartered or private boat. Undeveloped. Dockside & primitive beach campsites. Pit toilets, outdoor shower. (No electricity, no drinking water, no telephone, no concession.) Swim-beach, fish, boating. (Box 117 Port O'Connor 77982, tel 512/983-2215.)

A sturdy rope hanging from a cypress tree is always an invitation to a swing . . . and a splash!

From Colorado Bend State Park, Lake Buchanan is 20 miles south via the Colorado River. At present, facilities are quite primitive as portions of the park are being restored and allowed to revert to their natural condition.

SOUTH PADRE ISLAND

Adolph Thomae, Jr. Cameron County Park

From US 77: FM 1847 N 7 mi, right on FM 2925 6 mi. Entrance fee. Wheeled back-in camper or tent sites 35, with elec, water & sewage, fee. Tent sites 2, w/water, fee, limit 14 days on all camping; rsvns accepted on some sites. Nature trail, overlook tower, playground, picnic area, boat ramp, 2 lighted fishing piers, fish cleaning sta. (Box 2106, South Padre Island, 78597, tel 512/761-5493.)

SOUTH PADRE ISLAND

Andy Bowie Park

From E end Queen Isabella Causeway on South Padre Island: Park Rd 100 N 3.5 mi. On *Gulf of Mexico*. Primitive beach camping. Towing service. (NOTE: Drive only on moist, firm beach area; keep at least 25 ft from water; avoid dry, loose sand. Driving on sand dunes is prohibited by law.) Swim-beach; fish. (Box 2106, South Padre Island 78597, tel 512/761-5493.)

SOUTH PADRE ISLAND

Isla Blanca Park

From E end Queen Isabella Causeway on South Padre Island: Park Rd 100 S .8 mi. On *Gulf of Mexico*. Entrance fee. Wheeled camper sites 400 w/elec, water & sewage, fee. Screened shelters 18, fee, rsvns acptd. Dump sta, fl toilets, showers, day-use cabanas, picnic tables, groc, ice 6 restaurants, 2 boat ramps marina w/65 slips, bathhouse, laundry. Civic Center bldg accommodates 400, fee. Nondenominational chapel. Adjacent Pan Am Univ Marine Biology Lab, Queen Isabella State Fishing Pier. Swim-beach & pool; fish surf & jetties. (Box 2106, South Padre Island 78597, tel 512/761-5493.)

THREE RIVERS

Tips State Recreation Area

From US 281: Tex 72 W .4 mi. On *Frio River*, operated by City of Three Rivers. Picnic & fishing fee. Wheeled camper or tent sites 14; w/elec & water 8, fee; primitive tent sites 6, fee. Limit 14 days; rsvns acptd. Fl toilets, showers, dump sta, group picnic area. River fishing. (Box 398, Three Rivers 78071, tel 512/786-2528 or 786-3511.)

UTOPIA

Community Park

From FM 187: FM 1050 W .1 mi. On *Sabinal River*. Screened shelters 4, fee. Wheeled backin camper sites 5, fee; other camp area 10 acres, fee. Fl toilets, grills. Swim-river; fish, boat ramp, dance floor, adjacent baseball field & rodeo arena. (Utopia Community Park, PO Box 561, Utopia 78884, tel 512/966-2300.)

UVALDE

Nueces Park

From US 90: US 83 N 2 mi; Tex 55 NW 35 mi. On *Nueces River*. Wheeled camper sites 10 w/ elec, water & sewer, fee; w/elec & water 35, fee; tent sites 10, fee. Fl toilets, cold showers. Swim-river; fish, boat ramp, scenic views. Rsvns acptd for 10 sites or more. (Box 85, Camp Wood 78833, tel 512/597-3223.)

VICTORIA

RV Park

Within city at Red River & Vine. Wheeled camper sites 18 w/elec, water & sewage, fee. Adjacent to Riverside Park (zoo, fl toilets, grills, boat ramp & fish-Guadalupe River, concession stand, golf). (City Office, Box 1758, Victoria 77902, tel 512/573-2401.)

Region 4

Dumas 152
Borger
60
15
Pampa
Amarillo
Canyon
19
287
4
5 6
Vernon
Plainview
70
84
Lubbock
87
Snyder
180
Lamesa
14
Abilene
283 183
Cisco
Big Spring
12 Colorado City
1
208
277
11
13
10 El Paso
180
17 Midland
Odessa
18 San Angelo
9
Brownwood
Goldthwaite
20
16
83
Brady
10 Van Horn
Balmorhea
Fort Stockton
Menard
6 Fort Davis
2
10
Sonora
Alpine
385
163
Marathon
90
118
20
Comstock

1 5 10 20 30 40 50

Abilene State Recreation Area

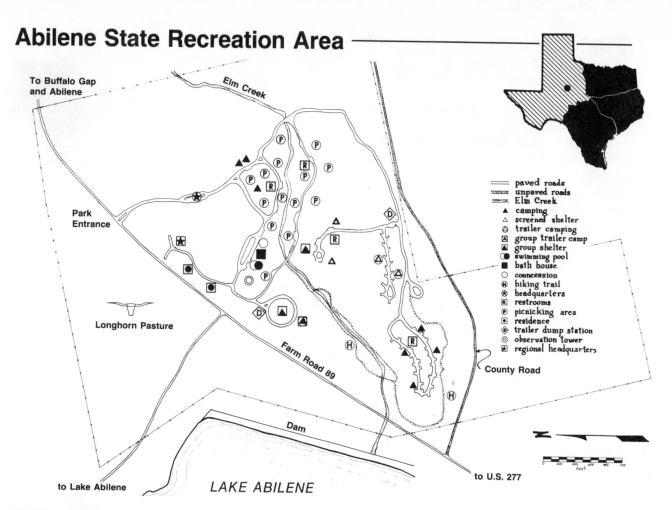

To Buffalo Gap and Abilene

Elm Creek

Park Entrance

Longhorn Pasture

Farm Road 89

Dam

to Lake Abilene

LAKE ABILENE

County Road

to U.S. 277

	paved roads
	unpaved roads
	Elm Creek
▲	camping
△	screened shelter
⊘	trailer camping
⊞	group trailer camp
◮	group shelter
◉	swimming pool
■	bath house
○	concession
Ⓗ	hiking trail
✳	headquarters
Ⓡ	restrooms
Ⓟ	picnicking area
▣	residence
◈	trailer dump station
◎	observation tower
▨	regional headquarters

Facilities & Activities

95 campsites
  12 with water only
  83 with water/electricity
8 screened shelters
restrooms
showers
trailer dump stations
group picnic area
group trailer area available (48 sites)
2 dining halls with kitchens (day-use only)
picnicking
swimming pool & bathhouse
1-mile hiking trail
concession
Texas Longhorn Herd

Location

Abilene State Recreation Area is located 16 miles southwest of Abilene off FM 89 in Taylor County. The 490-acre park borders the 614-acre Lake Abilene on the east.

For Information

Abilene State Recreation Area
Route 1, Box 940
Tuscola, TX 79562
915/572-3204

Texas longhorns are found at several state parks (see facilities summary at the back of this guide) and though they are accustomed to having visitors, it's best to give them a wide berth.

REGION 4

Balmorhea State Recreation Area

Location

Balmorhea State Recreation Area is located at Toyahvale, 4 miles southwest of Balmorhea near the foothills of the Davis Mountains off US 290. The park's scenic 43 acres, spring-fed swimming pool, Spanish-style buildings, lawns and trees provide a refreshing contrast to the flat desert plains to the north and east of the park.

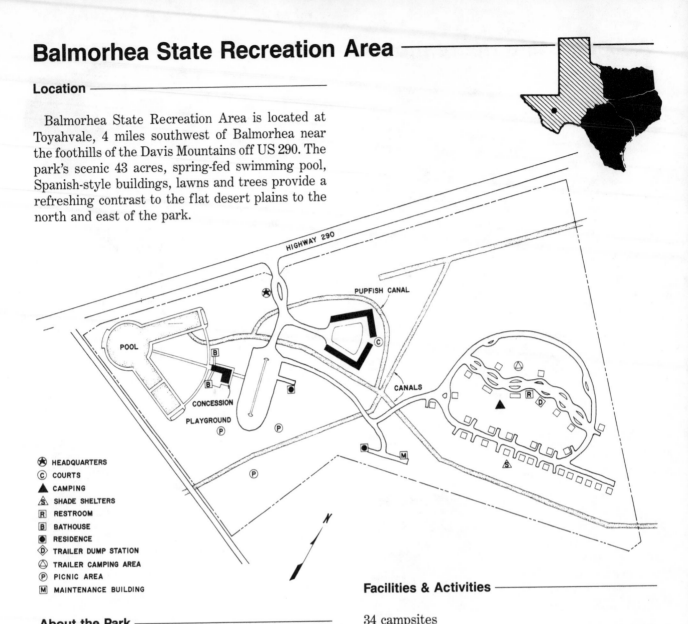

- ✪ HEADQUARTERS
- Ⓒ COURTS
- ▲ CAMPING
- ⬯ SHADE SHELTERS
- Ⓡ RESTROOM
- Ⓑ BATHOUSE
- ◉ RESIDENCE
- ◈ TRAILER DUMP STATION
- △ TRAILER CAMPING AREA
- Ⓟ PICNIC AREA
- Ⓜ MAINTENANCE BUILDING

About the Park

Balmorhea State Recreation Area and environs is often called the "Oasis of West Texas." San Solomon Springs, part of a group of artesian and gravity springs formed by subsurface faulting in the Balmorhea area, flow at the bottom of the world's largest spring-fed swimming pool. This 1¾ acre, 30-foot-deep natural pool has plenty of room for swimmers and offers a unique setting for scuba and skin-diving.

San Solomon Springs has provided water for campers for thousands of years. Artifacts indicate Indians used the spring before white men came to the area. In 1849, the springs were called Mescalero Springs for the Mescalero Apache Indians who watered their horses along its banks. The present name was given by the first settlers, Mexican farmers who used the water for irrigating crops.

Facilities & Activities

34 campsites
  6 with water only
  28 with water/electricity
18-unit San Solomon Springs Court
restrooms
showers
trailer dump station
picnicking
playground
swimming pool & bathhouse (fourth Friday in May through Labor Day)
concession (summer)

For Information

Balmorhea State Recreation Area
Box 15
Toyahvale, TX 79786
915/375-2370

Big Bend National Park

For Information

Park Superintendent
Big Bend National Park, TX 79834
915/477-2251

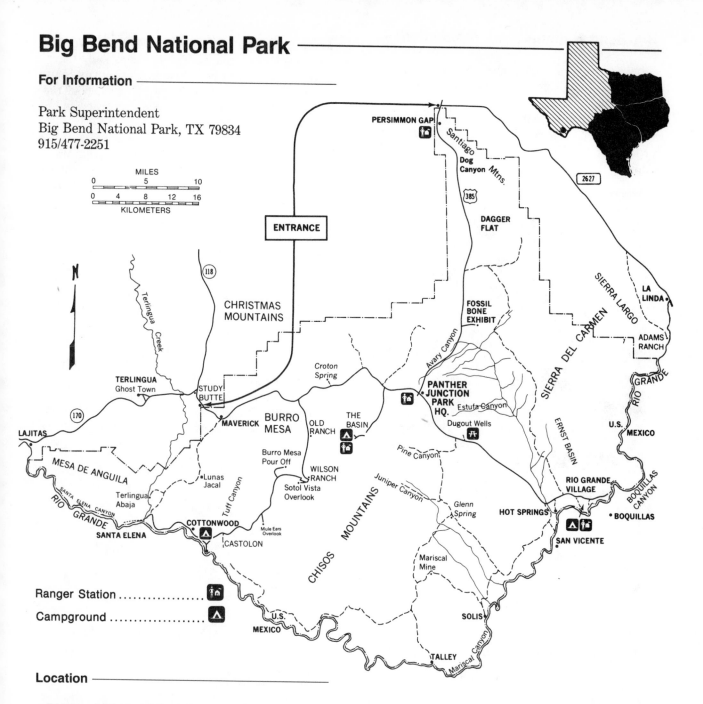

MILES
0   5   10
0   4   8   12   16
KILOMETERS

ENTRANCE

PERSIMMON GAP

Santiago Mtns.

Dog Canyon

385

DAGGER FLAT

2627

SIERRA LARGO

LA LINDA

FOSSIL BONE EXHIBIT

ADAMS RANCH

118

CHRISTMAS MOUNTAINS

Avary Canyon

SIERRA DEL CARMEN

RIO GRANDE

Croton Spring

PANTHER JUNCTION PARK HQ.

Estufa Canyon

TERLINGUA
Ghost Town

STUDY BUTTE

Dugout Wells

U.S.
MEXICO

170

MAVERICK

BURRO MESA

OLD RANCH

THE BASIN

Pine Canyon

ERNST BASIN

LAJITAS

Burro Mesa Pour Off

WILSON RANCH

Juniper Canyon

RIO GRANDE VILLAGE

BOQUILLAS CANYON

MESA DE ANGUILA

Lunas Jacal

Sotol Vista Overlook

Glenn Spring

HOT SPRINGS

BOQUILLAS

Terlingua Abaja

RIO GRANDE

Tuff Canyon

CHISOS MOUNTAINS

SANTA ELENA CANYON

COTTONWOOD

Mule Ears Overlook

SAN VICENTE

SANTA ELENA

CASTOLON

Mariscal Mine

U.S.
MEXICO

SOLIS

Ranger Station ....

Campground ....

TALLEY

Mariscal Canyon

Location

Big Bend National Park is accessible off of US 90 at Marathon via US 385 (69 miles), from Alpine via Texas 188 (108 miles), and from Marfa/Presidio via US 67 and FM 170 (156 miles). The park encompasses a vast area of 802,541 acres and is edged on three sides by the "big bend" of the Rio Grande, the international boundary between Mexico and the United States.

This huge park within the great curve of the Rio Grande is more suggestive of northern Mexico than the United States. Expanses of desert sweep away to remote horizons; mountain ranges rise abruptly above the flatlands; steep-walled canyons and

green, ribbonlike stretches of plants define the river course.

Winter is nippy in the mountains and comfortably warm during the day in the lowlands. Once or twice a year snow falls in the mountains.

Spring weather arrives early with a slow succession of bloom beginning in late February and reaching the mountain heights in May. Some desert plants bloom throughout the year.

Midsummer temperatures in the desert and river valley are likely to hover above 100° during the day. This is the best time of year to go to the mountains. In The Basin (5,400-foot elevation) daytime temper-

Big Bend National Park (continued)

atures average a comfortable 85°, and nights are cool. Autumn sunshine and air are usually gentle and warm.

Trains and transcontinental buses serve Alpine but there is now no regular public transportation to or through the park. Automobiles can be rented at Alpine.

The 7,325-foot Casa Grande, viewed from the Basin, may well be the most photographed peak in the park.

Primitive Camping

Numerous backcountry roadside campsites are located throughout the park. Most require a high clearance or 4-wheel-drive vehicle. No services or facilities are available at these primitive campsites. A backcountry permit is required to camp at these sites, and can be obtained free of charge at any ranger station.

Note: Back-country camping is by permit only. For more detailed maps of Big Bend National Park Trails, see pages 111–120 of *Hiking and Backpacking Trails of Texas*/3rd Ed. by Mickey Little, Lone Star Books/Gulf, 1990.

Activities

Horseback trips: Guided horseback trips are provided by the Chisos Remuda. Advance reservations required, 915/477-2374.

Swimming: Swimming in the Rio Grande is neither prohibited nor encouraged. However, it can be dangerous due to strong undercurrents or drop-offs.

Fishing: Fishing is allowed in the Rio Grande. No license is required. Catfish are commonly taken.

Wildlife: Seventy-five species of mammals, more than 400 species of birds, and 65 species of reptiles and amphibians have been recorded in the park.

Hiking: Hiking is the best way to experience, enjoy, and appreciate Big Bend National Park. Walks and hikes range from short self-guided trails to cross-park treks. A hiker's guide is sold at park headquarters.

Backpacking: A permit is required for all overnight trips, and can be obtained up to 24 hours in advance of the trip *in person only.*

River trips: The Rio Grande is a Wild and Scenic River for 191.2 miles along part of the park boundary and extending below. A free river permit is required for floating the river and is available at park headquarters and ranger stations. A river guide is sold at park headquarters. There are no equipment rentals in the park. Three options are available: (1) you can bring your own equipment; (2) you can rent equipment at Lajitas or Study Butte; or (3) you can hire guide service. Call or write the park for a list of river outfitters.

Campgrounds	Elevation (ft)	No. of Sites	*Camping Fee/Night	Toilets (flush or pit)	Picnic Table/Grill	Overhead Shelter
Basin Campground	5,400	63	$5	F	X	X
Cottonwood Campground	1,900	35	$3	P	X	
Rio Grande Village Class A Campground	1,850	100	$5	F	X	some
** Class B Campground			$3	P		
RV Park	Concessionaire operated 915/477-2293; full hook-up capability required; NO reservations					

Notes:
* Campground fees subject to change
** Used only when Class A campground, above, is full.
 Drinking water is available at all campsites.
 Dump stations are available at Basin Campground and Rio Grande Village Class A Campground.

Other Services

▲ Prepared food and lodging are available only in the Chisos Basin. Call 915/477-2291 for room reservations. Advance reservations recommended.

▲ Gas and groceries are available near all campgrounds. (No gas in the Chisos Basin.)

▲ Showers and laundry facilities are available only at the grocery store/service station at Rio Grande Village between 9:00 a.m. and 5:00 p.m.

Caprock Canyons State Park

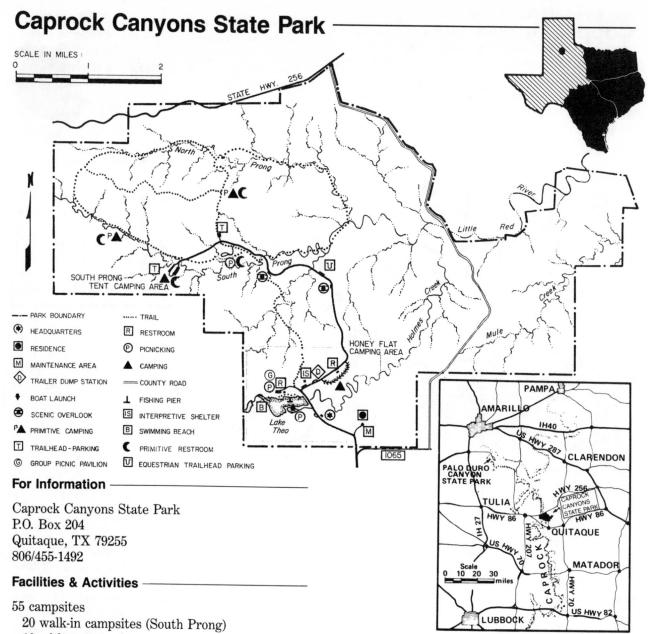

SCALE IN MILES:
0   1   2

STATE HWY. 256

North Prong

South Prong

SOUTH PRONG TENT CAMPING AREA

Little Red River

Holmes Creek

Mule Creek

HONEY FLAT CAMPING AREA

Lake Theo

1065

Legend:

- –––– PARK BOUNDARY
- ⊛ HEADQUARTERS
- ◉ RESIDENCE
- Ⓜ MAINTENANCE AREA
- ◇ TRAILER DUMP STATION
- ⚓ BOAT LAUNCH
- ⊛ SCENIC OVERLOOK
- ᴾ▲ PRIMITIVE CAMPING
- Ⓣ TRAILHEAD - PARKING
- Ⓖ GROUP PICNIC PAVILION
- ⋯⋯ TRAIL
- Ⓡ RESTROOM
- Ⓟ PICNICKING
- ▲ CAMPING
- ═══ COUNTY ROAD
- ⊥ FISHING PIER
- IS INTERPRETIVE SHELTER
- Ⓑ SWIMMING BEACH
- ☾ PRIMITIVE RESTROOM
- Ⓤ EQUESTRIAN TRAILHEAD PARKING

For Information

Caprock Canyons State Park
P.O. Box 204
Quitaque, TX 79255
806/455-1492

Facilities & Activities

55 campsites
  20 walk-in campsites (South Prong)
  10 with water only
  25 with water/electricity
primitive camping areas for backpackers
equestrian camping areas
restrooms
showers
trailer dump station
group picnic area
amphitheater
picnicking
playground
swimming beach
fishing pier
boat ramp
18 miles of hiking/horseback trails
interpretive exhibits

PAMPA

AMARILLO

IH40

US HWY 287

CLARENDON

PALO DURO CANYON STATE PARK

HWY 256

CAPROCK CANYONS STATE PARK

TULIA

HWY 86

HWY 86

IH 27

US HWY 70

HWY 207

QUITAQUE

MATADOR

CAPROCK

HWY 70

Scale
0 10 20 30 miles

LUBBOCK

US HWY 82

Location

Caprock Canyons State Park is located in southeastern Briscoe County three miles north of the town of Quitaque. The park contains 13,906 acres and extends from the caprock (the scenic and rugged escarpment that separates the tablelands of the Southern High Plains from the breaks and rolling plains to the east) eastward for a distance of about 8 miles. Although bordered on the north by SH 256, the park entrance is on the south and most easily accessible by traveling north through Quitaque on RR 1065. A feature attraction of the park is Lake Theo, which covers 120 acres at high level and provides opportunities for water-related activities.

Copper Breaks State Park

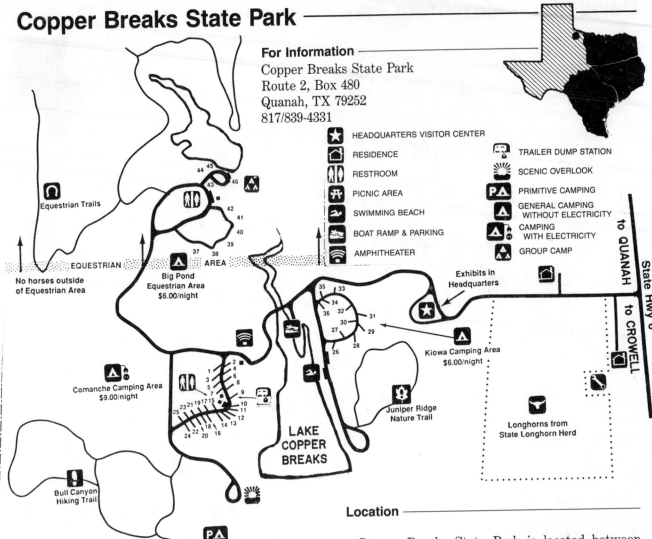

For Information

Copper Breaks State Park
Route 2, Box 480
Quanah, TX 79252
817/839-4331

⭐ HEADQUARTERS VISITOR CENTER

🏠 RESIDENCE

🚻 RESTROOM

⛱ PICNIC AREA

🏊 SWIMMING BEACH

🚤 BOAT RAMP & PARKING

🎭 AMPHITHEATER

🚽 TRAILER DUMP STATION

☀ SCENIC OVERLOOK

P△ PRIMITIVE CAMPING

△ GENERAL CAMPING WITHOUT ELECTRICITY

△ CAMPING WITH ELECTRICITY

△ GROUP CAMP

Equestrian Trails

No horses outside of Equestrian Area

EQUESTRIAN AREA

Big Pond Equestrian Area
$6.00/night

Comanche Camping Area
$9.00/night

Bull Canyon Hiking Trail

Primitive Camping Area
$4.00/night

LAKE COPPER BREAKS

Juniper Ridge Nature Trail

Kiowa Camping Area
$6.00/night

Exhibits in Headquarters

Longhorns from State Longhorn Herd

to QUANAH
to CROWELL
State Hwy 6

Facilities & Activities

40 campsites
  15 with water only
  35 with water/electricity
restrooms
showers
trailer dump station
group picnic area
group primitive camping area
amphitheater
picnicking
swimming beach
fishing piers
boat ramp
nature & hiking trails
equestrian area
Interpretive Center
Texas Longhorn Herd

Location

Copper Breaks State Park is located between Quanah and Crowell off of SH 6. The park contains 1,933 acres, primarily juniper breaks and grass-covered mesas, and a 60-acre lake formed by impoundment on Devil's Creek. The south boundary of the park is formed by the Pease River, a tributary of the Red River.

Teepee-like shade shelters give Copper Breaks State Park an Indian atmosphere.

Davis Mountains State Park

Location

Davis Mountains State Park is located 4 miles northwest of Fort Davis via SH 118, contains 1,869 acres and is adjacent to Fort Davis National Historic Site.

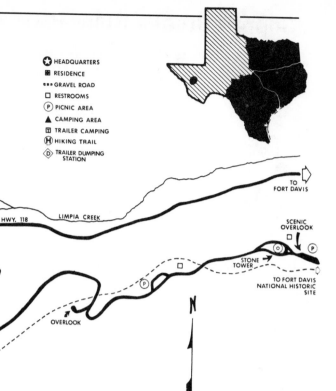

- ⊛ HEADQUARTERS
- ▥ RESIDENCE
- ▪▪▪ GRAVEL ROAD
- ☐ RESTROOMS
- Ⓟ PICNIC AREA
- ▲ CAMPING AREA
- ⊞ TRAILER CAMPING
- Ⓗ HIKING TRAIL
- Ⓓ TRAILER DUMPING STATION

Facilities & Activities

88 campsites
  41 with water only
  20 with water/electricity
  27 with water/electricity/sewage
39-room Indian Lodge, with heated pool
  & restaurant
restrooms
showers
trailer dump stations
group picnic area
amphitheater
picnicking
playground
Interpretive Center (summer)
4½ mile of hiking trails
scenic drive

For Information

Davis Mountains State Park
Box 786
Fort Davis, TX 79734
915/426-3337

The park's scenic drive provides panoramic views of the Davis Mountains.

Davis Mountains State Park   127

Fort Griffin State Historical Park

Facilities & Activities

20 campsites
  5 with water only
  15 with water/electricity
restrooms
showers
trailer dump station
group picnic area
amphitheater
picnicking
playground
fishing
1½ miles of nature trails
2½ miles of hiking trails
historical exhibit at Visitor Center
Fort Griffin ruins
Texas Longhorn Herd

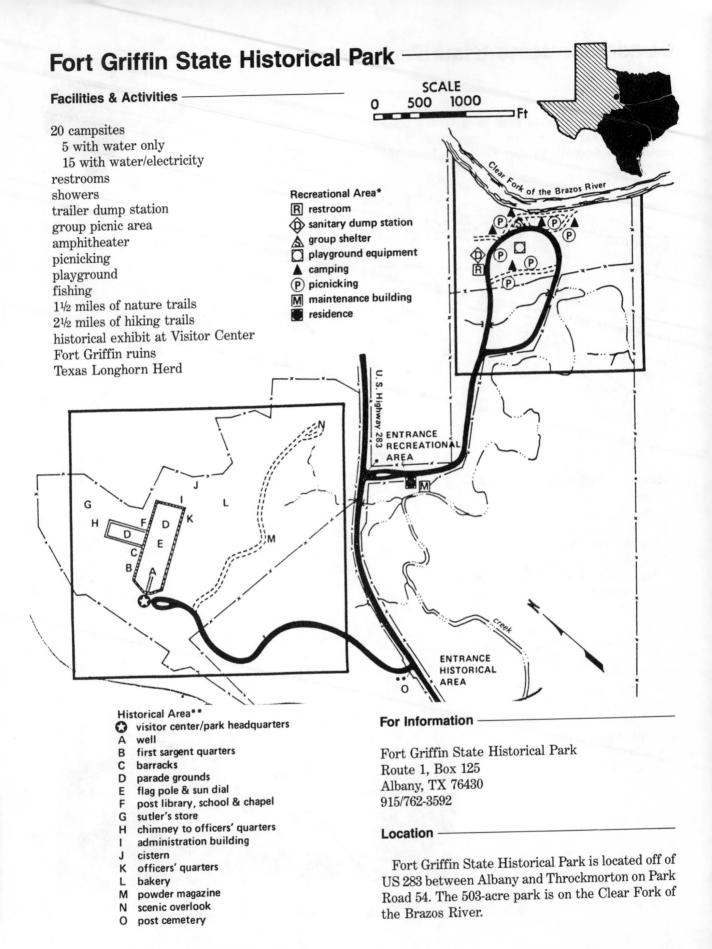

SCALE
0 500 1000 Ft

Recreational Area*
- R restroom
- ◇ sanitary dump station
- △ group shelter
- ☐ playground equipment
- ▲ camping
- Ⓟ picnicking
- M maintenance building
- ⬛ residence

Historical Area**
- ★ visitor center/park headquarters
- A well
- B first sargent quarters
- C barracks
- D parade grounds
- E flag pole & sun dial
- F post library, school & chapel
- G sutler's store
- H chimney to officers' quarters
- I administration building
- J cistern
- K officers' quarters
- L bakery
- M powder magazine
- N scenic overlook
- O post cemetery

For Information

Fort Griffin State Historical Park
Route 1, Box 125
Albany, TX 76430
915/762-3592

Location

Fort Griffin State Historical Park is located off of US 283 between Albany and Throckmorton on Park Road 54. The 503-acre park is on the Clear Fork of the Brazos River.

Guadalupe Mountains National Park

For Information

Guadalupe Mountains National Park
HC 60, Box 400
Salt Flat, TX 79847-9400
915/828-3251

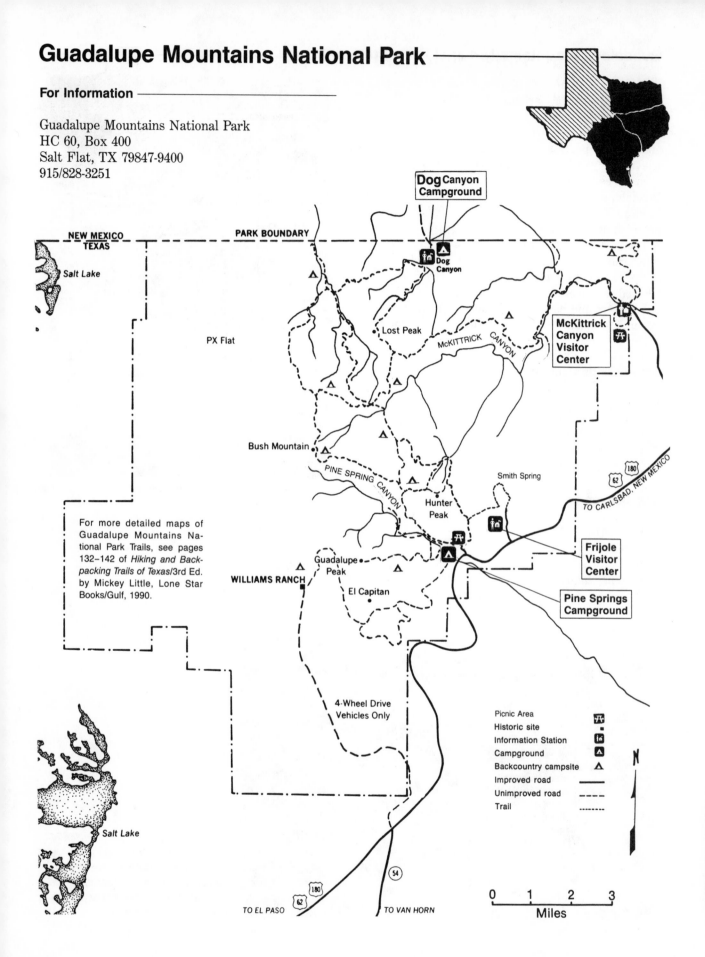

For more detailed maps of
Guadalupe Mountains Na-
tional Park Trails, see pages
132–142 of *Hiking and Backpacking Trails of Texas*/3rd Ed.
by Mickey Little, Lone Star
Books/Gulf, 1990.

Dog Canyon
Campground

McKittrick
Canyon
Visitor
Center

Frijole
Visitor
Center

Pine Springs
Campground

NEW MEXICO
TEXAS

Salt Lake

PARK BOUNDARY

PX Flat

Lost Peak

McKITTRICK   CANYON

Bush Mountain

PINE SPRING CANYON

Smith Spring

62 180

TO CARLSBAD, NEW MEXICO

Hunter
Peak

Guadalupe
Peak

WILLIAMS RANCH

El Capitan

4-Wheel Drive
Vehicles Only

Salt Lake

Picnic Area
Historic site
Information Station
Campground
Backcountry campsite
Improved road
Unimproved road
Trail

180
62

TO EL PASO

54

TO VAN HORN

0   1   2   3
Miles

N

Guadalupe Mountains National Park (continued)

Guadalupe Mountains National Park is located 55 miles southwest of Carlsbad, New Mexico and 110 miles east of El Paso, Texas on US 62/180.

The 77,500-acre park lies astride the most scenic and rugged portion of the Guadalupe Mountains. Elevations range from 3,650 feet at the base of the western escarpment to 8,749 feet on the summit of Guadalupe Peak, the highest point in Texas. The Capitan Reef is the most extensive fossil reef of Permian age complex on record.

The park contains over 80 miles of rugged mountain trails. Camping is permitted at designated campsites in the backcountry. Wood fires are not allowed, but containerized fuel stoves are permitted. Hikers and backpackers must carry all water. Permits for backcountry hiking and camping should

Backpackers are headed to the high-country from Dog Canyon Campground. Located near the New Mexico border, the campground is an access point to the park from the north via the Tejas Trail and the Bush Mountain Trail.

Pine Springs Campground

24 tent sites
29 sites for self-contained RVs
2 group sites (by reservation)
flush toilets/water nearby
picnic tables; no fires (only campstoves permitted)

Dog Canyon Campground

505/981-2418
15 tent sites
5 spaces for self-contained RVs
restrooms/water
picnic tables & grills (charcoal fires only)

McKittrick Canyon

915/828-3381
Day use area for picnicking and hiking.

The park contains over 80 miles of rugged mountain trails. Water is unavailable in the high-country, so careful planning is imperative; for overnight trips, a gallon per person per day is recommended.

Hords Creek Lake

For Information

Reservoir Manager
Hords Creek Lake
Glen Cove Route
Coleman, TX 76834
915/625-2322

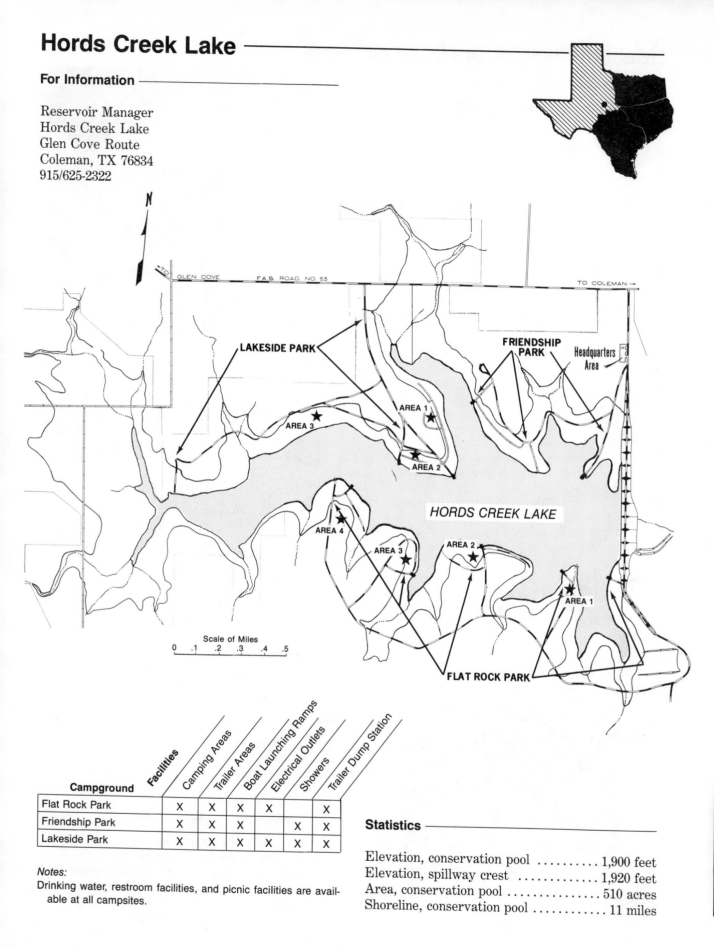

LAKESIDE PARK

FRIENDSHIP PARK

Headquarters Area

AREA 1

AREA 3

AREA 2

HORDS CREEK LAKE

AREA 4

AREA 3

AREA 2

AREA 1

FLAT ROCK PARK

TO GLEN COVE   F.A.S. ROAD NO. 53   TO COLEMAN →

Scale of Miles
0 .1 .2 .3 .4 .5

Campground	Facilities → Camping Areas	Trailer Areas	Boat Launching Ramps	Electrical Outlets	Showers	Trailer Dump Station
Flat Rock Park	X	X	X	X		X
Friendship Park	X	X	X		X	X
Lakeside Park	X	X	X	X	X	X

Notes:
Drinking water, restroom facilities, and picnic facilities are available at all campsites.

Statistics

Elevation, conservation pool .... 1,900 feet
Elevation, spillway crest .... 1,920 feet
Area, conservation pool .... 510 acres
Shoreline, conservation pool .... 11 miles

Hueco Tanks State Historical Park

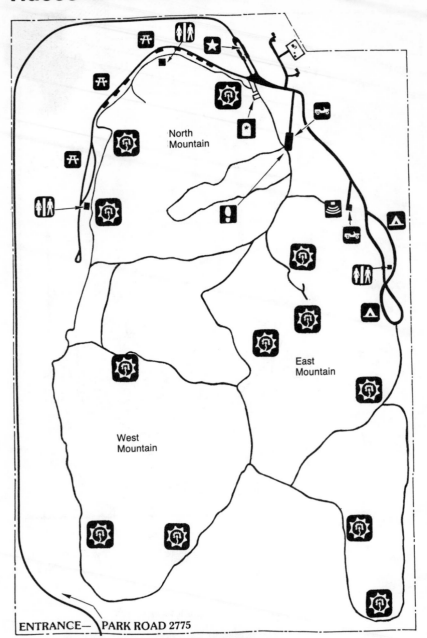

★	Headquarters
♨	Amphitheater
🌲	Picnic Area
⛺	Camping Area
🚻	Restroom
🖐	Pictograph Site
🅿	Parking
🏛	Ruins
🚶	Hiking Trail Head

North Mountain

East Mountain

West Mountain

ENTRANCE— PARK ROAD 2775

Facilities & Activities

20 campsites
  3 with water only
  17 with water/electricity
restrooms
showers
trailer dump station
group picnic area
picnicking
playground
hiking trail
historic structure
Indian pictographs

Indian rock art is found at more than 20 locations at Hueco Tanks.

For Information

Hueco Tanks State Historical Park
Rural Route 3, Box 1
El Paso, TX 79935
915/857-1135

Location

   Hueco Tanks State Historical Park is located 33 miles east of El Paso off of US 62/180 on FM 2775. On rocks are Indian pictographs 2,000 years old, and water from infrequent rains is "stored" in natural rock basins.

Lake Brownwood State Recreation Area

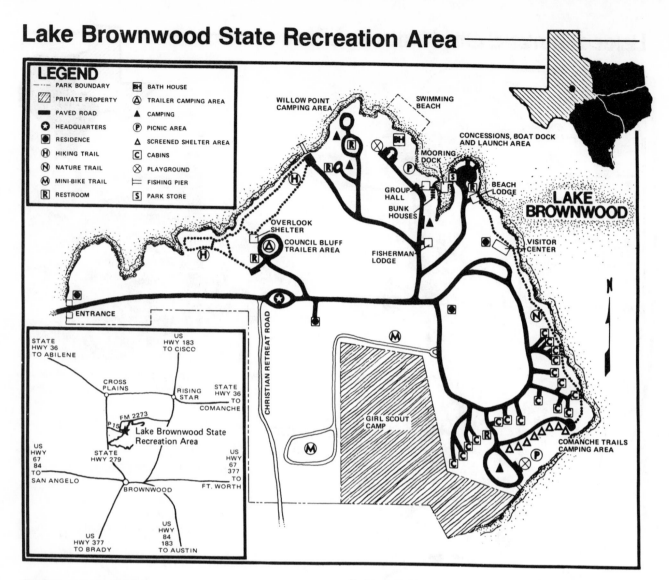

LEGEND

- – – – PARK BOUNDARY
- ▨ PRIVATE PROPERTY
- ▬ PAVED ROAD
- ✪ HEADQUARTERS
- ▣ RESIDENCE
- Ⓗ HIKING TRAIL
- Ⓝ NATURE TRAIL
- Ⓜ MINI-BIKE TRAIL
- Ⓡ RESTROOM
- ⊟ BATH HOUSE
- ⊕ TRAILER CAMPING AREA
- ▲ CAMPING
- Ⓟ PICNIC AREA
- △ SCREENED SHELTER AREA
- ⬚ CABINS
- ⊗ PLAYGROUND
- ⊨ FISHING PIER
- ⬚ PARK STORE

Facilities & Activities

87 campsites
  12 with water only
  55 with water/electricity
  20 with water/electricity/sewage
17 cabins
10 screened shelters
restrooms
showers
trailer dump stations
group facilities
  Beach Lodge
  Fisherman Lodge
  group camp: 4 bunkhouses & dining hall
  group recreation hall with kitchen (day-use only)
picnicking
playgrounds
swimming beach & bathhouse
water skiing

lighted fishing pier
fish cleaning facilities
boat ramps & docks
¾-mile nature trails
2 + miles of hiking trail
park store (seasonal)
Visitor Center

For Information

Lake Brownwood State Recreation Area
Route 5, Box 160
Brownwood, TX 76801
915/784-5223

Location

Lake Brownwood State Recreation Area is located 23 miles northwest of Brownwood via SH 279 and Park Road 15. The 538-acre park is located on the west shore of 7,300-acre Lake Brownwood.

Lake Colorado City State Recreation Area

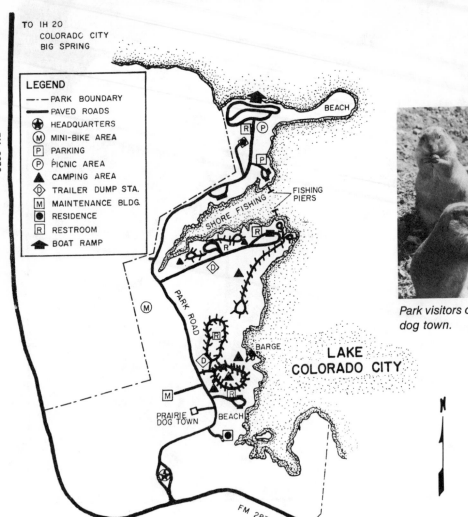

Park visitors of all ages enjoy visiting the prairie dog town.

Facilities & Activities

132 campsites
  53 with water only
  79 with water/electricity
restrooms
showers
trailer dump station
group picnic area
group dining hall
picnicking
swimming beach
water skiing
fishing piers
lighted fishing barge
boat ramp
prairie dog town

Location

Lake Colorado City State Recreation Area is located about 11 miles southwest of Colorado City off of IH 20 on FM 2836. The 500-acre park is on the southwest shore of the 1,655-acre Lake Colorado City.

For Information

Lake Colorado City State Recreation Area
Route 2, Box 232
Colorado City, TX 79512
915/728-3931

Lake E. V. Spence

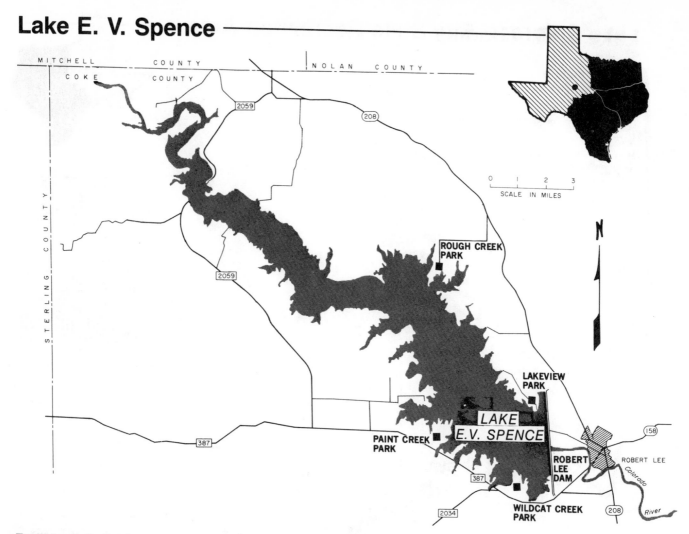

Facilities & Activities

(Available at the four parks named on the map)
tent and trailer sites
sanitary facilities
picnicking
boat ramp
fishing
boating
swimming
water skiing
concession facilities (only at Paint Creek
  Park & Wildcat Creek Park)

For Information

Lake E. V. Spence
Colorado River Municipal Water District
Box 869
Big Spring, TX 79721-0869
915/267-6341

Statistics

Elevation, full .... 1898.0 feet
Surface area, full .... 14,950 acres
Shoreline .... 137 miles

About the Lake

Lake E. V. Spence, with 14,950 surface acres and 137 miles of shoreline, is nestled in the scenic hills of Northwest Coke County.

The reservoir is one of the major water recreation areas of West Texas, with four large public areas containing complete facilities for camping, picnicking, and other recreation.

You can fish, boat, swim, and ski on the lake. A large, varied population of fishes, including the popular striped bass, will keep your lines tugging when you fish this lake.

Lake J. B. Thomas

For Information

Lake J. B. Thomas
Colorado River Municipal Water District
Box 869
Big Spring, TX 79721-0869
915/267-6341

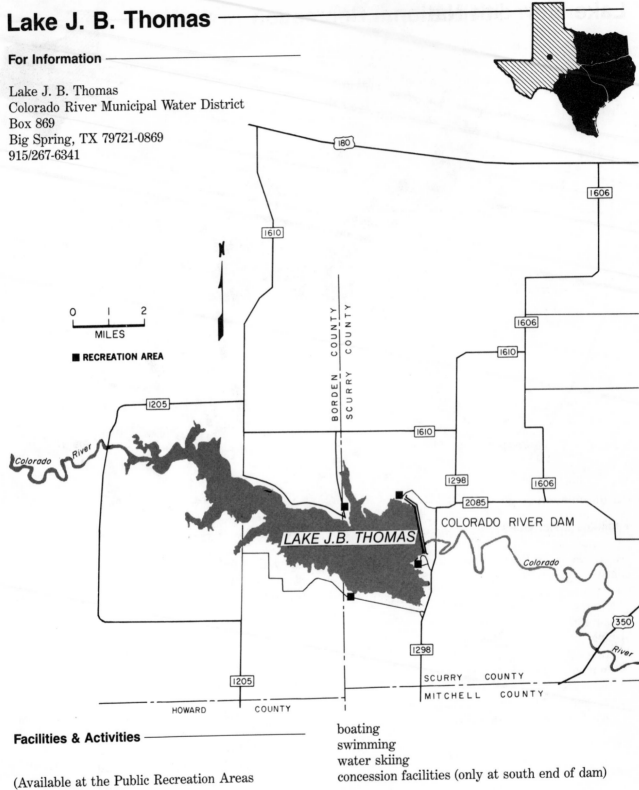

Facilities & Activities

(Available at the Public Recreation Areas
  indicated on map)
tent and trailer sites
sanitary facilities
picnicking
boat ramp
fishing

boating
swimming
water skiing
concession facilities (only at south end of dam)

Statistics

Elevation, full .... 2,258.0 feet
Surface area, full .... 8,000 acres
Shoreline .... 75 miles

Lake Meredith National Recreation Area

Statistics

Elevation, maximum capacity .. approx. 3,000 feet
Area .... 16,500 acres
Shoreline .... 100 miles

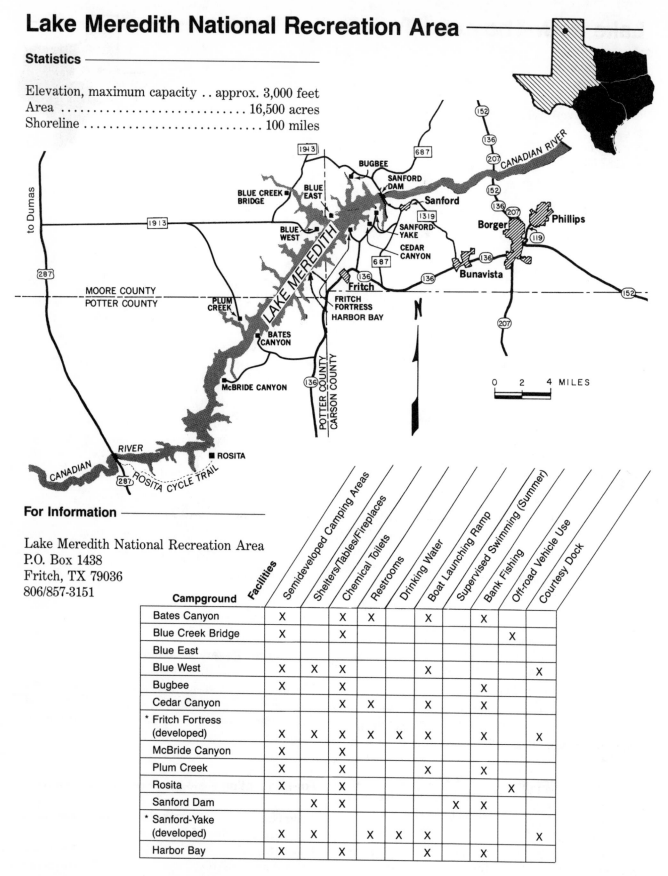

For Information

Lake Meredith National Recreation Area
P.O. Box 1438
Fritch, TX 79036
806/857-3151

Campground	Semideveloped Camping Areas	Shelters/Tables/Fireplaces	Chemical Toilets	Restrooms	Drinking Water	Boat Launching Ramp	Supervised Swimming (Summer)	Bank Fishing	Off-road Vehicle Use	Courtesy Dock
Bates Canyon	X		X	X		X		X		
Blue Creek Bridge	X		X						X	
Blue East										
Blue West	X	X	X			X				X
Bugbee	X		X				X			
Cedar Canyon			X	X		X		X		
* Fritch Fortress (developed)	X	X	X	X	X	X		X		X
McBride Canyon	X		X							
Plum Creek	X		X			X		X		
Rosita	X		X					X		
Sanford Dam		X	X				X	X		
* Sanford-Yake (developed)	X	X		X	X	X				X
Harbor Bay	X		X			X		X		

* Marina and sanitary dump

Lake Nasworthy and Twin Buttes Reservoir

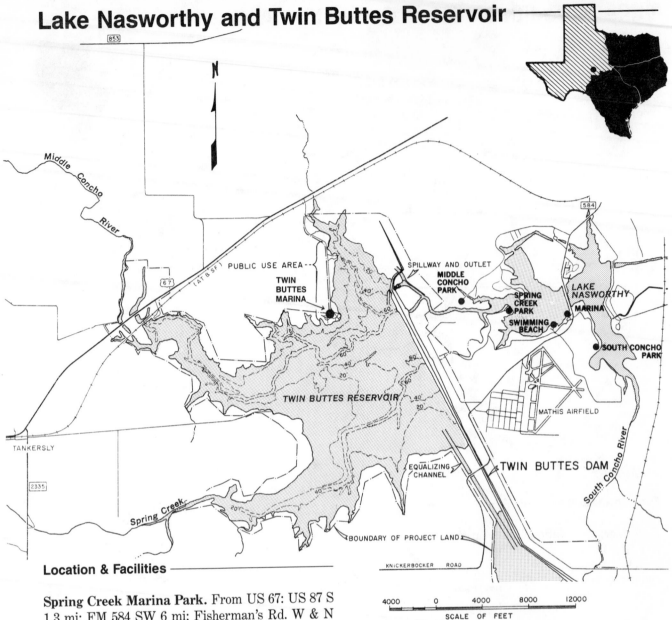

Location & Facilities

Spring Creek Marina Park. From US 67: US 87 S 1.3 mi; FM 584 SW 6 mi; Fisherman's Rd. W & N 1.5 mi. Concessionaire: tents or wheeled campers; full hook-ups available; flush toilets, showers, tackle & boat rental, grocery, snack bar, boat ramp; rsvns acptd. tel 915/944-3850.

Middle Concho Park. From US 67: US 87 S 1.3 mi; FM 584 SW 4.2 mi; Red Bluff Rd W & S 4 mi. Primitive camp area, flush toilets, no drinking water, boat ramp.

Twin Buttes Marina. From US 87: FM 2288 S 11 mi; US 67 W 3.5 mi. Concessionaire: primitive tent area; sites with electricity; flush toilets, picnic shelters, grocery, boat ramp. tel 915/942-9623.

Note: $1 fee charged to enter through the pay-gate located at both lakes on Saturday, Sunday and holidays from March through Labor Day.

Twin Buttes Reservoir Statistics

Elevation, conservation pool .... 1,940 feet
Elevation, spillway crest .... 1,969 feet
Area, conservation pool .... 10,000 acres

For Information

Lake Nasworthy and Twin Buttes Reservoir
Assistant Director of Public Works
P.O. Box 1751
San Angelo, TX 76902
915/657-4206

Monahans Sandhills State Park

For Information

Monahans Sandhills State Park
Box 1738
Monahans, TX 79756
915/943-2092

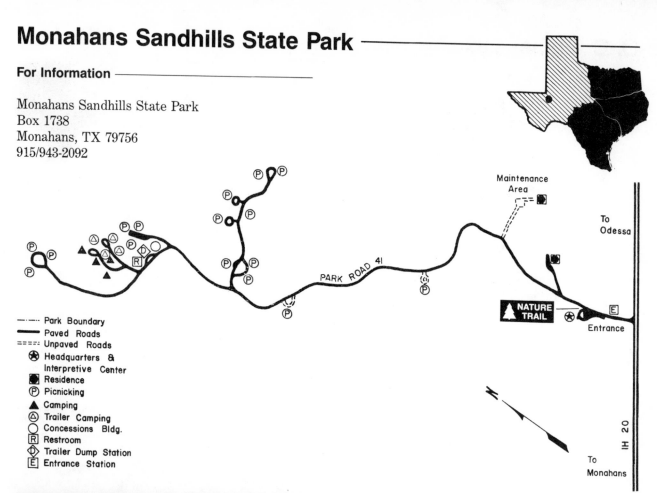

Park Boundary
Paved Roads
Unpaved Roads
Headquarters &
  Interpretive Center
Residence
Picnicking
Camping
Trailer Camping
Concessions Bldg.
Restroom
Trailer Dump Station
Entrance Station

Many of the sand dunes at the park are still active; they grow and change shape in response to prevailing winds.

Location

Monahans Sandhills State Park is located 6 miles northeast of Monahans off IH 20 on Park Road 41. The park contains 3,840 acres of wild-sculptured sand dunes up to 70 feet high, many of which are stabilized by Havard shinoak and other plants. Other dunes that are bare of vegetation constantly shift with the wind.

Facilities & Activities

24 campsites
  5 with water only
  19 with water/electricity
restrooms
showers
trailer dump station
picnicking
¼-mile nature trail
hiking in the sand dunes
sandsurfing
outdoor shower
concession (seasonal)
Interpretive Center

O. C. Fisher Lake

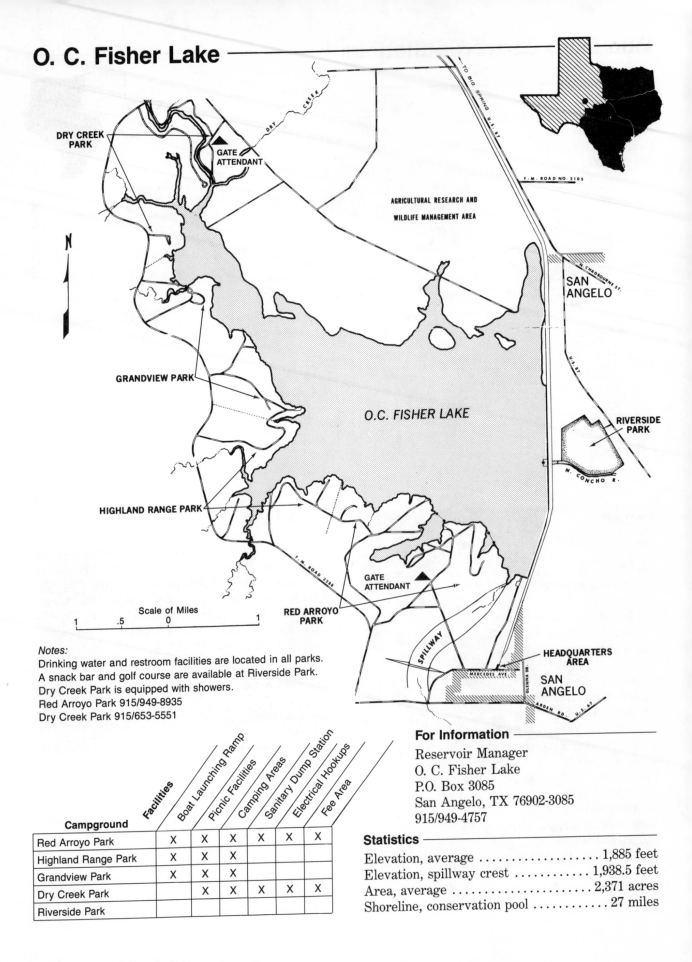

DRY CREEK PARK

GATE ATTENDANT

DRY CREEK

TO BIG SPRING U.S. 87

F.-M. ROAD NO. 2105

AGRICULTURAL RESEARCH AND
WILDLIFE MANAGEMENT AREA

N. CHADBOURNE ST.

SAN ANGELO

GRANDVIEW PARK

U.S. 87

O.C. FISHER LAKE

RIVERSIDE PARK

N. CONCHO R.

HIGHLAND RANGE PARK

F. M. ROAD 2288

GATE ATTENDANT

RED ARROYO PARK

SPILLWAY

HEADQUARTERS AREA

MERCEDES AVE.

SAN ANGELO

ARDEN RD. U.S. 87

Scale of Miles
1   .5   0   1

Notes:
Drinking water and restroom facilities are located in all parks.
A snack bar and golf course are available at Riverside Park.
Dry Creek Park is equipped with showers.
Red Arroyo Park 915/949-8935
Dry Creek Park 915/653-5551

Campground	Facilities	Boat Launching Ramp	Picnic Facilities	Camping Areas	Sanitary Dump Station	Electrical Hookups	Fee Area
Red Arroyo Park		X	X	X	X	X	X
Highland Range Park		X	X	X			
Grandview Park		X	X	X			
Dry Creek Park			X	X	X	X	X
Riverside Park							

For Information

Reservoir Manager
O. C. Fisher Lake
P.O. Box 3085
San Angelo, TX 76902-3085
915/949-4757

Statistics

Elevation, average . . . . 1,885 feet
Elevation, spillway crest . . . . 1,938.5 feet
Area, average . . . . 2,371 acres
Shoreline, conservation pool . . . . 27 miles

Palo Duro Canyon State Park

For Information

Palo Duro Canyon State Park
Route 2, Box 285
Canyon, TX 79015
806/488-2227

Map Legend

- **PARK BOUNDARY**
- **HISTORICAL MARKER**
- **RESIDENCES**
- **HEADQUARTERS**
- **STABLE**
- **VISITOR CENTER**
- **AMPITHEATRE**
- **TRADING POST (PARK STORE)**
- **SCENIC OVERLOOK**
- **DAY USE / PICNIC AREA**
- **RIVER CROSSINGS**
- **LIGHTHOUSE HIKING / EQUESTRIAN TRAIL**
- **REST AREA**
- **TRAILHEAD PARKING**
- **TENT CAMPING AREA**
- **MULTI - USE CAMPING (W / ELECTRICITY)**
- **TRAILER SITES**
- **RESTROOMS (NO SHOWERS)**
- **RESTROOMS W / SHOWERS**
- **TRAILER DUMP STATION**

Map labels: MESQUITE CAMPING AREA, CACTUS CAMPING AREA, SUNFLOWER CAMPING AREA, JUNIPER TRAILER CAMPING, FORTRESS CLIFF, FORTRESS CLIFF CAMPING AREA, HACKBERRY CAMPING AREA, CAPITOL PEAK, SANTANA'S FACE, SAD MONKEY RAILROAD, SUNDAY CANYON, DEVIL'S TOMBSTONE, CASTLE PEAK, LIGHTHOUSE PEAK, TRIASSIC PEAK, TIMBER CREEK CANYON, SPANISH SKIRTS, TO CANYON AND AMARILLO, SCALE 0 ¼ ½ ¾ 1 MILE

Facilities & Activities

116 campsites
  56 tent sites with water only
  60 with water/electricity
restrooms
showers
trailer dump station
group picnic area
Pioneer Amphitheater, 1,600-seat outdoor theater,
  site of summer performances of *Texas*, historical
  musical drama
picnicking
playground
hiking/horseback trails
horse rentals for trail rides
miniature train ride
Goodnight Trading Post (souvenirs & snacks)
Interpretive Center
Texas Longhorn Herd
scenic drive

Millions of years of geologic history are exposed in the park, creating a panorama of exceptional color and beauty.

Location

Palo Duro Canyon State Park is located approximately 12 miles east of Canyon on SH 217. From Amarillo, it is south on RR 1541, then 8 miles east on SH 217. More than 16,000 acres of canyon country are enclosed within Palo Duro.

Seminole Canyon State Historical Park

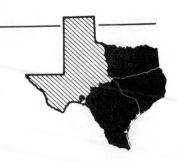

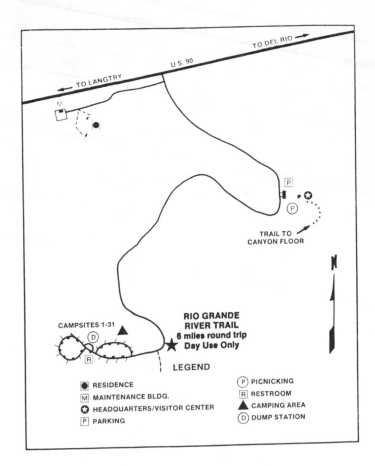

For Information

Seminole Canyon State Historical Park
P.O. Box 820
Comstock, TX 78837
915/292-4464

Facilities & Activities

31 campsites
  8 with water only
  23 with water/electricity
restrooms
showers
trailer dump station
picnicking
6-mile hiking trail
guided tour to Indian pictographs
Headquarters/Visitor Center exhibits

Location

Seminole Canyon State Historical Park is located in Val Verde County 45 miles west of Del Rio, a short distance downstream from the confluence of the Rio Grande with the Pecos River. The 2,173-acre park, with its rugged limestone terrain is noted for its sparse vegetation and deep canyons.

In the canyon is Fate Bell Shelter, which contains some of North America's oldest pictographs believed to have been painted as long as 8,000 years ago. Guided tours are conducted Wednesday thru Sunday at 10 a.m. and 3 p.m. to take visitors into the canyon to see these fine examples of rock art.

Guided tours of the Fate Bell Shelter give visitors an "up close and personal" view of Texas' ancient past.

Other Parks in Region 4*

ABILENE   **Johnson Park**
From I-20: FM 600 N 6.6 mi; FM 1082 E .6 mi. On *Lake Fort Phantom Hill*. Camp area 37 acres, prepared sites 5, limit 3 days. Fl toilets. No drinking water. Fish, boat ramp at E end of dam. (City Pk Dept, Box 60, Abilene 79604, tel 915/676-6218.)

ABILENE   **Seabee Park**
From I-20: FM 600 N 3.2 mi; local rd E. On *Elm Creek*. Camp area 40 acres, prepared sites 4, limit 3 days. Fl toilets. Fish, boat ramp. (City Pk Dept, Box 60, Abilene 79604, tel 915/676-6218.)

ALBANY   **Webb Park**
Within city, from US 180: Railroad St NW .3 mi. Wheeled backin camper sites 20 w/elec & water, fee. Picnic shelters, grills. Swim-pool; playground, ball field. (City Pk Dept, Box 595, Albany 76430, tel 915/762-3133.)

ANDREWS   **Florey Park**
From Tex 87: US 385 N 9.6 mi; local rd E 1 mi. In shady grove. Wheeled camper or tent sites 252; w/elec & water, 200; w/elec, water & sewage 52, fee, limit 4 days. Dump sta, fl toilets, grills, community center, pavilion (by rsvn 915/524-1401). Tennis, volleyball, basketball, croquet courts, playground. (Florey County Pk, Star HC 71, Box 5035, Andrews 79714, tel 915/523-4812.)

ANDREWS   **Municipal Trailer Park**
From US 385: Tex 115/176 (W. Broadway) W 7 blks. Wheeled backin camper sites 12 w/elec water & sewage; tent-trailer sites 10, limit 3 days. Fish, playground, prairie dog town. (Chamber of Commerce, 700 Broadway, Andrews 79714, tel 915/523-2695, or 523-4820.)

BALLINGER   **Ballinger City Park**
From Tex 158: Crosson St E .1 mi. On *Elm Creek*. Wheeled backin camper sites 8 w/elec & water, fee, limit 3 days. Dump sta, fl toilets, grills. Swim-pool; fish, playground. (Box 497, Ballinger 76821, tel 915/365-3511.)

BALLINGER   **Ballinger Lake Park**
From W city limit: Tex 158 NW 4.8 mi; FM 2111 S 1.2 mi; local rd W&S .7 mi. On *Lake Ballinger*. Wheeled camper or tent sites w/ elec & water 22, fee. Dump sta, fl toilets, picnic area. Swim-lake; fish, boat ramp, scenic views. (Box 497, Ballinger 76821, tel 915/365-3511.)

BIG LAKE   **Reagan County Park**
Within city, from US 67: Utah Ave N 11 blks. Wheeled camper sites 12; w/elec & water 4, w/ elec, water & sewage 1. Tent sites 6. Limit 3 days, donation. Dump sta, fl toilets, grills, ice, groc, laundry nearby. Swim-pool; bicycle trails, playground, tennis, volleyball. (Box 903, Big Lake 76932, tel 915/884-2014.)

BIG SPRING   **Comanche Trail Park**
From I-20: US 87 S 3.6 mi. Wheeled camper sites 9 w/elec & water, tent sites 10, fee, limit 3 days. Dump sta, fl toilets, cold showers, grills. Swim-pool; golf, tennis. (City Pk Dept, Box 391, Big Spring 79720, tel 915/263-8311.)

BIG SPRING   **Moss Lake Park**
From US 87: I-10 E 7.2 mi; Moss Lake Rd S 4.1 mi. On *Moss Lake*. Entrance fee. Wheeled camper or tent sites 21; w/elec 5; other camp area 200 acres. Closed Dec 15–Jan 15. Pit toilets, bait, picnic shelters, grills, snack bar, ice, groc. Swim-lake; fish, boat ramp, scenic views, nature trails, lighted fish docks, fish piers. (City Pk Dept, Rt 3, Box 225, Big Spring 79720, tel 915/393-5246.)

BLACKWELL   **Oak Creek Park**
From US 277: Tex 70 NW 1.5 mi; FM 3399 NE .7 mi. On *Oak Creek Lake*. 19 waterfront wheeled backin camper sites w/elec, water, fee. Other camp area 24 acres; permit required. Dump sta, fl toilets, bait, gas, ice, groc. Swim-lake; fish, boat ramp, skiing, scenic views. Rsvns acptd. (Sportsman's Lodge, Rt 1, Blackwell 79506, tel 915/282-2602.)

BORGER   **Huber Park**
Within city: 1300 Main St. Wheeled backin camper sites 10 w/elec & water, limit 3 days. Pit toilets, dump sta nearby. (City Pk, Box 5250, Borger 79008, tel 806/273-2883.)

BROWNFIELD   **Coleman Park**
Within city, US 62: Reppto St E 1 blk, First St S 1 blk. Wheeled backin camper sites 12 w/ elec, water & sewage, limit 4 days. Nearby park facilities include swimming pool (summer only); playground, tennis court. (Park Board, County Courthouse, Brownfield 79316, tel 806/637-6421.)

CANADIAN   **Lake Marvin Camp**
From US 60: FM 2266 E 14 mi. On *Lake Marvin*. Entrance fee. Wheeled camper or tent sites 23, fee, limit 14 days; cabins 3, fee. Pit toilets, boat rental, bait, picnic shelters, grills, snack bar, ice. Fish, nature trail. (Box 397, Canadian 79014, tel 806/323-5047.)

CHLDRESS   **City Park**
From courthouse: Main St N .2 mi. On *Groesbeck Creek* tributary. Fl toilets, picnic shelter. Swim-pool; playground, tennis, ball fields. (City Hall, Box 1087, Childress 79201, tel 817/937-3684.)

Greenbelt North, South
CLARENDON   **& West Marinas**
South Location, From US 287: Tex 70 N 4.5 mi; local rd W. **North Location**, Tex 70 N 5.5 mi; **West Location**, US 287 2.2 mi W, FM 3257 N 3.2 mi, local rd 1 mi. On *Greenbelt Lake*. Concessionaire: Entrance fee. Total of 108 hook-ups in 3 pks, fee. Other camp area 600 acres, fee. Trailer pk, mobile homes. Dump sta, fl toilets, picnic shelters, bait, ice. Swim-lake; fish, boat ramps. Jet ski, paddle boats, hover craft rentals at South Location. (Box 457, Clarendon 79226, tel 806/874-3900, or 874-5033.)

* Source: *Texas Public Campgrounds*, State Dept. of Highways and Public Transportation, Travel and Information Div., P.O. Box 5064, Austin, TX 78763.

In the yesteryears, Mule Ear Peaks was an important landmark to travelers through the lower Big Bend area; they are visible from the road to Castolon.

Palo Duro is one of eight state parks that has equestrian trails; horse rentals, for trail rides, are seasonal.

COLEMAN   **Press Morris Park**
From US 283/84: US 283 N 12.9 mi; FM 1274 W 2.4 mi. On *Lake Coleman*. Wheeled backin camper sites 13; w/elec 12, fee; other camp area 100 acres, limit 14 days. Fl & pit toilets, bait, picnic shelters. Swim-lake; fish, marina, gas, groc, boat ramp. (Box 592, Coleman 76834, tel 915/382-4635.)

COLORADO CITY   **Fisher Park**
From I-20: Tex 208 S 9 mi; local rd W 3 mi. On *Champion Lake*. Wheeled camper or tent sites 12; w/elec 9, w/water 3, fee; RV max length 28 ft; other camp area 35 acres, fee, limit 14 days. Fl toilets, bait, picnic shelters, grills, ice, groc. Swim-lake; trail bike area, fish, boat ramp, no skiing. (180 W. 3rd St, Colorado City 79512, tel 915/728-8100.)

COLORADO CITY   **Ruddick Park**
From I-20: Tex 208 S 14 blks; 7th St E 5 blks. On *Lone Wolf Creek*. Wheeled camper or tent sites 5; 1 with hookup; RV max length 28 ft; other camp area 50 acres, limit 14 days. Pit toilets, picnic shelters, grills. Swim-pool; fish, playground, scenic views, bicycle & nature trails. (180 W. 3rd St, Colorado City 79512, tel 915/728-5331.)

CRANE   **Crane County Campground**
From US 385: Airport Rd W to campground. Wheeled backin camper sites 5 w/elec & water, limit 3 days. RV max length 25 ft. Fl toilets, no drinking water, grills. (409 S. Gaston, Crane 79731, tel 915/558-2311.)

CROSBYTON   **Campground #1**
From US 82: FM 651 S 13.5 mi; FM 2794 E & S 8.6 mi. On *White River Lake*. Entrance fee. Wheeled camper or tent sites 20, fee. Limit 14 days, RV max length 25 ft. Fl toilets. Swim-lake; fish, boat ramps (fee). (Star Rt 2, Spur 79370, tel 806/263-4240.)

CROSBYTON   **Campground #2**
From US 82: FM 651 S 13.5 mi; FM 2794 E & S 8.6 mi; local rd NE 1.5 mi. On *White River Lake*. Entrance fee. Wheeled camper or tent sites 25; w/elec & water 10, fee, limit 14 days. RV max length 25 ft. Fl toilets. Swim-lake; fish. (Star Rt 2, Spur 79370, tel 806/263-4240.)

CROSBYTON   **Campground #3**
From US 82: FM 651 S 13.5 mi; FM 2794 E & S 7.2 mi; Lake Rd N. On *White River Lake*. Entrance fee. Wheeled camper or tent sites 25, fee. Limit 14 days, RV max length 25 ft. Fl toilets. Swim-lake; fish, boat ramps. (Star Rt 2, Spur 79370, tel 806/263-4240.)

CROSBYTON   **Campground #4**
From US 82: FM 651 S 13.5 mi; FM 2794 E & S 7.2 mi; Lake Rd N, 5 mi past Campground 3. On *White River Lake*. Entrance fee. Primitive camping only, fee, limit 14 days. Swim-lake; fish. (Star Rt 2, Spur 79370, tel 806/263-4240.)

CROSBYTON   **City Park**
US 82 at E city limit. Wheeled camper or tent sites 5, limit 3 days. Dump sta, grills. Swim-pool (fee); playground. (119 S. Ayrshire, Crosbyton 79322, tel 806/675-2301.)

DALHART   **Rita Blanca Lake Park**
From US 54: US 87/385 S 1 mi; FM 281 SW 1.5 mi. On *Rita Blanca Lake*. Wheeled camper sites 31 w/elec, water & sewage, fee; other camp area 1000 acres, fee, limit 14 days. Fl toilets, bait, picnic shelters, grills, snack bar, ice, groc. Fish, boat ramp, bike trail, playground, softball, horseshoe pitching, scenic views. (Rt 1, Box 1253, Dalhart 79022, tel 806/249-2450.)

DENVER CITY   **Yoakum County Park**
From Tex 83: Tex 214 N 5.9 mi. Wheeled backin camper sites 10 w/elec, fee, limit 3 days. Dump sta, fl toilets, grills. Playground, softball, croquet. (Box 172, Denver City 79323, tel 806/592-3166.)

DUMAS   **Texoma Park**
Within city: 500 W. 1st (US 87N). Wheeled camper sites 24 w/elec, limit 1 day. Closed in winter. Dump sta, fl toilets (Box 438, Dumas 79029, tel 806/935-4101.)

HAMLIN   **City Park**
Within city from 500 S. Central Ave: S. Central Ave W 5 blks; SW. 5th St 6 blks; SW. Ave E 1 blk. Camp area 13 acres, limit 7 days. Grills, swim-pool; playground, ball fields. (Drawer N, Hamlin 79520, tel 915/576-2711.)

HAMLIN   **South Park**
From US 83: FM 126 S 3.5 mi; local rd E .5 mi. On *South Lake*. Fishing permit, fee. Camp area 50 acres. Grills, fish, boat ramp, scenic views, no toilets or showers. (Drawer N, Hamlin 79520, tel 915/576-2711.)

HASKELL   **Haskell Park**
From US 380: Ave C S 6 blks. Wheeled backin camper sites w/water 10, w/water, elec & sewage 6, one night free, fee addnl nights. RV max length 25 ft. Dump sta, fl toilets, cold showers, grills. Swim-pool, tennis, playground. (Box 1003, Haskell 79521, tel 817/864-2333.)

IRAAN   **Alley Oop Park**
Within city, on US 190. Wheeled camper sites 10 w/water, fee, w/water, elec & sewage 6, fee, limit 7 days. Dump sta, grills. Adjoining county park has swimming pool, playground, tennis. (City Office, Box 457, Iraan 79744, tel 915/639-2301; rsvns not acptd.)

LAMESA   **Forrest Park**
Within city: 9th St and Bryan Ave. Wheeled camper sites 10 w/elec & water; other camp area 40 acres, limit 3 days. Dump sta, grills. Playground, ball field. (City Office, 310 S. Main, Lamesa 79331, tel 806/872-2124.)

LEVELLAND   **City-County Camp Site**
From Tex 114: US 385 S 3.3 mi. Wheeled camper sites w/elec & water 12, limit 3 days. Dump sta. Register w/city police. (Box 1010, Levelland 79336, tel 806/894-0113.)

LITTLEFIELD   **Bull Lake Campground**
From US 84: FM 54 E 7 mi. On *Bull Lake*. Camping sites with picnic shelters, grills, toilets; Swim-lake, fish, and scenic views. Fee. (City facility, Box 1267, Littlefield, 79339, tel 806/385-5161.)

LITTLEFIELD   **City Camp Site**
From US 84: US 385 N .3 mi. Wheeled backin camper sites 11 w/elec, water & sewage, limit 3 days. Picnic shelters, grills. (Box 1267, Littlefield 79339, tel 806/385-5161.)

LUBBOCK   **Buffalo Springs Lake**
From Loop 289: FM 835 E 4 mi. On *Buffalo Springs Lake*. Entrance fee. Wheeled camper sites 116; w/elec, water & sewage 46, fee; other camp areas 40 acres, fee, limit 14 days. Dump sta, fl toilets, showers, grills, snack bar, ice, groc. Fish, paddle boats, boat ramp, playground, scenic views. (Rt. 10, Box 400, Lubbock 79404, tel 806/747-3353.)

MULESHOE   **Muleshoe National Wildlife Refuge**
From Muleshoe: 20 mi S on SH 214, W for 2¼ mi on gravel road to designated campground. Primitive camping; toilets, drinkable water, nature trail, hiking. A wintering area for migratory waterfowl & sandhill cranes—number of cranes peaks between Dec. and mid-Feb., often with over 100,000 of the birds present at one time. (Refuge Manager, P.O. Box 549, Muleshoe, 79347, tel 806/946-3341.)

PAMPA   **Hobart Street Park**
From US 60: Tex 70 N. 1 mi. Wheeled camper sites 20; w/elec & water 15, limit 3 days. Dump sta, shelter, grills. Playground, volleyball, softball. (Box 2499, Pampa 79066-2499, tel 806/665-8481.)

Shumard Peak, in the Guadalupe Mountains National Park, is the third highest peak in the state; its elevation is 8,615 feet.

PERRYTON   **City Park**
Within city: US 83/FM 377. Wheeled backin camper sites 4 w/elec & water, limit 1 day. Dump sta, fl toilets, groc, laundry. Basketball court, playground. (Box 849, Perryton 79070, tel 806/435-4014.)

PLAINVIEW   **Broadway Street City Park**
Within city: SE First & Broadway. Wheeled camper sites 16 w/elec, fee, limit 3 days; tent sites 10, fee, limit 3 days. Dump sta, fl toilets, grills. Bike trails, playground, volleyball, softball. (Box 1870, Plainview 79072, tel 806/293-4171.)

SILVERTON   **Lake Mackenzie Park**
From Silverton: Tex 86/207 W 4 mi; Tex 207 N 7 mi to lake entrance. From Tulia, I-27: 23 mi E Tex 86; 7 mi N Tex 207 to entrance. On *Lake Mackenzie*. Entrance fee. Wheeled camper sites 38 w/elec & water, fee; tent sites, free; 25 picnic tables, (handicap tables). Group shelter by rsvn, fee. Dump sta, fl toilets, bait, shelters, tables, grills, snack bar, ice, groc. Swimlake; fish, 2 boat ramps, scenic views, nature trails. (Rt 1, Box 14, Silverton 79257, tel 806/633-4318.)

STINNETT   **Stinnett City Park**
Within city: 1 blk W of courthouse & 1 blk S. Wheeled backin camper sites 8, limit 3 days. Fl toilets, bait, grills, ice, groc nearby. Swimpool; playground, tennis, volleyball nearby. (Drawer 909, Stinnett 79083, tel 806/878-2422.)

SWEETWATER   **Lake Sweetwater Park**
From I-20: FM 1856 S 3.6 mi; FM 2035 E .4 mi. On *Lake Sweetwater*. Concessionaire: wheeled camper sites 19; 12 w/elec & water, fee; 7 w/ elec & water at water's edge, fee, other camp area 25 acres, fee. Dump sta, fl toilets, bait, grills, snack bar, ice, groc. Swim-lake; fish, boat ramp, playground, scenic views. (Rt 3, Box 255, Sweetwater 79556, tel 915/235-4648.)

SWEETWATER   **Lake Trammell Park**
From I-20: Tex 70 S 4 mi; FM 1809 2.8 mi & S 1.2 mi. On *Lake Trammell*. Primitive camp area 300 acres, fee. Fl toilets, bait, snack bar, ice. No swimming or skiing. Trail bike area, fish, boat ramp, scenic views. (Rt 1, Box 91, Sweetwater 79556, tel 915/235-5191.)

UMBARGER   **Buffalo Lake National Wildlife Refuge**
From US 60: FM 168 S 1.5 mi. Wheeled backin camper or tent sites 25. No elec or water, fee, limit 7 days. Other undeveloped tent areas available, limit 7 days. Fl & vault toilets, group shelters (rsvn req'd). Auto tour drive, park naturalist, nature trails. Golden Eagle Passports acptd. (US Fish & Wildlife Serv, Box 228, Umbarger 79091, tel 806/499-3382.)

WELLINGTON   **Collingsworth County Pioneer Park**
From Wellington: US 83 N 7 mi. On *Salt Fork of the Red River*. Wheeled camper sites 24 w/ water & elec, fee, limit 3 days. Dump sta, fl toilets, 1 large group shelter, 2 small covered picnic areas, grills, playground, scenic views. (Courthouse, Rm 1, 2nd Fl, Wellington 79095, tel 806/447-5408.)

Day hikers enjoy McKittrick Canyon of the Guadalupe Mountains National Park. (For detailed map of park trails, see Hiking and Backpacking Trails of Texas/3rd Edition by M. Little, Lone Star Books, Houston.)*

Appendix 1—
Camping Supplies/ Equipment Checklists

Camping Equipment Checklist

The following checklists are designed to guide you in planning your next camping trip. Your needs will vary according to the type, length, and destination of your trip, as well as personal preferences, number of persons included, season of the year, and budget limitations.

Obviously, all items on the checklists aren't needed on any one trip. Since using checklists helps you think more methodically in planning, these extensive lists should serve merely as a reminder of items you may need.

When using these checklists to plan a trip, the item may be checked (✔) if it needs to be taken. Upon returning, if the item was considered unnecessary, a slash could be used: ✘. If a needed item was forgotten, a zero could be used (0); if the item has been depleted and needs to be replenished, an encircling of the check could be used; (✔). This is of particular importance if you camp regularly and keep a camping box packed with staples that can be ready to go on a moment's notice.

Cooking equipment needs are quite dependent on the menu—whether you plan to cook and eat three balanced meals a day or whether you plan to eat non-cooked meals or snacks the entire trip. Many campers find it helpful to jot down the proposed menu for each meal on a 4″ × 6″ index card to help determine the grocery list as well as the equipment needed to prepare the meal. By planning this way, you'll avoid taking equipment you'll never use and you won't forget important items.

Typical Menu with Grocery and Equipment Needs

MEAL: Saturday breakfast		Number of Persons: 5
MENU	GROCERY LIST	EQUIPMENT
orange juice	Tang	camp stove
bacon	10 slices bacon	gasoline, funnel
eggs (scrambled)	8 eggs	folding oven
biscuits	1 can biscuits	frying pan
	peach jelly	baking pan
	honey	pitcher
	margarine	mixing bowl
	salt	cooking fork, spoon
	pepper	

Shelter/Sleeping:

___ Air mattresses
___ Air mattress pump
___ Cots, folding
___ Cot pads
___ Ground cloth
___ Hammock
___ Mosquito netting
___ Sleeping bag or bed roll
___ Tarps (plastic & canvas)
___ Tent
___ Tent stakes, poles, guy ropes
___ Tent repair kit
___ Whisk broom

Extra Comfort:

___ Camp stool
___ Catalytic heater
___ Folding chairs
___ Folding table
___ Fuel for lantern & heater
___ Funnel
___ Lantern
___ Mantels for lantern
___ Toilet, portable
___ Toilet chemicals
___ Toilet bags
___ Wash basin

Clothing/Personal Gear:

___ Bathing suit
___ Boots, hiking & rain
___ Cap/hat
___ Facial tissues
___ Flashlight (small), batteries
___ Jacket/windbreaker
___ Jeans/trousers
___ Pajamas
___ Pocket knife
___ Poncho
___ Prescription drugs
___ Rain suit
___ Sheath knife
___ Shirts
___ Shoes
___ Shorts
___ Socks
___ Sweat shirt/sweater
___ Thongs (for showering)
___ Toilet articles (comb, soap, shaving equipment, toothbrush, toothpaste, mirror, etc.)
___ Toilet paper
___ Towels
___ Underwear
___ Washcloth

Safety/Health:

___ First-aid kit
___ First-aid manual
___ Fire extinguisher
___ Insect bite remedy
___ Insect repellant
___ Insect spray/bomb
___ Poison ivy lotion
___ Safety pins
___ Sewing repair kit
___ Scissors
___ Snake bite kit
___ Sunburn lotion
___ Suntan cream
___ Water purifier

Optional:

___ Binoculars
___ Camera, film, tripod, light meter
___ Canteen
___ Compass
___ Fishing tackle
___ Frisbee, horseshoes, washers, etc.
___ Games for car travel & rainy day
___ Hobby equipment

___ Identification books: birds, flowers, rocks, stars, trees, etc.
___ Knapsack/day pack for hikes
___ Magnifying glass
___ Map of area
___ Notebook & pencil
___ Sunglasses

Miscellaneous:

___ Bucket/pail
___ Candles
___ Clothesline
___ Clothespins
___ Electrical extension cord
___ Flashlight (large), batteries
___ Hammer
___ Hand axe/hatchet
___ Nails
___ Newspapers
___ Pliers
___ Rope
___ Saw, bow or folding
___ Sharpening stone/file
___ Shovel
___ Tape, masking or plastic
___ Twine/cord
___ Wire
___ Work gloves

Cooking Equipment Checklist

**Food Preparation/
Serving/Storing:**

____ Aluminum foil
____ Bags (large & small,
    plastic & paper)
____ Bottle/juice can opener
____ Bowls, nested with lids for
    mixing, serving & storing
____ Can opener
____ Colander
____ Fork, long-handled
____ Ice chest
____ Ice pick
____ Knife, large
____ Knife, paring
____ Ladle for soups & stews
____ Measuring cup
____ Measuring spoon
____ Pancake turner
____ Potato & carrot peeler
____ Recipes

____ Rotary beater
____ Spatula
____ Spoon, large
____ Tongs
____ Towels, paper
____ Water jug
____ Wax paper/plastic wrap

Cooking:

____ Baking pans
____ Charcoal
____ Charcoal grill (hibachi or
    small collapsible type)
____ Charcoal lighter
____ Coffee pot
____ Cook kit, nested/pots &
    pans with lids
____ Fuel for stove (gas-
    oline/kerosene/liquid
    propane)

____ Griddle
____ Hot pads/asbestos gloves
____ Matches
    Ovens for baking:
____ Cast iron dutch oven
____ Folding oven for fuel
    stoves
____ Reflector oven
____ Tote oven
____ Skewers
____ Skillet with cover
____ Stove, portable
____ Toaster (folding camp
    type)
____ Wire grill for open fire

Eating:

____ Bowls for cereal, salad,
    soup
____ Cups, paper & styrofoam
____ Forks

____ Glasses, plastic
____ Knives
____ Napkins, paper
____ Pitcher, plastic
____ Plates (plastic, aluminum,
    paper)
____ Spoons
____ Table cloth, plastic

____ _____
____ _____

Clean-Up:

____ Detergent (Bio-degrad-
    able soap)
____ Dish pan
____ Dish rag
____ Dish towels
____ Scouring pad
____ Scouring powder
____ Sponge

Hiking/Backpacking Checklist

This list is not meant to be all inclusive or necessary for each trip. It is a guide in choosing the proper gear. Although this list was prepared for the hiker/backpacker, it is quite appropriate for anyone using the backcountry, whether they are traveling by foot, canoe, bicycle, or horse. Parentheses indicate those optional items that you may not want to carry depending upon the length of the trip, weather conditions, personal preferences, or necessity.

Ten Essentials for Any Trip:

____ Map
____ Compass
____ First-aid kit
____ Pocket knife
____ Signaling device
____ Extra clothing
____ Extra food
____ Small flashlight/extra
    bulb & batteries
____ Fire starter/candle/
    waterproof matches
____ Sunglasses

Day Trip (add to the above):

____ Comfortable boots or
    walking shoes
____ Rain parka or 60/40
    parka

____ Day pack
____ Water bottle/canteen
____ Cup
____ Water purification tablets
____ Insect repellant
____ Sun lotion
____ Chapstick
____ Food
____ Brimmed hat
____ (Guide book)
____ Toilet paper & trowel
____ (Camera & film)
____ (Binoculars)
____ (Book)
____ Wallet & I.D.
____ Car key & coins for
    phone
____ Moleskin for blisters
____ Whistle

Overnight or Longer Trips
(add the following):

____ Backpack
____ Sleeping bag
____ Foam pad
____ (Tent)
____ (Bivouac cover)
____ (Ground cloth/poncho)
____ Stove
____ Extra fuel
____ Cooking pot(s)
____ Pot scrubber
____ Spoon (knife & fork)
____ (Extra cup/bowl)
____ Extra socks
____ Extra shirt(s)
____ Extra pants/shorts
____ Extra underwear
____ Wool shirt/sweater
____ (Camp shoes)

____ Bandana
____ (Gloves)
____ (Extra water container)
____ Nylon cord
____ Extra matches
____ Soap
____ Toothbrush/powder/floss
____ Mirror
____ Medicines
____ (Snake bite kit)
____ (Notebook & pencil)
____ Licenses & permits
____ (Playing cards)
____ (Zip-lock bags)
____ (Rip stop repair tape)
____ Repair kit—wire, rivets,
    pins, buttons, thread,
    needle, boot strings

Appendix 2—
Facilities Summary of State Parks

This summary is designed to quickly show some special facilities and accommodations you'll find at state-operated parks and recreation areas. At a glance you should be able to tell which parks have screened shelters, primitive camping, group accommodations, swimming pools, equestrian/biking trails, golf courses, etc. Please note that this summary is *not* all-inclusive, i.e., it does not include all the parks in this guide, nor does it include all the types of camping, activities, etc. of the parks listed. For that information, consult the individual park descriptions on the pages cited.

Parks and Page Numbers	Screened Shelters	Cabins	Hotel-type Accommodations	Walk-in tent sites	Primitive campsites	Primitive camping areas for backpackers	Screened shelters in group camp	Sites in group trailer area	Group barracks, lodges	Swimming pool	Bicycle trails (designated)	Golf course	Miniature golf (seasonal)	Texas longhorn herd	Equestrian trails areas	Equestrian camping areas	Rental charges (seasonal)
Abilene, p. 121	8							40		X			X				
Balmorhea, p. 122			18-unit							X							
Bastrop, p. 54		12			X				4-bdrm. lodge; 4 dorms dh/rec hall w/kitchen	X		X					
Blanco, p. 90	7																
Bonham, p. 11									w/dining hall								
Brazos Bend, p. 56	14			X							X						
Buescher, p. 57	4							14	w/kitchen/dining hall								
Caddo Lake, p. 12	8	9															
Caprock Canyons, p. 125				X	X											X	
Choke Canyon (Calliham), p. 93	20									X							
South Shore, p. 93				X													
Cleburne, p. 13	6																
Colorado Bend, p. 96				X	X												
Copper Breaks, p. 126															X	X	

Parks and Page Numbers	Screened Shelters	Cabins	Hotel-type Accommodations	Walk-in tent sites, primitive campsites	Primitive camping areas for backpackers	Screened shelters in group camp	Sites in group trailer area	Group barracks, lodges	Swimming pool	Bicycle trails (designated)	Golf course	Miniature golf (seasonal)	Texas longhorn herd	Equestrian trails areas	Equestrian camping areas	Rental charges (seasonal)
Daingerfield, p. 14		3						Bass lodge								
Davis Mountains, p. 127			39-rm.													
Dinosaur Valley, p. 15					X									X	X	
Eisenhower, p. 16	35						37									
Enchanted Rock, p. 97				X	X											
Fairfield Lake, p. 17					X											
Falcon, p. 98	24															
Fort Griffin, p. 128													X			
Fort Parker, p. 61		12						4 dorms, rec hall, dh w/kitchen								
Fort Richardson, p. 18				X												
Galveston Island, p. 62	10						20									
Garner, p. 99	40	17				5				X		X				
Goliad, p. 100	5			X			24		X							
Guadalupe River, p. 102				X												
Hill Country, p. 103				X	X									X	X	
Huntsville, p. 64	30									X		X				
Inks, p. 104	22			X							X					
Kerrville-Schreiner, p. 105	16					7										
Lake Arrowhead, p. 21														X		
Lake Bob Sandlin, p. 22	20			X												
Lake Brownwood, p. 133	10	17						2 lodges, 4 bunkhouses, dining hall								
Lake Corpus Christi, p. 108	25			X												
Lake Lewisville, pp. 24, 33	38					14										
Lake Livingston, p. 67	10						50		X							

Parks and Page Numbers	Screened Shelters	Cabins	Hotel-type Accommodations	Walk-in tent sites	primitive campsites	Primitive camping areas for backpackers	Screened shelters in group camp	Sites in group trailer area	Group barracks, lodges	Swimming pool	Bicycle trails (designated)	Golf course	Miniature golf (seasonal)	Texas longhorn herd	Equestrian trails	Equestrian camping areas	Rental charges (seasonal)
Lake Mineral Wells, p. 25					X		15								X	X	
Lake Somerville, p. 68															X	X	
Birch Creek, p. 68					X			30									
Nails Creek, p. 69				X	X												
Lake Whitney, p. 30	48					1											
Lockhart, p. 110				X						X		X					
Lost Maples, p. 111					X												
Lyndon B. Johnson, p. 118										X				X			
Martin Creek Lake, p. 35	21			X													
Martin Dies, Jr. Walnut Ridge, p. 70	25																
Hen House Ridge, 70	21																
McKinney Falls, p. 112							6				X						
Meridian, p. 36	11			X			7										
Mustang Island, p. 113				X													
Palo Duro Canyon, p. 141															X	X	X
Pedernales Falls, p. 117					X												
Possum Kingdom, p. 39		6												X			
Purtis Creek, p. 41				X													
Rusk—Palestine, p. 42								46									
Sea Rim, p. 79				X													
Stephen F. Austin, p. 81	20									X	X						
Tyler, p. 43	35					1		30									

Index